RIGHT TO MANAGE:
LAW AND PRACTICE

RIGHT TO MANAGE: LAW AND PRACTICE

Piers Harrison
Harriet Holmes
Swita Kothari
Eleanor Murray
Hugh Rowan

WS
&H

Wildy, Simmonds & Hill Publishing

ISBN: 9780854903122

British Library Cataloguing in Publication Data

A catalogue record for this book is available from the British Library

First published in 2026 by

Wildy, Simmonds & Hill Publishing
Wildy & Sons Ltd
Lincoln's Inn Archway
Carey Street
London WC2A 2JD
www.wildy.com

Printed in Great Britain by CPI Group (UK) Ltd, Croydon CR0 4YY.

Contents

Table of Cases

References are to page numbers.

Table of Statutes

References are to page numbers.

Table of Statutory Instruments

References are to page numbers.

Table of Practice Directions

References are to page numbers.

Table of Forms and Guides

References are to page numbers.

Chapter 1

Introduction

1.1 When the right to manage was introduced by Chapter 1 of Part 2 of the Commonhold and Leasehold Reform Act 2002 (CLRA 2002), it represented a pivotal shift in the balance of power between landlords and leaseholders of residential properties in England and Wales. Previously, leaseholders with concerns as to the management of a property would have to rely on the fault-based application for appointment of a manager under Part II of the Landlord and Tenant Act 1987, or else look to collectively enfranchise the property under the Leasehold Reform, Housing and Urban Development Act 1993.

1.2 For the first time, leaseholders were given a statutory right to take over the management of their building without needing to prove fault, mismanagement or breach on the part of their landlord, or go to the expense of purchasing the underlying freehold. The right to manage is a right that may be exercised unilaterally, without the landlord's consent, and with limited grounds for objection.

1.3 The RTM process allows a company set up by qualifying leaseholders (the RTM company) to acquire responsibility for the management functions under the lease, including repairs, maintenance, insurance and service charge administration. Although the right does not transfer ownership or rent collection functions, it can significantly empower leaseholders to control how their building is run and how their money is spent.

1.4 Since its inception, the RTM regime has become an increasingly popular mechanism for leaseholders seeking more autonomy over the management of their homes, particularly in cases where managing agents appointed by landlords have proved unsatisfactory or unaccountable. However, the process is not without legal and procedural complexity. A strict set of statutory requirements governs eligibility, company formation, notice procedures, dispute resolution and the eventual handover of management functions. The courts and tribunals have developed a growing body of case law interpreting and refining the legislation, often in response to technical disputes or attempts to frustrate the statutory process.

1.5 This book aims to provide a comprehensive, practical and legally rigorous guide to the right to manage. It is written for lawyers, property managers, RTM company directors and leaseholders alike. The chapters that follow examine the origins and legislative framework of the RTM regime, the step-by-step process for acquiring the right, the consequences of acquisition, and the common pitfalls and procedural objections that arise in practice.

LAW REFORM

1.6 Initially, Chapter 1 was to refer to reforms proposed by the Law Commission in its enfranchisement consultation paper, *Leasehold home ownership: buying your freehold or extending your lease* (2018).[1] The book was so long in gestation that the report was published on 21 July 2020, *Leasehold home ownership: exercising the right to manage* (2020),[2] and some of those reforms have now been included in the Leasehold and Freehold Reform Act 2024.

1.7 The report highlights a number of key problems with the existing RTM regime, including:

(1) unpredictable and sometimes excessive costs of claiming the right to manage, particularly as the RTM company is liable for the landlord's costs as well as its own;
(2) restrictive qualifying criteria meaning it is not possible to claim the right to manage in respect of multiple blocks on an estate, buildings with more than 25% non-residential space or leasehold houses;

---

1 Law Com No 238.

2 Law Com No 393.

(3) information about the building and management functions being provided to the RTM company too late in the process, so that the leaseholders cannot always make informed decisions about claiming the right to manage or prepare for an efficient handover of management functions; and
(4) uncertainty as to how the right to manage applies to areas which are shared with other buildings, such as gardens and car parks.

1.8 The main changes introduced by the Leasehold and Freehold Reform Act 2024 are: (a) the change in the non-residential limit on RTM claims from 25% to 50% introduced by s 49 of the Leasehold and Freehold Reform Act 2024; and (b) the introduction of a more limited costs regime in ss 87A–87B of the CLRA 2002.

1.9 However, there were plenty of difficulties identified by the Law Commission which were not resolved by further legislation. The late provision of information to the RTM company remains problematic.

1.10 Some difficulty has been caused in borrowing the definition for premises to which the right to manage applies from the Leasehold Reform, Housing and Urban Development Act 1993. In particular, the requirement for a self-contained building or part of a building has proved problematic. The Law Commission had asked consultees whether they thought it sensible:

> to retain the existing requirements for a self-contained building or part of a building, but give the tribunal discretion to waive non-compliance where the acquisition of the RTM is not reasonably expected to cause particular practical problems for any interested party.

1.11 That suggestion was not taken forward and the Upper Tribunal (Lands Chamber) has considered the issues relating to the requirements of structural detachment and vertical division in a number of cases: *No 1 Deansgate (Residential) Limited v No 1 Deansgate RTM Company Limited*,[3] *Albion Residential Limited v Albion Riverside Residents RTM Limited*,[4] *CQN RTM Company Limited v Broad Quay North Block*

---

3 *No 1 Deansgate (Residential) Limited v No 1 Deansgate RTM Company Limited* [2013] UKUT 580 (LC), [2014] 1 P & CR DG18.

4 *Albion Residential Limited v Albion Riverside Residents RTM Limited* [2014] UKUT 6 (LC), [2014] 1 WLUK 141.

Freehold Limited[5] and most recently in *Courtyard RTM Company Limited v Rockwell Limited*.[6] Given the many different factual situations which can arise, this area seems likely to foster further litigation.

Buildings with different freeholders

1.12 Where parts of a building are owned by different freeholders and one of the parts is self-contained, then the building as a whole cannot currently be subject to the right to manage.[7] However, leaseholders can still apply for the right to manage the self-contained part or parts of the building. The Law Commission provisionally proposed that this restriction should be removed, so that the entire building could be managed together, by one RTM company, but that has not been taken forward.

Multi-building right to manage

1.13 Those familiar with the history of the right to manage will be aware that it was once thought that it was possible to have a single RTM company in relation to multiple buildings, but that concept was put to rest in *Triplerose Limited v Ninety Broomfield Road RTM Company Limited*.[8] This is so even where leaseholders pay into the same service charge fund or share appurtenant property, such as gardens or car parks.

1.14 Furthermore, the power of an RTM company in a multi-block estate was diminished by the decision of the Supreme Court in *FirstPort Property Services Limited v Settlers Court RTM Company Limited*[9] to the effect that where an RTM company took over the management of a block of flats which formed part of a larger estate containing other blocks, the CLRA 2002 did not provide for the RTM company to manage estate facilities shared by the blocks.

---

5 *CQN RTM Company Limited v Broad Quay North Block Freehold Limited* [2018] L & TR 26 (UT), [2018] L & TR 26 (UT).

6 *Courtyard RTM Company Limited v Rockwell Limited* [2025] UKUT 39 (LC), [2025] HLR 23.

7 CLRA 2002, Sch 6, para 2.

8 *Triplerose Limited v Ninety Broomfield Road RTM Company Limited* [2015] EWCA Civ 282, [2016] 1 WLR 275.

9 *FirstPort Property Services Limited v Settlers Court RTM Company Limited* [2022] UKSC 1, [2022] 1 WLR 519.

NOTICES

1.15 During the course of writing the book, there has been a fundamental sea change as to the approach to the validity of notices, a particularly litigious aspect of the RTM sphere. This was effected by the decision of the Supreme Court in *A1 Properties (Sunderland) Limited v Tudor Studios RTM Company Limited.*[10] This is covered in Chapter 5. The authors have attempted to state the law as at 1 September 2025.

---

[10] *A1 Properties (Sunderland) Limited v Tudor Studios RTM Company Limited* [2024] UKSC 27, [2025] AC 1075.

Chapter 2

RTM Companies, Membership and Governance

SUMMARY

2.1 A critical step towards exercising the right to manage is the formation of an RTM company. Section 73 of the Commonhold and Leasehold Reform Act 2002 (CLRA 2002) sets out strict requirements as to what constitutes an RTM company. This chapter considers the type of company that can be used for the purpose of an RTM claim, its Articles of Association, membership rules and voting rights.

RTM COMPANIES

2.2 Section 73(2) of the CLRA 2002 provides as follows:

> (2) A company is an RTM company in relation to premises if—
>
> (a) it is a private company limited by guarantee, and
> (b) its articles of association state that its object, or one of its objects, is the acquisition and exercise of the right to manage the premises.

2.3 An RTM company can be formed by leaseholders themselves, or they can instruct solicitors or company agents to do this for them. Guidance on how to form a company can be found on the Companies House website[1] and there are also interactive learning tools on how to set

1 www.gov.uk/limited-company-formation.

up property management companies on the Government's website.[2] It is possible to buy a shelf company, but its constitution may have to be adapted to comply with the requirements under the CLRA 2002.

2.4 An RTM company must be a private company limited by guarantee, as defined in section 3(3) of the Companies Act 2006. A company limited by guarantee does not have any shares or shareholders but, instead, it is owned by its members (also known as guarantors). The majority of companies limited by guarantee are not-for-profit companies, whose members will be required to contribute a sum of money to guarantee the company's debts (in the event that the company is wound up). The lack of any requirement to contribute towards an initial capital and its limited liability status makes it more attractive for leaseholders to participate and become members of an RTM company. Another practical benefit is that there is no requirement to transfer a share every time a member leaves (on the sale of his or her flat in the premises) and when a new member joins.

2.5 The RTM company must be registered at Companies House. This can be done by lodging the Memorandum of Association and an application for registration on Form IN01, which must contain the company's name, the type of company it is, set out the company's principal business activity and contain a registered address (which must be displayed on all public records).

2.6 Form IN01 must be accompanied by Articles of Association. RTM companies have model Articles of Association prescribed by the RTM Companies (Model Articles) (England) (Regulations) 2009 (SI 2009/2767) (2009 Regulations) (Prescribed Articles), which is considered in more detail at para 2.21.

2.7 Form IN01 must include a statement of guarantee (as set out in the Prescribed Articles) to bind future members of the company, a statement of initial significant control (if applicable pursuant to Part 21A of the Companies Act 2006), an election to keep information on a public central register and a statement of compliance with the requirements of the Companies Act 2006 generally.

---

2 www.gov.uk/government/publications/flat-management-and-right-to-manage-rtm-companies/about-flat-management-companies-rtm-companies-and-commonhold-associations.

2.8 The application for registration of a company must also be accompanied by a Memorandum of Association. Since the enactment of the Companies Act 2006, the role of a Memorandum of Association is reduced to a snapshot of the company's constitution in which the members confirm that they wish to form a company and to become members of that company. The Memorandum must be in a prescribed form set out in Schedule 2 to the Companies (Registration) Regulations 2008 (SI 2008/3014).

Commonhold association

2.9 Section 73(3) of the CLRA 2002 provides that a company is not an RTM company if it is a commonhold association (within the meaning of Part 1).

2.10 The definition of commonhold association is contained in section 34 of the CLRA 2002, which provides as follows:

> (1) A commonhold association is a private company limited by a guarantee—
>
> (a) the articles of which state that an object of the company is to exercise the functions of a commonhold association in relation to specified commonhold land, and
> (b) the statement of guarantee of which specifies £1 as the amount of the contribution required from each member in the event of the company being wound up.

2.11 A commonhold association is registered at Companies House and its Articles of Association are prescribed by the Commonhold Regulations 2004 (SI 2004/1829). The constitution of a commonhold association does not comply with the requirements of section 73 of the CLRA 2002 and therefore it cannot be used as a vehicle to acquire the right to manage. Further details about a commonhold association can be found in Schedule 3, which contains detailed provisions in relation to its Memorandum, Articles of Association and membership requirements.

Other RTM companies

2.12 Section 73(4) of the CLRA 2002 provides as follows:

(4) ... a company is not an RTM company in relation to premises if another company is already an RTM company in relation to the premises or to any premises containing or contained in the premises.

2.13 In order to avoid competing interests between numerous RTM claims, a company cannot be an RTM company in relation to premises if an RTM company already exists in respect of the premises or any premises contained in, or containing, the premises. This also prohibits the acquisition of the right to manage a whole building where an RTM company already exists in relation to a part of it, or a self-contained part of a building, or if an RTM company already exists in relation to the whole.[3]

2.14 In the case of *Triplerose Limited v Ninety Broomfield Road RTM Company Limited*[4] (which consisted of three conjoined appeals), the Court of Appeal determined that an RTM company could not acquire the right to manage more than one self-contained building (as defined in section 72 of the CLRA 2002). Thus, on an estate comprising multiple self-contained buildings, it was not possible for a single RTM company to acquire the right to manage the whole estate; the right to manage must be exercised separately in respect of each of the self-contained buildings.

2.15 Prior to this decision, numerous companies had sought and obtained confirmation that they had the right to manage more than one self-contained building (following the decision of the Upper Tribunal (Lands Chamber) in *Ninety Broomfield Road RTM Company Limited v Triplerose Limited*,[5] the same case which was reversed by the Court of Appeal).

2.16 However, the Court of Appeal's decision did not address the status of pre-existing RTM companies which had already acquired the right to manage more than one block. The status and rights of these companies are therefore now in doubt. Notwithstanding, the First-tier Tribunal (Property

---

3 *Fencott Limited v Lyttleton Court 114–34a RTM Company Limited* [2014] UKUT 27 (LC), [2014] 1 WLUK 641.

4 *Triplerose Limited v Ninety Broomfield Road RTM Company Limited* [2015] EWCA Civ 282, [2016] 1 WLR 275.

5 *Ninety Broomfield Road RTM Company Limited v Triplerose Limited* [2013] UKUT 606 (LC), [2013] 11 WLUK 826.

Chamber) has been reluctant to interfere in such cases.[6] It may be possible to justify the continued exercise of the right to manage on the basis of some species of estoppel.[7]

2.17 There are exceptions to the effect of section 73(4) of the CLRA 2002. For example, the Upper Tribunal (Lands Chamber) determined in the case of *Danescroft RTM Company Limited v Inspired Holdings Limited and Others*[8] that section 73(4) did not prevent an RTM claim where the landlord had previously formed an RTM company *purely* to prevent the tenants from creating an RTM company in respect of the same premises. The landlord, unbeknown to the tenants, had incorporated an RTM company a few months before the tenants, and objected to the tenants' claim on the grounds that there was already an RTM company in respect of the premises. The objective of the RTM company formed by the landlord was to manage Danescroft Estate, and the Upper Tribunal saw this as the landlord's attempt to retain control and management of the premises. On a purposive construction of the CLRA 2002, it could not have been intended that a landlord could take advantage of section 73(4) with a view to defeating any claim by a tenants' RTM company to acquire the right to manage.

2.18 The effect of *Ninety Broomfield* was more recently considered in *Assethold Limited v Eveline Road RTM Company Limited*,[9] in which the Court of Appeal held that it was possible to make an RTM claim in relation to a property which is itself a self-contained part of a building, notwithstanding that the property was comprised of two parts which were also self-contained parts of the same building. The case concerned a row of terraced houses, which could be divided and sub-divided multiple times within the meaning of section 72 of the CLRA 2002. The Court of Appeal

---

6 See for example *Williams Court (1–15) RTM Company Limited*, BIR/41UG/LRM/2016/0003 & -04, FTT (PC), 23 February 2017, unreported; *AB & R RTM Company Limited v Rovergrange Limited*, LON/00AM/LRM/2017/0005, FTT (PC), 12 April 2017, [2017] 4 WLUK 282; *Ramsbotton v Holding and Management (Solitaire) Limited*, CAM/31UB/ LSC/2019/0081, FTT (PC), 6 July 2020, unreported.

7 The authors note there are numerous issues with establishing such an estoppel in the face of a statute, and the point will need to be tested on appeal, see for example JA Andrews, 'Estoppels Against Statutes' [1966] MLR 1–15.

8 *Danescroft RTM Company Limited v Inspired Holdings Limited* [2014] L & TR 4.

9 *Assethold Limited v Eveline Road RTM Company Limited* [2024] EWCA Civ 187, [2024] Ch 204.

held that the CLRA 2002 did not require an RTM company to claim the smallest possible part satisfying the definition of self-contained premises.

2.19 The Prescribed Articles of an RTM company do not allow acquisition of any property. Therefore, if an RTM company is used to acquire the freehold of the premises, it will cease to be an RTM company.

ARTICLES OF ASSOCIATION

2.20 Section 74(3)–(7) of the CLRA 2002 provides as follows:

> (3) A RTM company may adopt provisions of the regulations for its articles [meaning the 2009 Regulations, as amended].
> (4) The [2009] regulations may include provision which is to have effect for a RTM company whether or not it is adopted by the company.
> (5) A provision of the articles of a RTM company has no effect to the extent that it is inconsistent with the [2009] regulations;
> (6) The [2009] regulations have effect in relation to articles—
>
> (a) irrespective of the date of the articles, but
> (b) subject to any transitional provisions of the [2009] regulations.
>
> (7) Section 20 of the Companies Act 2006 (default application of model articles) does not apply to a RTM company.

2.21 The Schedule to the 2009 Regulations contains a prescribed form of Articles of Association, the Prescribed Articles, and section 74(5) of the CLRA 2002 provides that the Prescribed Articles have effect whether or not they are adopted by the RTM company. There is no ability to contract out of the Prescribed Articles, although there is ability to add additional provisions to the Articles, as long as they are not inconsistent with the Prescribed Articles.

2.22 The Prescribed Articles must state that its object, or one of the objects of the RTM company, includes the acquisition and exercise of the right to manage the premises in question.

2.23 Article 2 of the Prescribed Articles states that the name of the RTM company should include the words 'RTM Company Limited'. However, in the case of *Fairhold Mercury Limited v HQ (Block 1) Action Management*

Company Limited,[10] the Upper Tribunal (Lands Chamber) confirmed that as long as an RTM company satisfies the criteria set out in section 73 of the CLRA 2002, it will be considered to be a valid RTM company even if it does not contain the letters 'RTM' in the company name.

2.24 An RTM company must relate to a specific premises to which Part 1 of the CLRA 2002 applies. Article 1(1) of the Prescribed Articles must specify the premises in respect to which the company intends to acquire and exercise the right to manage. If these premises are not premises to which Part 1 of the CLRA 2002 applies, the company will not be an RTM company. In the case of *Avon Ground Rents Limited v 51 Earls Court Square RTM Company Limited*,[11] the Upper Tribunal (Lands Chamber) was required to determine whether a company was an RTM company based on the description of the premises in its Articles. The premises were described as Flat 1-13, 51 Earls Court Square, London SW5 9DG. The freeholder claimed that the company was not a proper RTM company because the Articles described the premises as comprising only the flats in the building. The Upper Tribunal held that it was clear, using the reasonable person test, that the description of the premises in the Articles intended to apply to the whole building and the company was validly constituted as an RTM company.

2.25 A detailed analysis of the Articles of Association is outside the scope of this book; however, the authors refer to some key points emanating from the Articles in paras 2.27, 2.30 and 2.42–2.61.

Membership

2.26 Section 74 of the CLRA 2002 has a clear definition of persons who are entitled to be members of an RTM company. It provides as follows:

> (1) The persons who are entitled to be members of a company which is an RTM company in relation to premises are—
>
> (a) qualifying tenants of flats contained in the premises, and

---

10 *Fairhold Mercury Limited v HQ (Block 1) Action Management Company Limited* [2013] UKUT 487 (LC), [2014] L & TR 5.

11 *Avon Ground Rents Limited v 51 Earls Court Square RTM Company Limited* [2016] UKUT 22 (LC), [2016] 1 WLUK 174.

(b) from the date on which it acquires the right to manage (referred to in this Chapter as the 'acquisition date'), landlords under leases of the whole or any part of the premises.

2.27 Article 26 of the Prescribed Articles states that, before the RTM is exercised, no person other than a qualifying tenant is entitled to become a member of the RTM company. The opportunity to participate in the management of the premises is available to the qualifying tenant of each flat. After the RTM has been acquired, landlords who have leases of the whole or part of the premises are entitled to become members of the RTM company.

2.28 In the case of *Triplerose Limited v Mill House RTM Company Limited*,[12] the Upper Tribunal (Lands Chamber) accepted that it was common for the original members of an RTM company not to be qualifying tenants of flats in the premises which the company eventually aspires to manage. The Upper Tribunal determined that where an original subscriber, who was not a qualifying tenant, remained on a register of members when the RTM was exercised, it did not consider the entitlement of such an RTM company to seek to acquire the RTM is impaired in any way. However, steps should be taken to remove the original subscriber from the register of members.

2.29 It should also be noted that under section 81(2) of the CLRA 2002, an RTM company may have members who are not qualifying tenants of a flat in the premises and that their participation in giving a claim notice does not invalidate the claim as long as sufficient members (i.e. more than one half of the total number of flats) of qualifying tenants were members when the notice was given.

2.30 To become a member, an application form must be submitted to the Board of the RTM company in the form set out in Article 26(1) of the Prescribed Articles. Article 26(3) confirms that membership of the company is not transferable, although a member can withdraw from membership or cease to become a member in certain circumstances (see para 2.43).

---

12 *Triplerose Limited v Mill House RTM Company Limited* [2016] UKUT 80 (LC), [2016] L & TR 23.

Qualifying tenants

2.31 The definition of qualifying tenants is similar to the definition of a qualifying tenant for collective enfranchisement claims under Part 1 of the Leasehold Reform Housing and Urban Development Act 1993 and is considered in more detail in Chapter 3.

Membership of qualifying tenants

2.32 All qualifying tenants are entitled to be members of the RTM company at any time. Although the RTM company can be incorporated without having the sufficient number of qualifying tenants as its members, in order to exercise the RTM and to serve a valid claim under section 79 of the CLRA 2002, not less than one half of the qualifying tenants must be members of the RTM company at the date of the service of the claim notice.[13] Where there are only two qualifying tenants of flats contained in the premises, both must be members of the RTM company before the claim notice can be served.[14] After service of a valid claim notice, the number of qualifying tenants who are members can fall below the requisite majority of 50 per cent needed to exercise the RTM claim without any adverse consequence to the claim.

2.33 According to section 112(2) of the Companies Act 2006, a person is a member of an RTM company if that person has agreed to become a member and his or her name has been entered in the register of members. There are a string of cases which highlight the importance of creating and maintaining a register of members which should be available to submit as evidence before the tribunal if the RTM is challenged or if there is any doubt as to whether the RTM company is validly constituted at the date of the claim notice. Some of these cases are mentioned below.

2.34 In the case of *Trinity Court RTM Company Limited v Metropolitan Properties (SCG) Limited*,[15] which related to an RTM claim of a block of 98 flats, the RTM company could not produce to the Leasehold Valuation Tribunal a register of members in existence at the relevant date which

---

13 CLRA 2002, s 79.

14 CLRA 2002, s 79(4).

15 *Trinity Court RTM Company Limited v Metropolitan Properties (SCG) Limited*, LON/00AG/LEE/2006/0002, LVT, 7 March 2007, unreported.

satisfied the requirements of the Companies Act 2006 and the Prescribed Articles. The RTM claim was therefore rejected.

2.35 In the case of *Southall Court Residents Limited and Others v Buy Your Freehold Limited and Others*,[16] it was held by the Lands Tribunal that a person who is a qualifying tenant becomes a member of the RTM company on the date his or her name is entered on the register of members. In the absence of a register of members there was no evidence of members other than the original subscribers and, as a result, the RTM company did not fulfil the requirements of section 79(5) of the CLRA 2002. The RTM claim was therefore invalid.

2.36 In the more recent case of *Assethold Limited v 14 Stansfield Road RTM Company Limited*,[17] the Upper Tribunal (Lands Chamber) determined that a defect in the register of members would not be sufficient to prove failure to comply with section 79(5) of the CLRA 2002. However, it should be noted that the appellant's case on the membership point was dismissed on the grounds that it had failed to particularise the basis upon which it considered the register to be defective. The Upper Tribunal determined that the landlord must raise some preliminary doubt as to the register of members and cannot simply put an RTM company to proof. Hence, the approach in *Assethold* should not be considered a general rule, primarily because the appellant's case did not make any reference to any particular defects.

2.37 The fact that only qualifying tenants are initially entitled to be members of the RTM company means that third parties to leases such as management companies and guarantors are not entitled to join the RTM company. However, in the case of trustees who are qualifying tenants of a flat contained in the premises, they have the power to become members of an RTM company unless the trust instrument contains an exclusive direction to the contrary.[18]

---

16 *Southall Court Residents Limited and Others v Buy Your Freehold Limited and Others*, LRX/124/2007, LT, 23 July 2008, unreported, HHJ Reid QC.

17 *Assethold Limited v 14 Stansfield Road RTM Company Limited* [2012] UKUT 262 (LC), [2014] 43 EG 115 (CS).

18 CLRA 2002, s 109

Membership of landlord

2.38 The landlord of a premises, which is subject to an RTM claim, can only become a member of the RTM company after the RTM has been acquired.[19] It is difficult to see how a landlord can become a member of the RTM company any earlier, whilst the qualifying tenants are incorporating the RTM company and making preparations to mount an RTM claim against the landlord. The landlord is not required to have any leasehold interest in any of the flats within the premises to become a member.

2.39 The RTM is a no-fault process and therefore the landlord will have the same rights as any other members, i.e. the right to attend annual general meetings, the right to receive accounts, voting rights, etc. However, the Prescribed Articles were amended on 3 March 2025[20] to cap the voting rights exercisable by landlords under leases at one-third of the votes exercisable by qualifying tenants, thus limiting the ability of landlords to interfere with the RTM company's affairs. The amendments were made partly in consequence of section 49 of the Leasehold and Freehold Reform Act 2024, which increases the non-residential threshold that qualifies premises for the right to manage.

2.40 The degree to which any landlord may choose to interfere with an RTM company's affairs will depend on the facts of each case and the size of the premises. A disgruntled landlord could perhaps choose to become a member simply to obstruct the management of the premises, although whether the obstruction is effective will depend very much on the size of the premises and the number of votes allocated to the landlord.

2.41 If the landlord is really opposed to the idea of giving away control and management of the premises, it could make it more difficult for the RTM company to comply with its management functions or, indeed, use the complexities of company law and the Articles of the RTM company to jeopardise the smooth running of an RTM company. Any proceedings in the company courts are likely to be substantially more expensive than in the tribunal. This could pose a substantial threat to the interests of the rest of the members.

---

19 CLRA 2002, s 74(1)(b).

20 RTM Companies (Model Articles) (England) (Amendment) Regulations 2025 (SI 2025/130), regs 1(1), 2(2)(b).

Withdrawal and cessation of membership

2.42 Article 27(3) of the Prescribed Articles confers a right on the members to withdraw membership of the RTM company upon service of 7 days' notice, but such withdrawal cannot take place during the period between the service of the claim notice and the acquisition date (or if appropriate, the date of withdrawal or deemed withdrawal).

2.43 Article 26 of the Prescribed Articles confirms that no person shall be admitted to membership of the company unless that person is a qualifying tenant of a flat in the premises, or from the date after acquisition of the RTM, a landlord under a lease of the whole or any part of the premises. Article 27 confirms that a member who fails to satisfy these requirements for membership (set out in Article 26) shall cease to be a member of the company with immediate effect. If a member, who is a qualifying tenant or a landlord, dies or becomes bankrupt, and his personal representatives or trustees in bankruptcy do not apply for membership within 36 days, or if a member who is a qualifying tenant or landlord resigns from membership pursuant to Article 27(3), those persons shall cease to be members of the company with immediate effect unless they are otherwise entitled to be a member of the company by reason of their interest in some other flat or lease in the premises. All persons who are able to satisfy the qualification criteria in Article 26 are entitled to re-apply for membership of the company.

Directors of the RTM company

2.44 Article 22 of the Prescribed Articles provides that any person who is willing to act and is permitted by law to do so may be appointed a director. There does not appear to be any requirement for a director to be a member of the company (or, indeed, a resident of the premises), although in practice it is difficult to see why anyone would want to take on the burden of becoming a director unless that person had a vested interest in the premises. Usually, members of the RTM company will become directors, and in smaller premises where there are few members and no landlord members at all, it is often the case that all members become directors. This would allow all members (tenants) to have a say in the decision making. A member of the RTM company does not have an automatic right to become a director.

2.45 Article 10 of the Prescribed Articles allows directors to delegate powers conferred on them, which means that a director could employ professionals such as managing agents or accountants to become directors and to run the RTM company on a day-to-day basis. Articles 12–21 contain provisions relating to the decision making by directors of the RTM company.

2.46 The directors are responsible for the management of the company's business (i.e. in the case of an RTM company, the management of the premises).

2.47 The directors are responsible for the management of the premises.[21] The general rule about decision making by directors is that any decision of the directors must be either a majority decision at a meeting or a decision taken in accordance with Article 13 of the Prescribed Articles. Article 13 provides that a decision of the directors is taken in accordance with this Article when all eligible directors indicate to each other by any means that they share a common view on a matter. This decision may take the form of a resolution in writing or some other form indicating agreement in writing. However, a decision should not be taken in accordance with this Article if the eligible directors will not have formed a quorum at such a meeting. Article 14 sets out the process for calling a directors' meeting. Article 20 requires that the directors must ensure that the company keeps a record of all the decisions (whether taken unanimously or by a majority) for at least 10 years from the date of the decision recorded. Article 21 allows directors to make such rules they think fit on how decisions are made or about how such rules are to be recorded or communicated to the directors. However, the members may, by special resolution, instruct the directors to take or refrain from taking a specified action.[22]

2.48 Whether directors are entitled to remuneration will depend on individual circumstances. The Prescribed Articles state that directors shall not be entitled to any remuneration unless the consent of the members of the RTM company has been obtained in a general meeting. The Prescribed Articles further provide that the RTM company may pay reasonable expenses incurred by the directors. These are just some of the issues which

---

21 The Prescribed Articles, Art 8.

22 The Prescribed Articles, Art 9.

should be discussed between tenants at the outset when embarking upon the RTM process. Discussions should take place around the amount of time required by each member to run the RTM company and how the general management of the premises should be run, this will often depend on the size and the type of the building and how much time each tenant is willing to volunteer for the services. It should also be taken into account that any directors may be required to sign notices and other legal documents not only in the exercise of the RTM, but also in the subsequent management of the premises. Availability for such directors should be taken into account with regard to the day-to-day management and running of the premises. One of the unfortunate consequences of running an RTM company and managing the premises is the fact that neighbours and/or fellow tenants (who were once all on the same side against a landlord) could find themselves in conflict with each other if they do not agree on how the premises should be managed.

2.49 A person who is a director of the RTM company will cease to be a director as soon as he or she ceases to be a director by virtue of any provision of the Companies Act 2006 or is otherwise prohibited by law. If the director has a bankruptcy order made against him or her, or if any voluntary arrangements are made with the company's creditors or if there are medical grounds, then that person will cease to be a director. A director may simply notify the RTM company that he or she is resigning from office.

VOTING RIGHTS

2.50 Voting rights for members of the RTM company are governed by the Prescribed Articles and become hugely complicated if landlords have opted to become members of the company.

Quorum for general meetings

2.51 Article 29(2) of the Prescribed Articles confirms that the quorum for the meeting shall be 20 per cent of the members of the company entitled to vote upon the business to be transacted, or two members of the company so entitled (whichever is the greater) present in person or by proxy. Directors may attend and speak at general meetings, whether or not they are members. If the persons attending a general meeting within half an hour of the time at which the meeting was due to start do not constitute a quorum, or if during a meeting a quorum ceases to be present, the chairman of the meeting must adjourn it. If there are landlord members of the RTM company, they are entitled to vote and will form part of the quorum. If there are fewer qualifying tenants present at the general meeting, this could impact the outcome of a vote.

Voting rights if there are no landlord members

2.52 Article 33(2) of the Prescribed Articles states that if there are no landlord members of the RTM company, voting rights are based on a simple 'one flat, one vote system' irrespective of the size of the flats, proportion of service charge paid or otherwise. In respect of joint tenants of a single flat, whilst each of the joint tenants is entitled to become a member of the RTM company, any one of the joint members may cast the vote for the flat. If more than one joint member is present at the general meeting, the senior member casts the vote. The order in which the joint names are entered in the register of members governs the seniority, and this must be made clear by the qualifying tenants in their initial application for membership. The same provisions apply in the case of joint landlords.

Voting rights where there are landlord members

2.53 The existence of landlord members makes voting rights much more complicated. Article 33(3) of the Prescribed Articles contemplates that the voting rights need to be determined every time a vote is taken, and determination of voting rights is a two-stage process: (a) the company will first need to determine the votes available to be cast; and then (b) determine who may cast those votes. This will almost always lead to uncertainty as to how many votes are available to be cast until a vote actually comes to be taken at a meeting. If there are any empty residential units held directly out of the freehold title (i.e. not subject to a lease), the freeholder landlord would not be entitled to any votes for that unit unless and until the unit is let. The landlord members' votes do not vary depending on the number of qualifying tenants who have become members of the company, and the landlord members receive their votes even if tenant membership of the RTM company is low.

2.54 However, the Prescribed Articles were amended on 3 March 2025[23] to cap the voting rights exercisable by landlords under leases at one-third of the votes exercisable by qualifying tenants, thus limiting the ability of landlords to interfere with the RTM company's affairs.

Determination of votes available to be cast

Votes attributable to residential units

2.55 The number of votes available to each tenant will depend on the number of landlord members of the RTM company. Every residential unit in the premises is allocated a number of votes equal to the number of landlord members of the RTM company. For example, if there are two landlord members, each residential unit is allocated two votes. By contrast, the landlord members' votes do not vary depending on the number of qualifying tenants who have become members of the company; the landlord members receive their votes even if tenant membership of the RTM company is low. A residential unit is defined in Article 1 of the Prescribed Articles as a flat or any other separate set of premises which is constructed or adapted for use for the purposes of a dwelling and includes residential units which are not let to qualifying tenants, i.e. all residential units in the premises. The number of landlord members could vary from time to time depending on whether any vacant flat is sublet at any given time. This could also create uncertainty as to who may be entitled to become a member of the RTM company at any given time.

Votes attributable to non-residential units

2.56 Non-residential parts of the premises are also attributed votes in accordance with a formula set out in Article 33(3)(b) of the Prescribed Articles. The formula is as follows:

$$(\text{Total number of votes allocated to residential units}) \times \frac{A}{B}$$

Where:

A = total internal area of non-residential parts
B = total internal area of residential parts

---

23 RTM Companies (Model Articles) (England) (Amendment) Regulations 2025 (SI 2025/130), regs 1(1), 2(2)(b).

2.57 The A/B factor can never exceed a quarter, otherwise the premises would not qualify for a right to manage in the first place. Internal floor area is determined in accordance with paragraph 1(4) of Schedule 6 to the CLRA 2002. Calculations of the internal floor area are to be measured in square metres, fractions of floor area which are less than half a square metre are to be ignored and fractions of floor area in excess of half a square metre are to be counted as a whole square metre.

2.58 In Tanfield Chambers, *Service Charges and Management: Law and Practice* (Sweet & Maxwell, 5th edn, 2021), Chapter 34, it is stated at para 23-064:

> Detailed provision is made for calculating the internal areas and the rounding of the fractions of those areas, but no provision is made for any fractions of a vote which emerge from the application of the formula. It is unclear whether or not those fractions are lost – in principle that fraction of a vote might alter the outcome of a close vote.

The authors agree with this view, that a fraction of a vote could alter the outcome of a close vote. It is not clear why *rounding* of a fraction is provided for in the calculation of internal areas but not for any fractions of a vote.

Casting of the available votes

2.59 Where a residential unit has a qualifying tenant, only the qualifying tenant who is a member of the RTM company is entitled to cast the allocated votes. Where the residential unit is let to a non-qualifying tenant, the attributable votes are cast by the immediate landlord or, in the case of multiple leases, the landlord under the most inferior lease.[24] Article 33(3)(c) of the Prescribed Articles makes clear that the immediate landlord will not be entitled to the vote of a residential unit held by a qualifying tenant who is not a member of the RTM company. Therefore, any residential unit held by a qualifying tenant who is not a member of the RTM company will not be entitled to vote. Where a residential unit is not subject to any lease, the vote attributable to it may not be cast at all. Therefore, a freeholder with an empty flat may not cast any vote in respect of that flat, but if the flat is let on a tenancy then the votes may be cast.

---

[24] The Prescribed Articles, Art 33(3)(c).

A freeholder can manipulate the situation by granting a lease to an associated company or a connected person (as a non-qualifying tenant).

2.60 The votes allocated to any non-residential part which is subject to a lease are cast by the immediate landlord[25] and where a non-residential part has no lease, the votes are cast by the freeholder.[26] For the purposes of voting, there can only be one non-residential part. If that part is, in fact, a number of separate non-residential parts, Article 33(3)(d) of the Prescribed Articles provides for the votes allocated to be split in proportion to the respective internal floor areas. Any resulting entitlement to a fraction of a vote is to be ignored.

2.61 Any person who is a landlord under a lease or leases of the whole of any part of the premises and who is a member of the RTM company but is not otherwise entitled to any votes, is given one vote by Article 33(3)(e) of the Prescribed Articles. This is likely to apply to immediate landlords and landlords of external areas.

Errors and disputes over the voting system

2.62 Objections as to the eligibility to vote must be made at the general meeting where the vote is tendered and referred to the chairman of that meeting, whose decision is final.[27] In the cases of *Wall v London & Northern Assets*[28] and *Wall v Exchange Investment Corp*,[29] it was held that a decision by the chairman properly holding office under the Prescribed Articles is conclusive absent bad faith. However, the position is different where the chairman is not properly appointed.[30]

---

[25] The Prescribed Articles, Art 33(3)(d).

[26] The Prescribed Articles, Art 33(3)(d).

[27] The Prescribed Articles, Art 34.

[28] *Wall v London & Northern Assets* [1899] 1 Ch 550.

[29] *Wall v Exchange Investment Corp* [1926] 1 Ch 143.

[30] *Re Bradford Investments* [1991] BCLC 224.

Chapter 3

Qualifying for the Right to Manage

SUMMARY

3.1 This chapter considers the criteria which must be satisfied, both in terms of the premises as well as qualifying tenants, before a right to manage can be commenced. Those qualifying conditions are contained in sections 72 and 75 –77 of the Commonhold and Leasehold Reform Act 2002 (CLRA 2002).

3.2 The qualifying conditions are very similar to those for collective enfranchisement claims under Part I of Chapter I of the Leasehold Reform, Housing and Urban Development Act 1993 (as amended by the CLRA 2002) (LRHUDA 1993). The most significant difference between the two schemes is that, for the right to manage, there is no disqualification for a tenant who holds a long lease of more than two flats. Otherwise, there are more minor differences, with provisions being excluded/included from one scheme or the other.

QUALIFYING CONDITIONS

An introduction

3.3 Leaseholders can acquire the right to manage where the premises qualify and there are sufficient numbers of tenants or 'flats'.

3.4 Section 72(1) of the CLRA 2002 provides that the right may be exercised in relation to premises if:

(a) they consist of a self-contained building or part of a building, with or without appurtenant property,
(b) they contain two or more flats held by qualifying tenants, and
(c) the total number of flats held by such tenants is not less than two-thirds of the total number of flats contained in the premises.

3.5 This wording is identical to the qualifying conditions for a collective enfranchisement claim under section 3(1) of the LRHUDA 1993, save that the above definition includes reference to 'with or without appurtenant property'.

3.6 If there is any doubt as to whether qualifying conditions have been satisfied, a landlord who wishes to oppose the RTM claim must serve a counter-notice in accordance with section 84 of the CLRA 2002. In the absence of a counter-notice, there is deemed to be no objection to the RTM claim. Following service of a counter-notice disputing the RTM claim, it will be necessary to seek a declaration from the tribunal to determine whether the right has been successfully claimed. The Tribunal could of its own motion consider whether the statutory procedures have been correctly followed, as confirmed in the case of *Fairhold (Yorkshire) Limited v Trinity Wolf (SE16) RTM Company Limited.*[1]

3.7 In the case of *St Stephens Mansions RTM Company Limited v Fairhold NW Limited,*[2] the Upper Tribunal (Lands Chamber) suggested that where the qualifying conditions are not met, so that Chapter 1 of Part II of the CLRA 2002 does not apply to the premises, the appropriate Tribunal would lack jurisdiction to make a determination under section 84(3) that an RTM company was entitled to acquire the right. The authors' view is that this must be correct because, unless the premises in question are premises to which section 72 applies, none of the provisions of the Chapter have effect, including those which confer jurisdiction on the appropriate Tribunal.

---

1 *Fairhold (Yorkshire) Limited v Trinity Wolf (SE16) RTM Company Limited* [2013] UKUT 502 (LC), [2014] L & TR 6. See also *Albion Residential Limited v Albion Riverside Residents RTM Company Limited* [2014] UKUT 6 (LC), [2014] 1 WLUK 141 at [44].

2 *St Stephens Mansions RTM Company Limited v Fairhold NW Limited* [2014] UKUT 541 (LC), [2015] EGLR 15.

The first limb – premises to which the right to manage applies

3.8 RTM will apply to premises if they satisfy the requirements in section 72(2)–(6) of the CLRA 2002, which provides as follows:

> (2) A building is a self-contained building if it is structurally detached.
> (3) A part of a building is a self-contained part of the building if—
>
> (a) it constitutes a vertical division of the building,
> (b) the structure of the building is such that it could be redeveloped independently of the rest of the building, and
> (c) subsection (4) applies in relation to it.
>
> (4) This subsection applies in relation to a part of a building if the relevant services provided for occupiers of it—
>
> (a) are provided independently of the relevant services provided for occupiers for the rest of the building, or
> (b) could be so provided without involving the carrying out of works likely to result in a significant interruption in the provision of any relevant services for occupiers of the rest of the building.
>
> (5) Relevant services are services provided by means of pipes, cables or other fixed installations.
> (6) Schedule 6 (premises excepted from this Chapter) has effect.

3.9 The premises must, therefore, consist of either a 'self-contained building' or a 'self-contained part of a building', otherwise it will not qualify for the right to manage. This is necessary not only to establish whether or not the premises qualifies but also, more importantly, to establish the extent of the property over which the right to manage is claimed.

3.10 The test in question is a physical one. It is not one that concerns parties' entitlements or obligations in carrying out any development. A useful statement of principle can be found in Lewison LJ's decision in *Assethold v Eveline Road RTM Company Limited* as follows:[3]

---

3 *Assethold v Eveline Road RTM Company Limited* [2024] EWCA Civ 187, [2024] Ch 204 at [36].

Whether premises satisfy the definition of 'self-contained building or part of a building' is a purely physical test. The definition is concerned only with the structure of the built envelope, its internal structure, and the separability of services.

Self-contained building

3.11 A building is 'self-contained' if it is structurally detached (section 72(2)). Although there is little authority on the meaning of 'structurally detached' in this context, it is clear that the purpose of the CLRA 2002 was to enable an RTM company to manage premises which were self-contained and could be managed as a discrete unit.

3.12 It is not necessary for the building in question to be wholly detached from a neighbouring property, though when the building is physically constructed in this way, it will be much more obvious that it is 'structurally detached'. For if the building is structurally detached as a matter of fact, then it will always be a self-contained building for the purposes of section 72(2) of the CLRA 2002, even if it shares services or appurtenances with other blocks. That is why in the case of *Gala Unity Limited v Ariadne Road RTM Company Limited*,[4] the Upper Tribunal (Lands Chamber) (and the Court of Appeal) rejected the landlord's argument that the building was not self-contained due to the use of car-ports underneath two separate coach houses, a shared access road and visitors' parking spaces. The Upper Tribunal found that each building was undoubtedly self-contained since each building was, in fact, structurally detached.

3.13 Identifying whether a building is structurally detached for the purposes of section 72 of the CLRA 2002 can become more difficult when there are physical connections between the building over which the right to manage is claimed and neighbouring property.

---

4 *Gala Unity Limited v Ariadne Road RTM Company Limited*, decision of the Upper Tribunal (Lands Chamber) is reported at [2011] UKUT 425 (LC), [2012] 1 EGLR 99; the Court of Appeal decision is at [2012] EWCA Civ 1372, [2013] 1 WLR 988. Now overruled, on different grounds, by *FirstPort Property Services Limited v Settlers Court RTM Company Limited* [2022] UKSC 1, [2022] 1 WLR 519.

3.14 In *No 1 Deansgate (Residential) Limited v No 1 Deansgate RTM Company Limited*,[5] it was said that the correct approach to whether the building in question is 'structurally detached' is to determine whether there is any attachment of a structural nature, and not whether there was any attachment at all between the structures of the building and any neighbouring property.

3.15 In reaching its decision, the Upper Tribunal (Lands Chamber) rejected the landlord's argument that the building was physically connected to another by a strip of plastic weathering, distinguishing an earlier decision of Lord Wilberforce in *Parsons v Viscount Gage and Others (Henry Smiths Charity)*,[6] and interpreting the condition as requiring 'detachment of a structural nature' to be a question of fact and degree in each case. The Upper Tribunal went on to hold that, on the facts of that case, the building was structurally detached and self-contained, despite it being connected to neighbouring premises by weathering features introduced to cover gaps between the two buildings to prevent water ingress. Those features were not, so the Upper Tribunal held, attachments of a structural nature between the two buildings.

3.16 Neither the word 'building' nor the phrase 'structurally detached' is defined by statute or in the case law, but the test in *Deansgate* has since been applied, and those cases provide further guidance.

3.17 In *Albion Residential Limited v Albion Riverside Residents RTM Company Limited*,[7] a complex modern building, which shared an underground car park and a concrete foundation raft with another adjacent building, was held not to be 'self-contained'. The Upper Tribunal (Lands Chamber) held that each of these words should be given their ordinary meaning and that, in order to determine whether the premises is a structurally detached building, it is first necessary to identify the premises

---

5 *No 1 Deansgate (Residential) Limited v No 1 Deansgate RTM Company Limited* [2013] UKUT 580 (LC), [2014] 1 P & CR DG18.

6 *Parsons v Viscount Gage and Others (Henry Smiths Charity)* [1974] 1 WLR 435 was a case under the Leasehold Reform Act 1967. In determining whether the subject premises was to be treated as a 'house' for the purposes of that Act, Lord Wilberforce held that the expression 'structurally detached' was to mean 'detached from *any* structure'.

7 *Albion Residential Limited v Albion Riverside Residents RTM Company Limited* [2014] UKUT 6 (LC), [2014] 1 WLUK 141.

to which the RTM claim relates, and thereafter to consider whether they are structurally detached. It was clear to the Upper Tribunal that the building in *Albion Riverside* was neither structurally nor functionally detached, because the underground car park acted as support for the building over which the claim was made.

3.18 The *Deansgate* test was further clarified in the case of *CQN RTM Company Limited v Broad Quay North Block Freehold Limited*.[8] In that case, the Upper Tribunal (Lands Chamber) confirmed that the process to be followed was:

(a) to first identify the premises to which the RTM claim relates;
(b) to then identify which part of the premises are attached to some other building; and
(c) to form a view whether the nature and degree of that attachment to the relevant premises can be properly described as structurally detached.

3.19 In this particular case, the Upper Tribunal (Lands Chamber) had to determine whether a part of a ramp, situated under the premises in question but serving an underground car park which was predominately underneath two other blocks on the wider estate, prevented the premises from satisfying the 'structurally detached' criteria. The RTM company tried to argue that the physical connection with the neighbouring property was simply a case of two adjoining walls touching with no structural connection between them. The Upper Tribunal disagreed. Upholding the decision at first instance, it regarded the degree of attachment as going beyond a mere 'weathering feature' of the kind in issue in *Deansgate*. It went on to conclude that 'structural' in this context means 'appertaining or relating to be essential core fabric of the building'. It follows that if the 'essential core fabric of the building' over which the claim is made is attached to neighbouring property, then it is not likely to be regarded as self-contained. However, caution should be applied in relation to this 'essential core or fabric' test which (while it is intended to capture a distinction between structural features and others such as the merely decorative) may risk too much of a gloss on the statutory language.[9]

---

8 *CQN RTM Company Limited v Broad Quay North Block Freehold Limited* [2018] UKUT 183 (LC), [2018] L & TR 26 (UT).

9 *Consensus Business Group (Ground Rents) Limited v Palgrave Gardens Freehold Company Limited* [2020] EWHC 920 (Ch), [2020] 2 P & CR 13 at [121].

3.20 As can be seen from the above, the answer to whether a building is structurally detached (and thus self-contained) can be difficult to ascertain, and is not always going to be easily identifiable from plans or to the eyes of a lawyer. Prior to serving a claim notice, the authors consider it is advisable to obtain an expert opinion from a suitably qualified building surveyor or engineer, which identifies those parts of the premises which are attached to another building and to take expert advice on whether that attachment can be regarded as structural.

Self-contained part of a building

3.21 Premises will also qualify if it is a 'self-contained part of a building', namely if:

(a) it constitutes a vertical division of the building;
(b) the structure of the building is such that it could be redeveloped independently from the rest of the building; and
(c) the services provided for the occupiers of the building: (i) are provided independently of the rest of the building; or (ii) could be so provided without involving the carrying out of the works likely to result in a significant interruption in the provision of any relevant services for occupiers of the rest of the building (section 72(3)–(5)).

3.22 In the case of *Craftrule Limited v 41–60 Albert Palace Mansions (Freehold) Limited,*[10] a case under the LRHUDA 1993, the Court of Appeal held that the phrase 'self-contained part of a building' does not mean that the self-contained part of a building must be the smallest self-contained part of the building in question.

3.23 It was confirmed in *Assethold Limited v Eveline Road RTM Company Limited*[11] that the same reasoning applies to the right to manage with the effect that the 'part' can be the smallest self-contained part of a building or can include other eligible parts. An RTM company was entitled to make an RTM claim in relation to a property, which itself was a self-contained part of a building, notwithstanding that the property was comprised of two parts which were also self-contained parts of the same

---

10 *Craftrule Limited v 41–60 Albert Palace Mansions (Freehold) Limited* [2011] EWCA Civ 185, [2011] 1 P & CR 19.

11 *Assethold Limited v Eveline Road RTM Company Limited* [2024] EWCA Civ 187, [2024] Ch 204.

building. Applied, by way of illustration, to a row of mansion blocks, the right to manage can accordingly be claimed for the row as long as the blocks constitute non-detached buildings and so long as the row may reasonably be called one building (and are all in the same ownership).

VERTICAL DIVISION (SECTION 72(3)(A))

3.24 The requirement that, to be a self-contained part of a building, a part of a building must constitute a 'vertical division', is unqualified. There is, therefore, no test or notion of materiality and that test should not be imported from the Leasehold Reform Act 1967 (LRA 1967) legislation since the analogous provisions in that Act refer to 'a material part', whereas section 72(3)(a) of the CLRA 2002 does not. The question to be determined is whether, by including an area outside a line drawn vertically through the building, the relevant part of the building is physically a vertical division of the building. It is not whether the area in question was minimal in the context of the notice, or very small in relation to the total floor area.

3.25 The meaning of vertical division of a building was considered in the case of *Re Holding and Management (Solitaire) Limited.*[12] *Solitaire* was a case in which the building was divided down one vertical plane at ground level and the upper three floors, but down a different vertical plane at basement level where an underground car park ran beneath the subject property and other adjoining premises. The Lands Tribunal held that the building did not constitute a vertical division and therefore the premises did not qualify for the right to manage. Applying the reasons set out above, the Lands Tribunal considered section 72(3) of the CLRA 2002 as requiring a straight vertical division from basement to the roof of the premises. The requirement that the parts of the building must constitute a vertical division is absolute, and any deviation from the vertical line (save which is genuinely *de minimis*) will exclude that part of the building from the scope of the right to manage. In *Solitaire*, a deviation from verticality amounting to some 2 per cent (two car parking spaces and a shutter door which ran under the neighbouring building) was considered not to be minimal. No guidance was given, however, as to how to draw the line between what is and is not to be regarded as minimal.

---

12 *Re Holding and Management (Solitaire) Limited* [2008] L & TR 16.

3.26 The Upper Tribunal (Lands Chamber) again considered the vertical division test in *Courtyard RTM Company Limited v Rockwell Limited.*[13] Martin Rodger KC highlighted that the effect of this provision was to limit the acquisition of the right to manage to premises which do not overlap or underlap the remainder of the building of which they form part. The line is a notional one.

3.27 Notably, the vertical division only relates to the premises in question and the rest of the building. In other words, there does not have to be a clear vertical division between the relevant premises and all other property; only between the relevant premises and the 'building' of which it is part. Therefore, the fact that there may be overhanging balconies or other projections is not a relevant consideration.[14]

3.28 The fact that a notional dividing line passes through a solid structure running perpendicular to that dividing line is no obstacle to the premises constituting a vertical division of the building.[15] In the *Courtyard* case the relevant structure was an undivided basement slab, which was held not to prevent the premises from qualifying. However, the fact that there was an open plan, undivided car park shared between blocks did prevent the premises from qualifying.

3.29 That said, the existence of an underground car park alone will not always invalidate an RTM claim. *Chelsea Bridge Wharf RTM Company Limited v Fairhold Artemis Limited*[16] was another claim involving an underground car park. The First-tier Tribunal (Property Chamber) accepted that most of the buildings were not structurally detached (and so they would not have qualified individually), although it found, as a matter of fact, that together they all were structurally independent, including the car park, and so could satisfy one limb of section 72(3) of the CLRA 2002. As regards the car park, the First-tier Tribunal distinguished *Re Holding*

---

13 *Courtyard RTM Company Limited v Rockwell Limited* [2025] UKUT 39 (LC), [2025] HLR 23.

14 Ibid, at [50].

15 Ibid, at [60].

16 *Chelsea Bridge Wharf RTM Company Limited v Fairhold Artemis Limited,* LON/00DJ/LRN/2011/0013, LVT, no date, unreported.

and Management (Solitaire) Limited[17] on the facts and concluded in the instant case that the car park was a separate building.

3.30 Given the complex physical layouts of buildings, particularly blocks of flats and mansion blocks, identifying a 'self-contained part of a building' can be complex. The authors would recommend obtaining expert evidence in relation to whether the existence of a car park, which runs beneath a number of properties, is likely to affect the structure of the premises and whether it could be argued that those premises themselves comprise a self-contained part of a building.

3.31 A word of warning to practitioners: where several blocks are, in fact, structurally connected and integral to one another such that they are one single set of premises for the purposes of section 72(1) of the CLRA 2002, serving separate claim notices in relation to each block would result in each claim being invalid (since none of the blocks are self-containing buildings and none of them are self-contained parts of a building either, not being vertically divided). A row of mansion blocks is a series of self-contained parts of a building. The effect of section 72(3)(a) is that each block can acquire the right to manage independently if there is a physical vertical division, but if there is a significant overlap between parts of a building, then the right to manage cannot be acquired separately for any of those parts alone.

REDEVELOPED INDEPENDENTLY (SECTION 72(3)(B))

3.32 The term 'independent redevelopment' is not defined. There is no guidance within the CLRA 2002 (or the case law) as to whether the notion of development is limited to 'operational development' or may extend to material changes of use which may constitute development for the purposes of the Town and Country Planning Act 1990.

3.33 It is considered that the part of the building must be capable of being demolished and/or rebuilt without causing damage to the structure of the neighbouring part. This test was derived by the Leasehold Valuation Tribunal from the definition of 'redevelopment' under section 23(2) of the LRHUDA 1993.[18]

---

17 *Re Holding and Management (Solitaire) Limited* [2008] L & TR 16.

18 *Stamford Hill Mansions RTM Company Limited v Daejan Properties Limited*, LON/008N/LRN/2007/007, LVT, 1 October 2007, unreported, at [32] and [36].

3.34 In the more recent case of *Parkgate (1–6) RTM Company Limited v Ground Rents (Regis) Limited*,[19] the relevant part of the building comprised four self-contained flats. They shared a chimney stack with the neighbouring premises. The question arose as to whether the building could be redeveloped independently, thus allowing the application to qualify for the right to manage. The First-tier Tribunal (Property Chamber) considered the fact that the building could be and was divided into self-contained flats was, in itself, enough to demonstrate that that part of the building could be redeveloped.

3.35 Whether or not a part of a building is capable of being redeveloped independently is likely to be a question of fact which, where contested, will likely need to be proved with reliance on suitable expert evidence.

HAS OR COULD HAVE INDEPENDENT SERVICES (SECTION 72(4))

3.36 As well as being a vertical division and capable of being redeveloped independently, the relevant part of the building must either have, or be capable of having, independent services. The relevant services must therefore be:

(a) … provided independently of the relevant services provided for occupiers of the rest of the building, or
(b) could be so provided without involving the carrying out of works likely to result in a significant interruption in the provision of any relevant services for occupiers of the rest of the building.

3.37 Relevant services in this context are those 'provided by means of pipes, cables or other fixed installations' (section 72(5) of the CLRA 2002). They would therefore include the electricity, gas and water supply, but probably not shared vertical lifts or security systems.

3.38 If, on the facts, the part of the building which seeks to acquire the right to manage has services which are provided independently of the rest of the building, then this part of the test is satisfied without further enquiry. But if the part of the building does not have independent services, the question is whether the services could be rendered independent without

---

[19] *Parkgate (1–6) RTM Company Limited v Ground Rents (Regis) Limited*, CAM/00KF/LRM/2015/0002 & 3, FTT (PC), 14 September 2015, unreported, at [49].

'significant interruption' to the provision of the services to the rest of the building.

3.39 The Upper Tribunal (Lands Chamber) has, in the RTM context, provided a five-part test for determining whether services could be made independent.[20] The court or tribunal is required to:

(1) identify the services provided to occupiers of the part of the building of which the right to manage is claimed ('the RTM part') which are in issue because they are not provided independently;
(2) consider whether the services can be provided independently to the RTM part independently of their provision to the remainder of the building;
(3) ascertain the works required to separate the respective parts of the services supplying the RTM part and the remainder of the building, so that such services will thereafter be supplied to each part independently of the other;
(4) assess the interruption to the services provided to the remainder of the building which will be caused by carrying out the works; and
(5) decide whether that interruption would be 'significant'.

3.40 'Significant' takes into account the duration of the interruption and the severity of its effect on the non-RTM residents. This is a question of fact and degree. Generally speaking, the longer the duration of the interruption, the more likely it is to be regarded as 'significant', although one should also have regard to the seriousness of the interruption. Furthermore, the significance does not depend on any subjective inconvenience caused to an occupier, i.e. hence it being held in *Oakwood Court (Holland Park) Limited v Daejan Properties Limited*[21] that works to a central heating system are not to be regarded as less significant if conducted during the summer.

3.41 It is for the RTM company to prove that the works to separate the service could be done without resulting in a significant interruption.

---

20 *St Stephens Mansions RTM Company Limited v Fairhold NW Limited* [2014] UKUT 541 (LC), [2015] EGLR 15 at [47]–[48]. See also the enfranchisement case concerning similar provisions of *Oakwood Court (Holland Park) Limited v Daejan Properties Limited* [2007] 1 EGLR 121.

21 *Oakwood Court (Holland Park) Limited v Daejan Properties Limited* [2007] 1 EGLR 121.

Usually, expert evidence would be put forward to explain how the services could be made independent and the effect of doing so.

3.42 Services which have separate meters, or where separate meters can be installed without major work, are or can be rendered independent (and so will meet this criterion).[22]

3.43 In *Oakwood Court*, the Upper Tribunal (Lands Chamber) considered 8 hours of interruption to the heating supply to be a 'significant interruption', even when the works could have been scheduled in the summer. However, in the more recent RTM case of *84–91 Windmill Gate RTM Limited v HML Hawksworth Limited*,[23] the First-tier Tribunal (Property Chamber) suggested that an interruption to the water supply for one day would not have been significant, given similar interruptions had been required previously for the water tank to be chlorinated.

3.44 In *St Stephens Mansions RTM Company Limited v Fairhold NW Limited*,[24] which concerned a shared water supply, the Upper Tribunal (Lands Chamber) found that the test had been satisfied. It was held to be irrelevant that the RTM company proposed to continue with the current arrangements and to co-operate with the owners or managers of the remainder of the building in providing services on a common basis rather than independently. That case highlights the necessity to consider issues relating to the separation of services on a purely practical basis, focusing on the construction and configuration of premises, rather than on the rights of their occupiers.

The second limb – number and proportion of 'flats'

3.45 The second aspect to the qualifying criteria relates to the number and proportion of flats which are to be held by 'qualifying tenants' before a valid claim can be made.

---

22 *Parkgate (1–6) RTM Company Limited v Ground Rents (Regis) Limited*, CAM/00KF/LRM/2015/0002 & 3, FTT (PC), 14 September 2015, unreported; *Timken Way RTM Company Limited v Sinclair Garden Investments (Kensington) Limited*, CAM/34UF/LOA/2012/0001, LVT, 3 August 2012, unreported.

23 *84–91 Windmill Gate RTM Limited v HML Hawksworth Limited*, County Court (Central London), 18 December 2006, unreported.

24 *St Stephens Mansions RTM Company Limited v Fairhold NW Limited* [2014] UKUT 541 (LC), [2015] EGLR 15.

3.46 To qualify for the right to manage, the building must contain at least two flats held by qualifying tenants, and two-thirds of the total number of flats in the building must be held by qualifying tenants (section 72(1)(b) of the CLRA 2002). The effect of the minimum number of flats requirement is to exclude from the right to manage:

(a) houses;
(b) buildings containing only two flats where only one of them is held on a long lease to a qualifying tenant and the other is either not let to a qualifying tenant (for example on a short lease) or let at all; and
(c) buildings containing one flat held by a qualifying tenant and other space that is not 'flats'.

3.47 We explain the meaning of 'qualifying tenant' in more detail in paras 3.62–3.68, but broadly speaking it means a leaseholder who has a lease of more than 21 years.

Meaning of 'flat'

3.48 The definition of the flat is contained in section 112(1) of the CLRA 2002. It provides as follows:

> 'flat' means a separate set of premises (whether or not on the same floor)—
>
> (a) which forms part of a building,
> (b) which is constructed or adapted for use for the purposes of a dwelling, and
> (c) either the whole or a material part of which lies above or below some other part of the building,

3.49 'Dwelling' is also defined in section 112(1) of the CLRA 2002 as follows:

> 'dwelling' means a building or part of a building occupied or intended to be occupied as a separate dwelling,

3.50 The definition is concerned with physical configuration. It is an objective test, not a question of what, subjectively, the developer or builder intended when carrying out the works to construct or adapt it, or how an owner for the time being intends to make use of the premises.[25]

3.51 The meaning and effect of the first limb in section 112(1)(a) of the CLRA 2002 is obvious: the premises must form part of a building and they can be situated entirely on one floor, duplex or multi-plex. The effect is to include as 'flats' maisonettes which comprise a single separate set of premises.

3.52 Likewise, the third limb is straightforward, at least conceptually. It requires the entire or a material part of the horizontal plane of the flat to lie above or below another part of the building.

3.53 What has been more contentious in the RTM context, and formed part of recent consideration by the President of the Upper Tribunal (Lands Chamber),[26] is the second limb, i.e. whether the premises are 'constructed or adapted for use for the purposes of a dwelling'. The relevant question is whether the premises in question is constructed or adapted for use for the purposes of a dwelling, where 'dwelling' has the defined meaning of something which is, in fact, occupied or is to be occupied 'as a separate dwelling'.

3.54 The case of *Q Studios (Stoke) RTM Company Limited v Premier Grounds Rents No 6 Limited and Another*[27] concerned a purpose-built block of studio accommodation. The block contained 292 study studios, which contained en-suite facilities, a sitting area, double bed and a small kitchen. Each studio unit had been sold on long leases to investors, with the intention of sub-letting them to students on short lets once they were built. The RTM company sought the right to manage on the basis that the studios were each 'flats' held by qualifying tenants.

3.55 The proposition by the respondent landlord in the *Q Studios* case was that the effect of the words 'separate dwelling' was intended to have

---

25 *Q Studios (Stoke) RTM Company Limited v Premier Grounds Rents No 6 Limited and Another* [2020] UKUT 197 (LC), [2021] L & TR 9 (*Q Studios*) at [65] per Fancourt J, following the reasoning of the Court of Appeal in the enfranchisement case of *Aldford House Freehold Limited v Grosvenor (Mayfair) Estate* [2019] EWCA Civ 1848, [2020] Ch 270.

26 In *Q Studios*, ibid.

27 *Q Studios*, ibid.

the same meaning as the expression has in the Rent Acts. It was said that it had the following effect: (a) if the premises are let or intended to be let on terms that provide for the use of shared living accommodation, then the premises could not be regarded as occupied or intended to be occupied as a separate dwelling, and so are not a dwelling and thus cannot be a 'flat' as defined in section 112(1) of the CLRA 2002; and (b) if the premises are intended to be the home of neither the lessee nor the sub-occupier, then that is not used for the purposes of a dwelling since 'dwelling' connotes use as a home. The respondent relied, in support of its argument, on case law concerning the meaning of 'dwelling' and 'separate dwelling' in the wider landlord and tenant context, particularly of the Rent Acts and an alleged infringement of the Protection from Eviction Act 1977.

3.56 In reaching its decision, the Upper Tribunal (Lands Chamber) observed that the statutory context of Part 2 of the CLRA 2002 is 'quite different'. The President (Fancourt J) said:[28]

> 69. … It is concerned with allowing those with the greatest financial stake and long-term interest in a building to have control of its management. This tribunal, in the *Ezekwe* case, decided that in the Landlord and Tenant Act 1985 there was no requirement for a dwelling (defined as 'a building or part of a building occupied or intended to be occupied as a separate dwelling…') to be occupied as someone's home. …
>
> 70. It seems to me that if, in the context of the 1985 Act, a 'dwelling' does not necessarily connote a 'home', that conclusion will apply more strongly in the 2002 Act, which has the statutory purpose that I have just identified. It has nothing to do with protecting lessees in their homes and is concerned to reflect substantial ownership of a building or part of a building by long leaseholders. For those purposes, the test is whether there are sufficient flats in the building let to qualifying tenants. Whether something is a 'flat' depends on what it was constructed or adapted for use for the purposes of. This is a question of the physical characteristics of the premises in question, not a question of whether it is the occupier's home. I therefore reject the argument that a 'flat' must be occupied or intended to be occupied as a home.

3.57 Fancourt J went on to explain that the focus is not on what the premises are 'let as' but on what, objectively viewed, they are constructed or adopted for use as. It follows from the tribunal's reasoning that if essential living accommodation is provided separate from those premises

---

28 *Q Studios*, ibid.

and as shared common space for use by the occupiers of the premises and others, then they will not be a 'dwelling' and thus are not a 'flat' for the purposes of the CLRA 2002. But if the premises comprise all the usual facilities required for residential living, then it will be regarded as a 'dwelling'. Whether it is also a 'flat' will depend upon whether the other two limbs are satisfied.

3.58 On the facts in *Q Studios*, the fact that a lounge/cinema, gym and laundry provided extra shared facilities which the occupiers of the individual units (flats) within the building were entitled to use did not prevent the units themselves being regarded as flats. The units had 'ample living accommodation for occupation as a separate dwelling' and could be regarded themselves as separate dwellings and constructed for that purpose.[29] They were held to each be 'flats' within the meaning of section 112(1) of the CLRA 2002.

3.59 The effect of the outcome in that case is that it is now clearer that the right to manage could extend beyond buildings traditionally regarded as susceptible to a right to manage (such as mansion blocks), to student letting accommodation or even care homes, if they are designed and held in a way which would meet the criteria as explained in *Q Studios.*

3.60 A part of the premises (a storeroom) on a different floor from a flat, but used in conjunction with it, has been held not to be part of the flat, but rather to be an appurtenance.[30]

3.61 The question of whether premises satisfy the definition of a 'flat' is judged by, and will depend very much on, the physical integration as at the date on which a claim is made.

Qualifying tenants

3.62 Section 75 of the CLRA 2002 deals with qualifying tenants and provides as follows:

---

[29] *Q Studios*, ibid at [82]–[84].

[30] *Cadogan v McGirk* [1996] 73 P & C R 483.

(1) This section specifies whether there is a qualifying tenant at the flat for the purposes of this Chapter and, if so, who it is.
(2) Subject as follows, a person is a qualifying tenant of a flat if he is tenant of the flat under a long lease.
(3) Subsection (2) does not apply where the lease is a tenancy to which Part 2 of the Landlord and Tenant Act 1954 (c. 56) (business tenancies) applies.
(4) Subsection (2) does not apply where—

    (a) the lease was granted by sub-demise out of a superior lease other than a long lease,
    (b) the grant was made in breach of the terms of the superior lease, and
    (c) there has been no waiver of the breach by the superior landlord.

(5) No flat has more than one qualifying tenant at any one time; and subsections (6) and (7) apply accordingly.
(6) Where a flat is being let under two or more long leases, a tenant under any of those leases which is superior to that held by another is not the qualifying tenant of the flat.
(7) Where a flat is being let to joint tenants under a long lease, the joint tenants shall (subject to subsection (6)) be regarded as jointly being the qualifying tenant of the flat.

3.63 A qualifying tenant is, therefore, a tenant under a long lease (within the meaning of section 76 of the CLRA 2002)[31] unless expressly excluded. The exclusions are: (a) a business tenancy to which the Landlord and Tenant Act 1954 applies; and (b) where the long lease was granted out of a superior lease in breach of the terms of the superior lease (and where that breach has not been waived).

3.64 No flat can have more than one qualifying tenant at one time (section 75(5) of the CLRA 2002). So, where there is a chain of long leases, it is the tenant who holds the long lease which is lowest down the chain which qualifies. For example, where there is a 999-year virtual freehold, out of which was granted a 125-year lease followed by a 30-year sub-under lease, it is the tenant of the 30-year sub-under lease which would be the 'qualifying tenant'.

---

31 See paras 3.71–3.83.

JOINT TENANTS

3.65 Where a flat is let to joint tenants under a long lease, the joint tenants (together) shall be regarded as jointly being the qualifying tenant of the flat (section 75(7) of the CLRA 2002). All joint tenants must act together to readily participate in an RTM claim.

3.66 Section 112(5) of the CLRA 2002 states that:

> (5) Where two or more persons jointly constitute either the landlord or the tenant or qualifying tenant in relation to the lease of a flat, any reference in this Chapter to the landlord or the tenant or qualifying tenant is (unless the context otherwise requires) a reference to both or all of the persons who jointly constitute the landlord or the tenant or qualifying tenant, as the case may require.

3.67 It was held in the case of *Assethold Limited v 7 Sunny Gardens Road RTM Company Limited*[32] that where the qualifying tenant dies and the lease passes to the personal representatives, they are the qualifying tenants.

3.68 Whilst each of the joint tenants is entitled to become a member of the RTM company, any one of the joint members may cast a vote for the flat, and if more than one joint member is present at the AGM, it is usually the senior member who casts the vote. See Chapter 2 regarding voting rights.

Trustees

3.69 Trustees who are qualifying tenants may take part in RTM companies. Where trustees are qualifying tenants, their powers under the trust instrument include the power to be a member of a RTM company for the purpose of acquisition and exercise of the right to manage, unless the trust instrument contains an explicit direction to the contrary (section 109(1)–(2) of the CLRA 2002). Trustees can exercise the power conferred by section 109 with the same consent, or on the same direction, as may be required for the exercise of their powers (or ordinary powers) of investment.

---

[32] *Assethold Limited v 7 Sunny Gardens Road RTM Company Limited* [2013] UKUT 509 (LC), [2013] 44 EG 99 (CS).

3.70 Section 109(4) of the CLRA 2002 goes on to provide as follows:

> (4) The purposes—
>
> (a) authorised for the application of capital money by section 73 of the Settled Land Act 1925 (c.18), and
> (b) authorised by section 71 of that Act as purposes for which monies may be raised by mortgage,
>
> include the payment of any expenses incurred by a tenant for life or statutory owner as a member of an RTM company.

Long lease (sections 76 and 77)

3.71 Sections 76 and 77 of the CLRA 2002 supplement section 75, and provide for what is a 'long lease' for the purposes of the CLRA 2002. Those provisions are set out in full below, but their general effect is as follows.

3.72 Only where tenants have a long-term interest in the premises are they given the right to manage. They must be tenants under a 'long lease'. The basic definition is that it must be a lease for a term exceeding 21 years. It was held in *Roberts v Church Commissioners*[33] that the term cannot be backdated, i.e. the term must expire more than 21 years after the date of the grant of the lease. There is no requirement that a lease must be at a low rent and there are no requirements as to rateable value.

3.73 The words 'lease' and 'tenancy' have the same meaning for the purposes of the CLRA 2002 (section 112(1)) and both words include a sub-lease or sub-tenancy, and an agreement for a lease or tenancy (or sub-lease or sub-tenancy, as the case may be). A tenancy at will or sufferance is not included.

3.74 A lease is 'long' if it either: (a) is granted for a term of years exceeding 21 years, whether or not that lease is terminable before the end of that term by notice, re-entry or otherwise; (b) is for a term fixed by law under a grant with a covenant or obligation for perpetual renewal (but is not a lease by sub-demise from one which is not a long lease); (c) takes

---

33 *Roberts v Church Commissioners* [1972] 1 QB 278 (CA).

effect under section 149(6) of the Law of Property Act 1925 (for example a lease for an uncertain term, à la *Mexfield Housing Co-operative Limited v Berrisford*[34]); (d) was granted under Part V of the Housing Act 1985 in pursuance of the right to buy; (e) is a shared ownership lease but only where the tenant's total share is 100 per cent (as defined in section 76(3) of the CLRA 2002); or (f) it was granted in under the right to acquire provisions (section 17 of the Housing Act 1996).

3.75 The requirement under section 76(2)(e) of the CLRA 2002 in relation to shared ownership leases was clarified in the case of *Avon Ground Rents Limited v Canary Gateway (Block A) RTM Company Limited*.[35] In that case it was successfully argued that a tenant with a shared ownership lease – provided it had been granted for a term of years certain exceeding 21 years – fell within section 76(2)(a), even if the tenant's share was less than 100 per cent. This means that the provision in section 76(2)(e) is now only of relevance in cases of shared ownership leases granted for a term of less than 21 years.

3.76 In the case of *Corscombe Close Block 8 RTM Company Limited v Roseleb Limited*,[36] the Upper Tribunal (Lands Chamber), following the courts in the LRHUDA 1993 case of *Richmond Housing Partnership v Brick Farm Management Limited*,[37] has improved the construction of a shared ownership lease, shared equity lease or other form of stair casing leases as a qualifying tenancy. As long as the lease is granted for a term exceeding 21 years, it will qualify under section 76(2)(a) of the CLRA 2002 and it is not necessary to go on to consider section 76(2)(e).

3.77 Special provision is made in section 77 of the CLRA 2002 in respect of certain long leases.

3.78 Where a long lease held by a lessee comes to an end and the lessee acquires a subsequent tenancy (whether by express grant or by implication

---

34 *Mexfield Housing Co-operative Limited v Berrisford* [2011] UKSC 52, [2012] 1 AC 955.

35 *Avon Ground Rents Limited v Canary Gateway (Block A) RTM Company Limited* [2023] EWCA Civ 616, [2023] 1 WLR 3516.

36 *Corscombe Close Block 8 RTM Company Limited v Roseleb Limited* [2013] UKUT 81 (LC), [2013] L & TR 16.

37 *Richmond Housing Partnership v Brick Farm Management Limited* [2005] EWHC 1650 (QB), [2006] HLR 3.

of law), the new tenancy will be treated as a long lease (section 77(2) of the CLRA 2002). Where the term of the original lease does not exceed 21 years but the lease contains a covenant or obligation for renewal without payment of a premium, and when that renewal has been granted (on one or more occasions), bringing the total of the term to 21 years, the term originally granted is deemed to be one of more than 21 years (section 77(3)).

3.79 If a long lease is or was continued after its expiry either by virtue of Part 1 of the Landlord and Tenant Act 1954 or by Schedule 10 to the Local Government and Housing Act 1989, or was continued for any period under the Leasehold Property (Temporary Provisions) Act 1951, it remains a long lease during that period by virtue of section 77(4) of the CLRA 2002. If the lease is one to which Part 2 of the Landlord and Tenant Act 1954 (business lease) applies, then it is excluded from the RTM process.

3.80 The effect of section 77(5) of the CLRA 2002 is that where the same flat is held under two or more separate leases, having the same landlord and the same tenant, and the property comprised in one of the leases is the whole or part of the flat (with or without appurtenant property) whilst the property comprised in the other lease or leases is either a part of the flat (with or without appurtenant property) or appurtenant property only, both leases are taken to be a single long lease of the property comprised in such of those leases as are long leases. Section 112(6) confirms that the date of commencement of the single long lease is taken to be the earliest date of commencement of the term of the lease.

3.81 There is no occupancy condition nor any minimum period the lease must have been held before the status of qualifying tenant is acquired, nor are there any restrictions on the number of flats which may be held by the same qualifying tenant. This can be contrasted in the LRHUDA 1993, which excludes tenants from being qualifying tenants if they own more than two flats in the premises to which the claim applies. Large duplex or lateral conversions which consist of two flats converted into one large flat will count as one flat even if the flats are held on two separate leases and even if there is a covenant to reinstate at the end of the lease term into two separate flats.

3.82 Section 76 of the CLRA 2002 provides as follows:

(1) This section and section 77 specify what is a long lease for the purpose of this Chapter.
(2) Subject to section 77, a lease is a long lease if—

(a) it is granted for a term of years certain exceeding 21 years, whether or not it is (or may become) terminable before the end of that term by notice given by or to the tenant, by re-entry or forfeiture or otherwise,
(b) it is for a term fixed by law under a grant with a covenant or obligation for perpetual renewal (but is not a lease by sub-demise from one which is not a long lease),
(c) it takes effect under section 149(6) of the Law of Property Act 1925 (c. 20) (leases terminable after a death or marriage or the formation of a civil partnership),
(d) it was granted in pursuance of the right to buy conferred by Part 5 of the Housing Act 1985 (c. 68) or in pursuance of the right to acquire on rent to mortgage terms conferred by that Part of that Act,
(e) it is a shared ownership lease, whether granted in pursuance of that Part of that Act or otherwise, where the tenant's total share is 100 per cent, or
(f) it was granted in pursuance of that part of that Act as it had effect by virtue of section 17 of the Housing Act 1996 (c. 52) (the right to acquire).

(3) 'Shared ownership lease' means a lease—

(a) granted on payment of a premium calculated by reference to a percentage of the value of the demised premises or the cost of providing them, or
(b) under which the tenant (or his personal representatives) will or may be entitled to a sum calculated by a reference, directly or indirectly, to the value of those premises.

(4) 'Total share', in relation to the interest of a tenant under a shared ownership lease, means his initial share plus any additional share or shares in the demised premises which he has acquired.

3.83 Section 77 of the CLRA 2002 supplements section 76 as follows:

(1) A lease terminable by notice after a death, a marriage or the formation of a civil partnership is not a long lease if—

(a) the notice is capable of being given at any time after the death or marriage of, or the formation of a civil partnership by, the tenant,
(b) the length of the notice is no more than three months, and
(c) the terms of the lease preclude both its assignment otherwise than by virtue of section 92 of the Housing Act 1985 (assignments by way of exchange) and the sub-letting of the whole of the demised premises.

(2) Where the tenant of any property under a long lease, on the coming to an end of the lease, becomes or has become tenant of the property or part of it under any subsequent tenancy (whether by express grant or by implication of law), that tenancy is a long lease irrespective of its terms.

(3) A lease—

(a) granted for a term of years certain not exceeding 21 years, but with a covenant or obligation for renewal without payment of a premium (but not for perpetual renewal), and
(b) renewed on one or more occasions so as to bring to more than 21 years the total of the terms granted (including any interval between the end of a lease and the grant of a renewal),

is to be treated as if the term originally granted had been one exceeding 21 years.

(4) Where a long lease—

(a) is or was continued for any period under Part 1 of the Landlord and Tenant Act 1954 (c. 56) or under Schedule 10 to the Local Government and Housing Act 1989 (c. 42), or
(b) was continued for any period under the Leasehold Property (Temporary Provisions) Act 1951 (c. 38),

it remains a long lease during that period.

(5) Where in the case of a flat there are at any time two or more separate leases, with the same landlord and the same tenant and—

(a) the property comprised in one of those leases consists of either the flat or a part of it (in either case with or without appurtenant property), and
(b) the property comprised in every other lease consists of either a part of the flat (with or without appurtenant property) or appurtenant property only,

there shall be taken to be a single long lease of the property comprised in such of those leases as are long leases.

Sub-leases

3.84 As explained in para 3.64, no flat can have more than one qualifying tenant (section 75(5) of the CLRA 2002). Accordingly, it is the tenant which holds the long lease lowest in the chain of ownership which is the qualifying tenant. Any superior long leaseholders do not qualify. The 'qualifying' long lease does not, however, have to be the occupational lease. If the occupational lease is for a term of less than 21 years, then the intermediate long lessee will qualify. Further, it is possible for the owner of an intermediate lease to be a qualifying tenant of a flat if there are no inferior long leases in respect of that flat, despite the fact that an intermediate lease includes other property (section 112(4)). This approach was adopted in the LRHUDA 1993 case of *Howard de Walden Estate Limited v Aggio*.[38]

Exceptions – leases which do not qualify

3.85 As mentioned above, there are categories of leases which are excepted from qualification from the right to manage.

3.86 The first (in section 75(3) of the CLRA 2002) is where the lease is a tenancy to which Part 2 of the Landlord and Tenant Act 1954 applies. It was held in the LRHUDA 1993 case of *Bishopsgate Foundation v Curtis*[39] that business tenancies are only business tenancies under the Landlord and Tenant Act 1954 if business use is being carried on at the relevant time (i.e. at the date of the claim), and even if the actual use was in breach of the terms of the lease, the tenant met the qualification requirements. However, contrast this with the Court of Appeal decision in *Henley v Cohen*,[40] in which it was held that the lessees could not rely on their own breaches of covenants to bring the property within the definition of 'lease' for the purpose of the LRA 1967. This is considered further in para 3.110.

3.87 The second is where the long lease was granted by sub-demise out of a superior lease in breach of the terms of the superior lease and there has been no waiver of breach by the superior landlord. If the waiver has been waived by the superior landlord, the lease granted by sub-demise out of a superior lease is no longer excluded.

---

38 *Howard de Walden Estate Limited v Aggio* [2008] UKHL 44, [2009] 1 AC 39.

39 *Bishopsgate Foundation v Curtis* [2004] 3 EGLR 57.

40 *Henley v Cohen* [2013] EWCA Civ 480, [2013] HLR 28.

3.88 The third category (section 77(1) of the CLRA 2002) is a lease terminable by notice after a death or marriage and where the notice is: (a) capable of being given at any time after the death or marriage of the tenant; (b) the length of the notice is no more than 3 months; and (c) the terms of the lease preclude: (i) its assignment otherwise than by virtue of section 92 of the Housing Act 1985 (assignments by way of exchange); and (ii) the sub-letting of the whole of the demised premises. Further details on the notice provisions are set out in the case of *Skinns v Greenwood*.[41]

MULTIPLE PREMISES

3.89 Can an RTM company manage only one building or can it manage the whole estate/multiple blocks? In 2013, the Upper Tribunal (Lands Chamber) answered that question in the affirmative. However, in 2015, the Court of Appeal overturned that decision, answering the question 'no'.

3.90 We have already seen that, under section 72 of the CLRA 2002, the requisite proportion of qualifying leaseholders of flats can form an RTM company to acquire the right to manage 'a self-contained building or part of a building'. In the case of *Triplerose Limited v Ninety Broomfield Road RTM Company Limited*,[42] the freeholder owned two purpose-built, structurally detached, blocks of flats together with parking spaces, garden areas and a cycle and bin store. The RTM company, Ninety Broomfield Road RTM Company Limited, was set up to acquire the right to manage both blocks and served a separate notice of claim in respect of each block. There were sufficient qualifying tenants in each block to make the claim. The landlord argued that the company was only entitled to manage one building and that, consequently, the claim was invalid.

3.91 The Upper Tribunal (Lands Chamber)[43] adopted a purposive approach. It said that the 'main objective' of the statutory provisions was to 'grant long leaseholders the right to take over the management of their building without having to prove fault or pay compensation'. It said that

---

41 *Skinns v Greenwood* [2002] EWCA Civ 424, [2002] HLR 50 (a case under the LRHUDA 1993 but likely to be followed in the RTM context).

42 *Triplerose Limited v Ninety Broomfield Road RTM Company Limited* [2015] EWCA Civ 282, [2016] 1 WLR 275.

43 *Ninety Broomfield Road RTM Company Limited v Triplerose Limited* [2013] UKUT 606 (LC), [2013] 11 WLUK 826.

managing a number of self-contained buildings and shared appurtenant property could 'only' be achieved by adopting a purposive construction. Thus, it said, one RTM company could acquire the right to manage more than one set of premises so long as each set of premises qualified for the right to manage, i.e. it contained the requisite number of qualifying tenants and was 'self-contained'.

3.92 The landlord appealed to the Court of Appeal. It argued that the purpose of the legislation was to allow qualifying leaseholders to take over the management of their own block via their RTM company. It was not intended to allow anyone else to do so. Moreover, said the landlord, the statutory provisions could only be construed as meaning that there had to be one RTM company for each exercise of the right – i.e. one for each block – and the 'premises' had to have the same meaning throughout and could not stretch to multiple buildings.

3.93 The Court of Appeal agreed with the landlord.[44] It held that:

(1) section 72(1) of the CLRA 2002 provides that the right to manage applies to premises only if they satisfy three separate conditions, one of which is that the premises consist of 'a self-contained building or part of a building'. The right does not, therefore, apply to a number of blocks or self-contained buildings in an estate but to a single self-contained building;
(2) section 74 provides that the persons who are entitled to be members of the RTM company are qualifying tenants of flats contained in those premises;
(3) accordingly, as it was put by Gloster LJ:

> If a company is an RTM company in relation to premises A, only qualifying tenants of premises A, and the relevant landlords of premises A, are entitled to be members of that RTM company. Section 74 does not envisage that qualifying tenants of premises B, and the relevant landlords of premises B, are also entitled to be members of that RTM company.

(4) there were practical problems with the Upper Tribunal (Lands Chamber)'s construction. For example, where two blocks of different sizes were managed by one RTM company, the members belonging

---

44 *Triplerose Limited v Ninety Broomfield Road RTM Company Limited* [2015] EWCA Civ 282, [2016] 1 WLR 275.

to the larger block would tend to dominate decisions referrable to the smaller block.

3.94 This decision forms part of a series of decisions in which the 'purposive' approach to construing the CLRA 2002 was rejected in favour of a more literal construction of the statutory language. It presented an opportunity for landlords to claim that the RTM company managing multiple blocks is invalid, since prior to the decision of the Court of Appeal (and particularly after the Upper Tribunal (Lands Chamber)'s decision), RTM companies had acquired management over multiple blocks. It likewise presented (and presents) leaseholders who consider the right to manage is not properly managing an estate to seek a declaration that the right to manage is invalid. That said, for many estates, the decision in *Triplerose* is unlikely to cause much practical difficulty because, if tenants really want the whole estate to be managed by a single RTM company, there is nothing to stop neighbouring RTM companies from agreeing to delegate management to one RTM company within their number.

APPURTENANT PROPERTY

3.95 Section 72(1) of the CLRA 2002 confirms that this Chapter applies to premises 'with or without appurtenant property'. In relation to a building or part of a building (or a flat), 'appurtenant property' means any garage, outhouse, garden, yard that is belonging to, or usually enjoyed with, the building or part of a flat.[45] It is worth noting the contrast with the right to acquire the freehold of appurtenant property in collective enfranchisement claims, where the right is not absolute and can be satisfied by the grant of permanent rights.

3.96 The definition of 'appurtenant property' was comprehensively considered by the Supreme Court in *FirstPort Property Services Limited v Settlers Court RTM Company Limited*.[46] Overturning the Court of Appeal's decision in *Gala Unity Limited v Ariadne Road RTM Company*

---

45 See the definition of 'appurtenant property' in CLRA 2002, s 112(1).

46 *FirstPort Property Services Limited v Settlers Court RTM Company Limited* [2022] UKSC 1, [2022] 1 WLR 519.

Limited,[47] it was held that appurtenant property needs to be appurtenant exclusively to the premises over which the right to manage is claimed. As a result, the right to manage does not extend to shared or estate facilities. This decision has resolved a large number of practical difficulties that arose as a result of the *Gala Unity* case, which in effect provided for shared management of certain communal areas.

3.97 In the *Gala Unity* case, the Upper Tribunal (Lands Chamber) also held that it is not necessary to specify the appurtenant property in the claim notice, or even state that the claim includes appurtenant property.[48] This point was not overturned in *FirstPort*. From a practical point of view, this could cause confusion if it is not immediately apparent from the claim notice the extent of the premises over which management functions are to be exercised by the right to manage. Furthermore, given that the right to manage has a right over land, capable of being noted on the Land Register and capable of being acquired without being challenged by either the landlord, the court or tribunal, it is surprising that it is unnecessary to identify areas of appurtenant land over which the right to manage is claimed.

3.98 In the case of *Pineview Limited v 83 Crampton Street RTM Company Limited*,[49] it was held that a claim will not be invalidated simply because there is another claim notice in force which purports to cover the same property, or another RTM company which states that its objective is to acquire the right to manage in respect of premises which includes the same appurtenant property. The Upper Tribunal (Lands Chamber) thus decided that the build area, access road and garden which were enjoyed with the flats comprised in another block (in this case two coach houses) would constitute appurtenances, and the fact that the occupiers of another property also enjoyed those appurtenances does not mean that they are outside of the definition in section 112(1) of the CLRA 2002.

3.99 This decision contradicts section 73(4) of the CLRA 2002, which states that 'a company is not a RTM company in relation to premises

---

47 *Gala Unity Limited v Ariadne Road RTM Company Limited* [2012] EWCA Civ 1372, [2013] 1 WLR 988.

48 *Gala Unity Limited v Ariadne Road RTM Company Limited* [2011] UKUT 425 (LC), [2012] 1 EGLR 99.

49 *Pineview Limited v 83 Crampton Street RTM Company Limited* [2013] UKUT 598 (LC), [2014] 1 EGLR 65.

if another company is already a RTM company in relation to the premises or to any premises containing or contained in the premises' and section 81(3) which provides that 'where any premises have been specified in a claim notice, no subsequent claim notice which specifies the premises, or any premises containing or contained in the premises, may be given so long as the earlier claim notice continues in force'.

3.100 The Upper Tribunal (Lands Chamber) has, since the decision in *Pineview*, been twice invited to determine a claim notice invalid for want of specifying appurtenant property.[50] The most recent instance[51] was before the President of the Upper Tribunal, who considered there was no reason to depart from the decisions in *Pineview* and *Miltonland*, and therefore the claim notice was not defective for failure to specify any appurtenant property.

3.101 There is no requirement that the appurtenant property 'be let' with the building or any part of it. Instead, it must be an appurtenance that is belonging to, or usually enjoyed with, the building or part of a flat, and could include parking spaces which are merely held on licences by a qualifying tenant of a flat in the premises, as well as external areas over which the lessees have rights in the nature of easements.

PREMISES EXCLUDED FROM THE RIGHT TO MANAGE

3.102 Section 72(6) of the CLRA 2002 states the following:

> (6) Schedule 6 (premises excepted from this Chapter) has effect.

3.103 Paragraph 1 of Schedule 6 to the CLRA 2002 provides as follows:

> **Buildings with substantial non-residential parts**
>
> 1(1) This Chapter does not apply to premises falling within section 72(1) if the internal floor area—

---

50 *Miltonland Limited v Platinum House (Harrow) RTM Company Limited* [2015] UKUT 236 (LC), [2016] L & TR 9 and *Q Studios*, above, n 24 at [96] and [99]–[103] per Fancourt J.

51 *Q Studios*, above, n 24.

(a) of any non-residential part, or
(b) (where there is more than one such part) of those parts (taken together),

exceeds 50%[52] of the internal floor area of the premises (taken as a whole).

(2) A part of premises is a non-residential part if it is neither—

(a) occupied, or intended to be occupied, for residential purposes, nor
(b) comprised in any common parts of the premises.

(3) Where in the case of any premises any part of the premises (such as, for example, a garage, parking space or storage area) is used, or is intended for use, in conjunction with a particular dwelling contained in the premises (and accordingly is not comprised in any common part of the premises), it shall be taken to be occupied, or intended to be occupied, for residential purposes.
(4) For the purpose of determining the internal floor area of a building or of any part of a building, the floor or floors of the building or part shall be taken to extend (without interruption) throughout the whole of the interior of the building or part, except that the area of any common parts of the building or part shall be disregarded.

3.104 It is common for a number of properties to have non-residential premises on the ground and basement levels (usually commercial premises for retail) and residential flats to be contained on the floors above. Premises containing non-residential premises will only be excluded from the right to manage if the proportion of the non-residential parts exceeds 50 per cent of the total internal floor area.

3.105 Two county court decisions under the LRHUDA 1993 set out a detailed explanation of the method of calculating the floor areas.[53] The method of calculation is adopted from section 4(2). Section 4(3) requires communal areas to be disregarded. First, the total areas not occupied, or

[52] Prior to 3 March 2025 this figure was set at 25 per cent. Amended by Leasehold and Freehold Reform Act 2024, s 49.

[53] *Indiana Investments Limited v Taylor* [2004] 3 EGLR 63 and *Marine Court (St Leonards on Sea) Freeholders Limited v Rother District Investments Limited* [2008] 1 EGLR 39.

intended to be occupied, for residential purposes are measured, excluding the common parts. The use of the words 'intended to be occupied' makes it clear that a flat which is not occupied, but built for residential use, will count as part of the residential element. The figure so calculated will then compare to the total internal floor area of the premises, excluding the common parts. If the first measured area exceeds 50 per cent of the total internal floor area of the premises, excluding the common parts, then the property is excluded from the right to manage.

3.106 The first step is to consider what is the floor area being referred to. This was considered in *Interface Properties Limited v 307 Barking Road RTM Company Limited*,[54] where the Upper Tribunal (Lands Chamber) determined that the use of the definite article before 'internal floor area' did not mean that it was assumed that all parts of the building had a floor; it was a question of fact what that area is in order to do the calculation required by paragraph 1 of Schedule 6 to the CLRA 2002. The Upper Tribunal went on to consider what was required of a floor. There is no express stipulation in Schedule 6 that the space concerned must be in use or potentially useful; rather, a floor is a physical and obvious thing comprising a continuous surface. Hence, a space that might have a floor installed within it one day is not part of the internal floor area of the premises.

3.107 The next step is to identify all those parts of the premises, other than the common parts, which are not occupied for residential purposes, or intended to be so occupied. In the case of *Connaught Court RTM Company Limited v Abouzaki Holdings Limited*,[55] the Lands Tribunal held that the question as to whether a part or parts of a property are occupied or intended to be occupied for residential purposes, is essentially a question of fact.

3.108 Occupation for residential purposes is wider than occupation as a resident. In the case of *Gaingold Limited v WHRA RTM Company Limited*,[56] the Lands Tribunal held that residential accommodation used by staff employed by the occupier of commercial premises was nonetheless

---

54 *Interface Properties Limited v 307 Barking Road RTM Company Limited* [2024] UKUT 383 (LC), [2024] 12 WLUK 26.

55 *Connaught Court RTM Company Limited v Abouzaki Holdings Limited* [2008] 3 EGLR 175.

56 *Gaingold Limited v WHRA RTM Company Limited* [2006] 1 EGLR 81.

occupied for residential purposes. Subsequently, in the case of *Westbrook Dolphin Square Limited v Friends Life Limited*,[57] the High Court held that no degree of permanence of residence is required, such that even very short-term lets can be counted for residential purposes. Contrast this with the case of *Smith and Another v Jafton Properties Limited*,[58] in which it was held that use of the premises for short-stay accommodation for business travellers was not residential occupation in the context of the LRHUDA 1993. Similarly, in *Triplerose v Beattie*,[59] it was held that use of a property for short-term lets on 'AirBnB' and 'Booking.com' was not use as a 'private dwelling'. It is considered that the burden of proof is on the landlord to show that the premises is excluded on the balance of probabilities.

3.109 In considering what constitutes common parts, it should be noted that paragraph 1(3) of Schedule 6 to the CLRA 2002 provides that garages, parking spaces, storage spaces or any other part of premises used or intended for use in conjunction with a particular dwelling count towards the residential element. In the case of *Panagopoulos v Cadogan*,[60] it was held that a caretaker's flat was both residential and a common part, irrespective of whether the obligation under the lease to provide a caretaker requires a caretaker to be resident. Common parts constitute areas of a building that are available for a shared use and benefit. It is not necessary that the lessees have access to those parts. In the case of an underground car park, the parking spaces which are allocated to individual flats would be regarded as being occupied for residential purposes, whilst a concourse and access ways, etc would be regarded as common parts (and therefore disregarded from any calculation of the internal floor area of the premises). In the case of *Marine Court (St Leonards on Sea) Freeholders Limited v Rother District Investments Limited*,[61] it was held that common parts are regarded as common parts even when solely used by commercial lessees.

---

57 *Westbrook Dolphin Square Limited v Friends Life Limited* [2014] EWHC 2433 (Ch), [2015] 1 WLR 1713.

58 *Smith and Another v Jafton Properties Limited* [2013] 2 EGLR 104 (CC).

59 *Triplerose v Beattie* [2020] UKUT 180 (LC), [2020] L & TR 32.

60 *Panagopoulos v Cadogan* [2010] EWCA Civ 1259, [2011] Ch 177.

61 *Marine Court (St Leonards on Sea) Freeholders Limited v Rother District Investments Limited* [2008] 1 EGLR 39.

3.110 In the case of *KW RTM Company Limited v Lemonland (Kings Wharf) Limited*,[62] the tribunal, following the county court decision in the LRHUDA 1993 case of *Bishopsgate Foundation v Curtis*,[63] held that even if the use of residential purpose was in breach of the intended use, the actual use and occupation for residential purposes satisfied the residential purposes requirement. In contrast, in *Henley v Cohen*,[64] the Court Appeal held that the lessees could not rely on their own breaches of covenant to bring the property within the definition of a house for the purposes of the LRA 1967.

3.111 The phrase 'intended for residential purposes' is not defined. It is considered that a flat which has been left vacant for a long time would be included as residential premises. In order to rebut the presumption, it would be necessary to prove that the intention had been formed to change to non-residential use in the future. In the case of any premises without any identifiable existing or previous use, the onus will be on the qualifying tenants to prove that there is an intention to use a premises for residential purposes at some point in the future and this will be done by demonstrating that planning permission has been obtained for change of use.

3.112 It is worth noting the decision of the Supreme Court in *Sequent Nominees Limited v Hautford Limited*.[65] There the Supreme Court held (by a majority of three to two) that it was reasonable for a landlord to refuse an application for change of planning use from commercial to residential. The landlord was concerned that if they gave consent this would increase the prospect of a successful claim to enfranchise under the LRA 1967. It was held by Lord Briggs that the risk of enfranchisement was the quintessential type of consideration rendering reasonable the refusal of consent.

Building with self-contained parts in different ownership

3.113 Paragraph 2 of Schedule 6 to the CLRA 2002 provides as follows:

---

62 *KW RTM Company Limited v Lemonland (Kings Wharf) Limited*, LON/00AN/LEE/2006/0003, LVT, 16 April 2007, unreported.

63 *Bishopsgate Foundation v Curtis* [2004] 3 EGLR 57.

64 *Henley v Cohen* [2013] EWCA Civ 480, [2013] HLR 28.

65 *Sequent Nominees Limited v Hautford Limited* [2019] UKSC 47, [2020] AC 28.

> 2 Where different persons own the freehold of different parts of premises falling within section 72(1), this Chapter does not apply to the premises if any of those parts is a self-contained part of a building.

3.114 The effect of paragraph 2 is that where different persons own the freehold of different parts of the premises, the right to acquire the right to manage does not apply to the premises as a whole if any of those parts owned by those different persons is itself a self-contained part of a building. In other words, the lessees have to narrow the RTM claim to the individually owned parts and cannot make a single claim to the whole.

3.115 By contrast, there is no requirement in the LRHUDA 1993 that the building has to be owned by a single freeholder. However, section 4(3A) confirms that the lessees are required to enfranchise the smallest self-contained part where there is more than one freeholder.

Resident landlords

3.116 Paragraph 3 of Schedule 6 to the CLRA 2002 provides as follows:

> 3(1) This Chapter does not apply to premises falling within section 72(1) if the premises—
>
> (a) have a resident landlord, and
> (b) do not contain more than four units.
>
> (2) Premises have a resident landlord if—
>
> (a) the premises are not, and do not form part of, a purpose-built block of flats (that is, a building which, as constructed, contained two or more flats),
> (b) the relevant freeholder, or an adult member of a relevant freeholder's family, occupies a qualifying flat as his only or principal home, and
> (c) sub-paragraph (4) or (5) is satisfied.
>
> (3) A person is a relevant freeholder, in relation to any premises, if he owns the freehold of the whole or any part of the premises.
> (4) This sub-paragraph is satisfied if—
>
> (a) the relevant freeholder, or
> (b) the adult member of his family,

has throughout the last twelve months occupied the flat as his only or principal home.

(5) This sub-paragraph is satisfied if—

(a) immediately before the date when the relevant freeholder acquired his interest in the premises, the premises were premises with a resident landlord, and
(b) he, or an adult member of his family, entered into occupation of the flat during the period of 28 days beginning with that date and has occupied the flat as his only or principal home ever since.

(6) 'Qualifying flat', in relation to any premises and a relevant freeholder or an adult member of his family, means a flat or any other unit as a dwelling—

(a) which is contained in the premises, and
(b) the freehold of the whole of which is owned by the relevant freeholder.

(7) Where the interest of a relevant freeholder in any premises is held on trust, the references in sub-paragraphs (2), (4) and (5)(b) to a relevant freeholder are to a person having an interest under the trust (whether or not also a trustee).

(8) A person is an adult member of another's family if he is—

(a) the other's spouse or a civil partner,
(b) a son, daughter, son-in-law or daughter-in-law of the other, or of the other's spouse or civil partner, who has attained the age of 18, or
(c) the father or mother of the other or of the other's spouse or civil partner;

and 'son' and 'daughter' include stepson and stepdaughter ('son-in-law' and 'daughter-in-law' being construed accordingly).

3.117 The intention is to protect the interests of landlords who convert their home into flats. The exception applies only to premises containing no more than four units, thus purpose-built blocks are not caught by this exemption. For the exception to apply, the relevant freeholder or an adult member of a relevant freeholder's family must occupy a qualifying flat as his or her only or principal home. The person is a relevant freeholder if he or she owns the freehold of the whole or any part of the premises and has throughout the last 12 months occupied the flat as his or her only or principal home.

3.118 A qualifying flat is a flat or other unit used as a dwelling in the specified premises, the freehold of which is owned by the relevant freeholder. The exception is extended to the freeholder's spouse or civil partner, children (including stepchildren), children-in-law and parents.

3.119 Paragraph 3(5) of Schedule 6 to the CLRA 2002 makes provision for the exemption to continue to apply in the case of purchase by one resident landlord from another. For the exemption to apply, the premises must have a resident landlord immediately before the date the new freeholder acquires its interest in the premises, and the new freeholder (or an adult member of his or her family) must enter into occupation of the flat during the period of 28 days beginning with that date and continue to occupy the flat as his or her only or principal home thereafter. This will enable an incoming freeholder to preserve an existing exemption from the right to manage, achieved by reason of the residence of its predecessor.

Owned by local housing authority

3.120 Paragraph 4 of Schedule 6 to the CLRA 2002 provides as follows:

> 4(1) This Chapter does not apply to premises falling within section 72(1) if a local housing authority is the immediate landlord of any of the qualifying tenants of flats contained in the premises.
> (2) 'Local housing authority' has the meaning given by section 1 of the Housing Act 1985 (c. 68).

3.121 There is no right to manage in respect of any premises if the immediate landlord of any qualifying flats is a local housing authority. The entire premises will be excluded if there is even one qualifying flat in the whole building, whose immediate landlord is a local authority.

3.122 Paragraph 4(2) of Schedule 6 to the CLRA 2002 incorporates the definition in section 1(1) of the Housing Act 1985, which would include a local authority as a district council, a London borough council, the Common Council of the City of London, a Welsh county council or county borough council, or the council of the Isle of Scilly.[66]

---

66 Words inserted in the Housing Act by Local Government (Wales) Act 1994 (c 19), Sch 8, para 5(1).

Premises in relation to which rights previously exercised

3.123 Paragraph 5 of Schedule 6 to the CLRA 2002 provides as follows:

> 5(1) This Chapter does not apply to premises falling within section 72(1) at any time if—
>
> (a) the right to manage the premises is at that time exercisable by an RTM company, or
>
> (b) that right has been so exercisable but has ceased to be so exercisable less than four years before that time.
>
> (2) Sub-paragraph (1)(b) does not apply where the right to manage the premises ceased to be exercisable by virtue of section 73(5).
>
> (3) The appropriate tribunal may, on an application made by a RTM company, determine that sub-paragraph 1(b) is not to apply in any case if it considers that it would be unreasonable for it to apply in the circumstances of the case.

3.124 The right to manage cannot be exercised in respect of any premises which is already subject to an RTM scheme. This is reinforced by section 73(4) of the CLRA 2002, which provides that a company cannot be an RTM company in relation to a premises if an RTM company already exists in respect of those premises or any premises contained in, or containing, the premises. This is to prevent competing RTM claims being exercised in respect of a premises.

3.125 In the case of *Danescroft RTM Company Limited v Inspired Holdings Limited and Others*,[67] the Leasehold Valuation Tribunal was required to determine whether a landlord can set up an RTM company before the lessees could, so as to defeat the lessee's claim. In the first instance, the Leasehold Valuation Tribunal found in favour of the legitimate RTM company holding the landlord's company to be a sham. The Leasehold Valuation Tribunal granted permission to appeal to the Upper Tribunal (Lands Chamber) on account of the question of law. However, the matter has since settled.

3.126 Paragraph 5(1)(b) of Schedule 6 to the CLRA 2002 confirms that an RTM claim cannot proceed in respect of premises which was subject

---

[67] *Danescroft RTM Company Limited v Inspired Holdings Limited and Others* [2013] 3 EGLR 155, [2014] L & TR 4.

to a right to manage but has ceased to be so exercisable in fewer than 4 years prior to the claim. However, the exclusion in paragraph 5(1)(b) can be overturned by a Tribunal if it considers that it would be unreasonable for it to apply in the circumstances of any particular given facts. The exclusion in paragraph 5(1)(b) applies if the freehold of any premises is transferred to an RTM company and it ceases to be an RTM company by virtue of section 73(5).

3.127 Section 105 of the CLRA 2002 deals with the cessation of management. Section 105(3) provides that the right to manage ceases to be exercisable where:

> (a) a winding-up order is made, or a resolution for voluntary winding-up is passed, with respect to the RTM company, or the RTM company enters administration,
> (b) a receiver or a manager of the RTM company's undertaking is duly appointed, or possession is taken, by or on behalf of the holders of any debentures secured by a floating charge, of any property of the RTM company comprised in or subject to the charge,
> (c) a voluntary arrangement proposed in the case of the RTM company for the purposes of Part 1 of the Insolvency Act 1986 (c. 45) is approved under that Part of the Act, or
> (d) the RTM company's name is struck off the register under section 1000, 1001 or 1003 of the Companies Act 2006.

In those circumstances the First-tier Tribunal (Property Chamber) can determine that the 4-year exclusion does not apply to a claim if it is satisfied that it would be unreasonable for the exclusion to apply.

Crown Land

3.128 Section 108 of the CLRA 2002 provides as follows:

> (1) This Chapter applies in relation to premises in which there is a Crown interest.
> (2) There is a Crown interest in premises if there is in the premises an interest or estate—
>
> > (a) which is comprised in the Crown Estate,
> > (b) which belongs to Her Majesty in Right of the Duchy of Lancaster,
> > (c) which belongs to the Duchy of Cornwall, or

(d) which belongs to a government department or is held on behalf of Her Majesty for the purposes of a government department.

(3) Any sum payable under this Chapter to an RTM company by the Chancellor of the Duchy of Lancaster may be raised and paid under section 25 of the Duchy of Lancaster Act 1817 (c. 97) as an expense incurred in improvement of land belonging to Her Majesty in right of the Duchy.

(4) Any sum payment under this Chapter to an RTM company by the Duke of Cornwall (or any other possessor for the time being of the Duchy of Cornwall) may be raised and paid under section 8 of the Duchy of Cornwall Management Act 1863 (c. 49) as an expense incurred in permanently improving the possessions of the Duchy.

This confirms that the right to manage applies to premises despite the existence of a Crown estate in the subject premises.

Chapter 4

Claiming the Right to Manage – Giving Notice

SUMMARY

4.1 This chapter examines how to claim the right to manage under the Commonhold and Leasehold Reform Act 2002 (CLRA 2002). It begins by considering participation in the right to manage, service of the notice of invitation to participate (NITP) and the relevant case law. Thereafter, it examines service of the claim notice and the relevant case law relating to the validity of notices. As will be seen in the discussion in this chapter, disputes as to the validity of notices are a frequent cause for litigation in this area of law, and the case law shows how the approach of the courts to the validity of statutory notices has changed in respect of non-compliance with the requirements of the CLRA 2002.

PARTICIPATION IN THE RIGHT SCHEDULE

4.2 Unlike a collective enfranchisement claim under the Leasehold Reform Housing and Urban Development Act 1993 (LRHUDA 1993), the CLRA 2002 ensures that entitlement to exercise the right to manage is 'inclusive'. It confers the right for all qualifying tenants to join the RTM company and requires the RTM company to serve an express notice of that right to membership on all qualifying tenants of flats in the building. The CLRA 2002 specifically enables each qualifying tenant to become a member of the RTM company if they wish and, unlike the collective enfranchisement procedure under the LRHUDA 1993, individual qualifying tenants cannot be excluded from membership of the RTM company under the CLRA 2002. The relevant notice is the NITP.

4.3 'Membership' means becoming a member of the company in the formal company law sense. The subscribers of a company's memorandum are deemed to have agreed to become members of the company, and on its registration become members and must be entered as such in its register of members (section 112(1) of the Companies Act 2006). Every other person who agrees to become a member of a company, and whose name is entered in its register of members, is a member of the company (section 112(2)).

4.4 Every company must keep a register of its members (section 113 of the Companies Act 2006) and the register must be kept available for inspection (section 114).

4.5 Where a landlord is a qualifying tenant of a flat in the building, the landlord is also entitled to be a member of the RTM company and must be served with an NITP. From the date on which it acquires the right to manage (referred to in this chapter as the 'acquisition date'), landlords under leases of the whole or any part of the premises are also entitled to become members (section 74 of the CLRA 2002).

4.6 Service of the NITP is the first step in the process to claim the right to manage and must be completed in advance of service of the claim notice.

WHO MUST BE SERVED WITH NOTICE OF INVITATION TO PARTICIPATE?

4.7 Section 78 of the CLRA 2002 relates to notice inviting participation. Section 78(1) states as follows:

> (1) Before making a claim to acquire the right to manage any premises, an RTM company must give notice to each person who at the time when the notice is given—
>
> (a) is the qualifying tenant of a flat contained in the premises, but
> (b) neither is nor has agreed to become a member of the RTM company.

4.8 The remaining requirements as to the content of the NITP are contained in section 78(2)–(6) of the CLRA 2002.

VALIDITY OF NOTICES

4.9 Before exploring the consequence of failing to serve an NITP, it is convenient to examine the law on the validity of notices more generally. The case of *A1 Properties (Sunderland) Limited v Tudor Studios RTM Company Limited*[1] re-cast the law in relation to the validity of notices where there has been a failure to comply with a statutory requirement. It is worth mapping out the road to the decision in *A1 Properties*, as many older cases have been decided under different principles. The 'old approach' to statutory notices and statutory requirement in general was to focus on statutory interpretation and to ask whether the provision was 'mandatory' or 'directory'. If a statutory requirement was found to be 'mandatory', the consequence of non-compliance was said to be invalidity. If the requirement was 'directory', then some lesser consequence or, perhaps, no consequence, might follow from non-compliance. There was no middle position where it could be inferred that Parliament had intended that the consequences of non-compliance ought to depend on any resultant prejudice.

4.10 In the case of *R v Soneji*,[2] the House of Lords abrogated that approach stating that 'the emphasis ought to be on the consequences of non-compliance, and posing the question whether Parliament can fairly be taken to have intended total invalidity'. In some cases, on its true construction a statute might require strict compliance, or it might explicitly provide the consequence of non-compliance, but there was also a middle position where the consequence would depend on whether there had been 'substantial compliance', which was to be decided by having regard to the resultant consequence or prejudice. *Soneji* was a case in the criminal law sphere concerned with the effect of the expiry of a time limit on the validity of a confiscation order, but was thought to be of universal effect.

---

1 *A1 Properties (Sunderland) Limited v Tudor Studios RTM Company Limited* [2024] UKSC 27, [2025] AC 1075.

2 *R v Soneji* [2005] UKHL 49, [2006] 1 AC 340.

4.11 In the case of *Natt v Osman*,[3] an enfranchisement case, the Court of Appeal made a distinction between the public law context and statutes which confer a property or similar right. *Soneji* applied in the former but not in the latter. In the property law context, the correct approach to non-compliance was a question of statutory construction. One should consider the statutory scheme and whether compliance with the statutory requirement in question was necessary in that context. Actual prejudice, i.e. the prejudice flowing from the non-compliance with the statutory requirement in the instant case, was held to be irrelevant. On that basis, breach of a requirement should lead to the same result in every case (facts relating to actual prejudice being irrelevant). This had the advantage of certainty in that one could judge the validity of a non-compliant notice without knowing the underlying facts relating to prejudice.

4.12 In the case of *Elim Court RTM Company Limited v Avon Freeholds Limited*,[4] the Court of Appeal purported to apply *Natt v Osman* but opened the door to the same statutory provision having a different meaning in different factual contexts. The question in that case was the same question as arose in *A1 Properties*, i.e. whether a failure to serve an RTM claim notice on a landlord would invalidate the acquisition of the right to manage. The Court of Appeal held that it would not, if, on the facts of the case, the landlord in question did not have management powers.

4.13 In *A1 Properties*, the Supreme Court held that in the event of failure to comply with a provision prescribing an action to be taken before a power could be exercised, the correct approach was to ask whether the legislature intended that a breach of that provision should result in total invalidity, *R v Soneji* followed. The proper approach, set out at [61], was to focus on:

> (a) the purpose served by the requirement as assessed in light of a detailed analysis of the particular statute and (b) the specific facts of the case, having regard to whether any (and what) prejudice might be caused or whether any injustice might arise if the validity of the statutory process is affirmed notwithstanding the breach of the procedural requirement.

---

3 *Natt v Osman* [2014] EWCA Civ 1520, [2015] 1 WLR 1536.

4 *Elim Court RTM Company Limited v Avon Freeholds Limited* [2017] EWCA Civ 89, [2018] QB 571.

In the instant case, the Supreme Court's decision was that the failure did not render the transfer of the right to manage void, but rather voidable unless or until the tribunal approved the transfer scheme.

4.14 As to *Natt v Osman*, the Supreme Court held at [61] that it:

> needs to be considered and applied with some caution, particularly in its suggestion that cases where it becomes necessary to infer the intended consequences of non-compliance can for that purpose be divided into distinct and watertight categories and its apparent suggestion (para 31) that in the second category the possibility of a middle position as identified in *Soneji* between outright validity or outright invalidity is excluded.

4.15 But the Supreme Court did not overrule *Natt v Osman* or say that the Court of Appeal reached the wrong conclusion in that case. On the contrary, the import of the decision is that it was correctly decided, and that although the Court of Appeal was wrong to deny the existence of the 'middle position', *Natt v Osman* itself was not a 'middle position' case. Furthermore, many other property cases would not be. Lord Briggs and Lord Sales said as follows in their joint judgment at [62] (with which the others agreed):

> This does not mean that application of procedural rules in every statutory context turns on detailed examination of the consequences arising from the particular facts of the case, nor that a test of substantial compliance is properly to be applied in relation to every procedural rule. Examination of the purpose served by a particular statutory procedural rule may indicate that Parliament intended that it should operate strictly, as a bright line rule, so that any failure to comply with it invalidates the procedure which follows.

4.16 So, there will be statutory provisions where strict compliance is required because the statutory requirement is a 'bright line rule'; and, where that is not the case, the statute may specify the consequence of non-compliance is something less than invalidity; and, in the middle, there will be cases where substantial compliance may suffice. The first step of categorisation into one of these three categories is a question of statutory construction. If one concludes that substantial compliance would suffice, then one turns to focus on the purpose of the provision in question – whether it has been substantially complied with and what, if any, prejudice has been caused.

CONSEQUENCE OF FAILURE TO SERVE NOTICE OF INVITATION TO PARTICIPATE

4.17 Section 79(2) of the CLRA 2002 provides that the claim notice to acquire the right to manage may not be given unless each person required to be given an NITP has been served at least 14 days prior. Given that the consequence of non-compliance with section 78(1) is specifically stated in section 79(2), it might well be thought that there is no scope for arguments based on the doctrine of 'substantial compliance' (see paras 4.9–4.16) as to the consequence of failing to serve a valid NITP. As a result of the decision of the Court of Appeal in *Avon Freeholds Limited v Cresta Court E RTM Co Limited*,[5] that is not the law. The case law leading up to that result is summarised below.

4.18 In the case of *Sinclair Gardens Investments (Kensington) Limited v Oak Investments RTM Company Limited* (*Sinclair Gardens* (2005)),[6] a landlord sought to resist the acquisition of the right to manage because a qualifying tenant had not been given an NITP. The President of the Lands Tribunal said that the purpose of the service of that notice was to ensure that all qualifying tenants have the opportunity to participate in the process. Where that has not been done, 'the principal question for the tribunal will be whether the qualifying tenant has in practice such awareness of the procedures as the statute intended him to have'. On the facts, the tenant had not been prejudiced by the failure to serve an NITP and the claim notice was held to be valid. In the case of *Avon Freeholds Limited v Regent Court RTM Company Limited* (*Regent Court*),[7] the then President of the Lands Chamber followed a similar approach concluding that the tenants who had not been given the notice had not been prejudiced and that the procedure was not invalidated.

4.19 In contrast, in the case of *Avon Ground Rents Limited v Canary Gateway (Block A) RTM Company Limited*,[8] the first of these cases decided post-*Natt v Osman*, the President (Fancourt J) treated section 79(2) of the CLRA 2002 as a bright line rule stating:

---

5 *Avon Freeholds Limited v Cresta Court E RTM Co Limited* [2025] EWCA Civ 1016.

6 *Sinclair Gardens Investments (Kensington) Limited v Oak Investments RTM Company Limited* [2005] RVR 426 (*Sinclair Gardens* (2005)).

7 *Avon Freeholds Limited v Regent Court RTM Company Limited* [2013] UKUT 213 (LC), [2013] L & TR 23 (*Regent Court*).

8 *Avon Ground Rents Limited v Canary Gateway (Block A) RTM Company Limited* [2020] UKUT 358 (LC), [2020] 12 WLUK 459.

> 90. … it appears to me that Parliament did intend failure to give s.78 notices as required to invalidate a claim notice and that s.79(2) should not be interpreted as merely a stipulation as to when a claim notice may be served. The natural and ordinary reading of s.79(2) is that a purported claim notice that is served otherwise than in accordance with its terms will be invalid.

4.20 In *Avon Freeholds Limited v Cresta Court E RTM Company Limited*,[9] Judge Elizabeth Cooke held that *Sinclair Gardens* (2005) and *Regent Court* were inconsistent with *obiter dicta* in *A1 Properties* that, 'Section 79(2) imposes a clear consequence of failure in good time to give participation notices: no valid claim notice can be given to anyone'. But she did not follow *Canary Gateway* on the basis that there was in the decision of the Supreme Court in *A1 Properties* 'ample indication … that it was not the intention of Parliament for a landlord to be able to thwart a right to manage scheme on the basis of the windfall presented by a procedural failure that did not directly affect it'. Her decision was overturned on appeal in *Avon Freeholds Limited v Cresta Court E RTM Co Limited*.[10] Sir Launcelot Henderson, with whom the two other judge agreed said as follows in his judgment:

> [the] approach [of the judge below] overlooks the fundamental point that this is a case where the consequence of non-compliance with the requirement to give a participation notice to Ms O'Connor is prescribed by section 79(2) of the CLRA, namely that 'The claim notice may not be given', or as the Supreme Court put it in *A1 Properties* at [69] 'no valid claim notice can be given to anyone'. That simple language means what it says, and gives rise (objectively) to no absurdity, so it was the duty of the UT, as it is the duty of this court, to apply it accordingly.

FORM AND CONTENT OF THE NOTICE OF INVITATION TO PARTICIPATE

Basic requirements

4.21 The basic requirements of the NITP are set out in section 78(2) of the CLRA 2002, which states as follows:

> (2) A notice given under this section (referred to in this Chapter as a 'notice of invitation to participate') must—

---

[9] *Avon Freeholds Limited v Cresta Court E RTM Company Limited* [2024] UKUT 335 (LC), [2025] 1 WLR 1262.

[10] *Avon Freeholds Limited v Cresta Court E RTM Co Limited* [2025] EWCA Civ 1016.

> (a) state that the RTM company intends to acquire the right to manage the premises,
> (b) state the names of the members of the RTM company,
> (c) invite the recipients of the notice to become members of the company, and
> (d) contain such other particulars (if any) as may be required to be contained in notices of invitation to participate by regulations made by the appropriate national authority.

4.22 In addition, section 78(3) of the CLRA 2002 states as follows:

> (3) A notice of invitation to participate must also comply with such requirements (if any) about the form of notices of invitation to participate as may be prescribed by regulations made so far.

4.23 The contents and form of the NITP are governed by both the CLRA 2002 and subordinate regulations. The relevant regulations are referred to at section 78(2)(d) and (3), and are known as the Right to Manage (Prescribed Particulars and Forms) (England) Regulations (SI 2010/825) (2010 England Regulations). These have subsequently been amended by paragraphs 41–44 of Schedule 2 to the Transfer of Tribunal Functions Order 2013 (SI 2013/1036). In this text, references to regulations will relate to the 2010 England Regulations unless otherwise stated. See Appendix 1 for the 2010 England Regulations.

4.24 The NITP must be in writing and there is a prescribed form with prescribed notes which must be attached to the NITP when served. This is as prescribed by regulation 8(1) of the 2010 England Regulations. Please note that the 2010 England Regulations apply to premises in England only. Equivalent regulations apply in Wales, namely the Right to Manage (Prescribed Particulars and Forms) (Wales) Regulations 2011 (SI 2011/2684) (W287) (2011 Wales Regulations). See Appendix 2 for the 2011 Wales Regulations.

Additional content of the notice of invitation to participate

4.25 Regulation 3 of the 2010 England Regulations prescribes 'additional content' for the NITP in addition to the requirements stated in section 78(2)(a)–(c) of the CLRA 2002. This content is contained in the prescribed form. When preparing the NITP, the authors suggest that careful attention be given to the particulars contained in regulation 3(2)(a)–(j) (see para 4.26).

Additional content prescribed by regulation 3

4.26 Regulation 3 of the 2010 England Regulations prescribes as follows:

> 3. (1) A notice of invitation to participate shall contain, in addition to the statements and information referred to in section 78(2)(a) to (c) of the 2002 Act (notice inviting participation), the particulars mentioned in paragraph (2).
>
> (2) The particulars referred to in paragraph (1) are—
>
> (a) the RTM company's registered number, the address of its registered office and the names of its directors and if applicable, secretary;
>
> (b) the names of the landlord and any third party;
>
> (c) a statement that, subject to the exclusions mentioned in sub-paragraph (e), if the right to manage is acquired by the RTM company, the company will be responsible for—
>
> (i) the discharge of the landlord's duties under the lease; and
>
> (ii) the exercise of his powers under the lease,
>
> with respect to services, repairs, maintenance, improvements, insurance and management;
>
> (d) a statement that, subject to the exclusion mentioned in sub-paragraph (e)(ii), if the right to manage is acquired by the RTM company, the company may enforce untransferred tenant covenants;
>
> (e) a statement that, if the right to manage is acquired by the RTM company, the company will not be responsible for the discharge of the landlord's duties or the exercise of his powers under the lease—
>
> (i) with respect to a matter concerning only a part of the premises consisting of a flat or other unit not subject to a lease held by a qualifying tenant; or
>
> (ii) relating to re-entry or forfeiture;
>
> (f) a statement that, if the right to manage is acquired by the RTM company, the company will have functions under the statutory provisions referred to in Schedule 7 to the 2002 Act;
>
> (g) a statement that the RTM company intends or, as the case may be, does not intend, to appoint a managing agent; and—

(i) if it does so intend, a statement—

(aa) of the name and address of the proposed managing agent (if known); and
(bb) if it be the case, that the person is the landlord's managing agent; or

(ii) if it does not so intend, the qualifications or experience (if any) of the existing members of the RTM company in relation to the management of residential property;

(h) a statement that, where the RTM company gives a claim notice, a person who is or has been a member of the company may be liable for costs incurred by the landlord and others in consequence of the notice;
(i) a statement that, if the recipient of the notice (of invitation to participate) does not fully understand its purpose or implications, he is advised to seek professional help; and
(j) the information provided in the notes to the form set out in Schedule 1 to these Regulations.

4.27 The particulars at regulation 3(2) of the 2010 England Regulations are intended to provide the qualifying tenants with adequate background information as to the more significant issues that will arise when the right to manage is exercised and are provided to allow the recipient to make an informed decision as to whether to become a member of the RTM company. It is considered that the most important is regulation 3(2)(g), whereby the RTM company is required to state in the NITP whether it intends to appoint a managing agent. If it does not intend to appoint a managing agent, it must state the qualifications or experience (if any) of the existing members of the RTM company relating to managing residential property (regulation 3(2)(g)(ii)). Section 78(3) of the CLRA 2002 states that the NITP must comply with requirements as to the form of notice in the regulations.

4.28 Regulation 8(1) of the 2010 England Regulations provides that 'Notices of invitation to participate shall be in the form set out in Schedule 1 to these Regulations'. The prescribed form is set out at para 4.32. Regulation 3(1) provides that an NITP 'shall contain, in addition to the statements and information referred to in section 78(2)(a) to (c) of the 2002 Act … the particulars mentioned in paragraph (2)'. All of that information is prompted for in the prescribed form and thus will be included if the prompts are properly addressed. In addition, on service the information contained in the prescribed notes to the Form must also be included as per regulation 8(2)(g). To avoid a challenge as to validity of the NITP and the subsequent claim once served, it is essential to use the prescribed form contained in Schedule 1 (or in the equivalent 2011 Wales Regulations) and attach the prescribed notes.

4.29 When serving the NITP, section 78(4) of the CLRA 2002 states as follows:

> (4) A notice of invitation to participate must either—
>
> (a) be accompanied by a copy of the articles of association of the RTM company, or
> (b) include a statement about inspection and copying of the articles of association of the RTM company.

4.30 In addition, section 78(5) of the CLRA 2002 requires that:

> (5) A statement under subsection (4)(b) must—
>
> (a) specify a place (in England or Wales) at which the articles of association may be inspected,
> (b) specify as the times at which they may be inspected periods of least two hours on each of at least three days (including a Saturday or Sunday or both) within the seven days beginning with the day following that on which the notice is given,
> (c) specify a place (in England or Wales) at which, at any time within those seven days, a copy of the articles of association may be ordered, and
> (d) specify a fee for the provision of an ordered copy, not exceeding the reasonable costs of providing it.

4.31 If the NITP includes the statement under subsection (4)(b), section 78(6) goes on to state that the NITP will nevertheless be treated as not having been given to the tenants if the tenants are not subsequently allowed to undertake an inspection or provided with a copy in accordance with the statement. This is a key point to consider and necessary arrangements must be made to allow inspection if required.

Schedule 1: Form of notice of invitation to participate

4.32

RIGHT TO MANAGE (PRESCRIBED PARTICULARS AND FORMS) (ENGLAND) REGULATIONS 2010/825

SCHEDULE 1
FORM OF NOTICE OF INVITATION TO PARTICIPATE

To [*name and address*] (See Note 1 below)

1. *[*name*] 'RTM company' ('the company'), a private company limited by guarantee, of [*address of registered office*], and of which the registered number is [*number under Companies Act 2006*], is authorised by its articles of association to acquire and exercise the right to manage [*name of premises to which notice relates*] ('the premises'). The company intends to acquire the right to manage the premises.

2. The company's articles of association accompany this notice.

*The company's articles of association may be inspected at [*address for inspection*] between [*specify times*]. (See Note 2 below) At any time within the period of seven days beginning with the day after this notice is given, a copy of the articles of association may be ordered from [*specify address*] on payment of [*specify fee*]. (See Note 3 below)

**Delete one of these statements, as the circumstances require.*

3. The names of—

(a) the members of the company;
(b) the company's directors; and
(c) if the company has a secretary, the name of that person

are set out in the Schedule below.

4. The names of the landlord and of the person (if any) who is party to a lease of the whole or any part of the premises otherwise than as landlord or tenant are [*specify*].

5. Subject to the exclusions mentioned in paragraph 7, if the right to manage is acquired by the company, the company will be responsible for—

(a) the discharge of the landlord's duties under the lease; and
(b) the exercise of his powers under the lease,

with respect to services, repairs, maintenance, improvements, insurance and management.

6. Subject to the exclusion mentioned in paragraph 7(b), if the right to manage is acquired by the company, the company may enforce untransferred tenant covenants. (See Note 4 below)

7. If the right to manage is acquired by the company, the company will not be responsible for the discharge of the landlord's duties or the exercise of his powers under the lease—

(a) with respect to a matter concerning only a part of the premises consisting of a flat or other unit not subject to a lease held by a qualifying tenant; or
(b) relating to re-entry or forfeiture.

8. If the right to manage is acquired by the company, the company will have functions under the statutory provisions referred to in Schedule 7 to the Commonhold and Leasehold Reform Act 2002. (See Note 5 below)

9. *The company intends to appoint a managing agent within the meaning of section 30B(8) of the Landlord and Tenant Act 1985. [*If known, give the name and address of the proposed managing agent here. If that person is the current managing agent, that fact must also be stated here.*]

*The company does not intend to appoint a managing agent within the meaning of section 30B(8) of the Landlord and Tenant Act 1985. [*If any existing member of the company has qualifications or experience in relation to the management of residential property, give details in the Schedule below.*]

**Delete one of these statements, as the circumstances require.*

10. If the company gives notice of its claim to acquire the right to manage the premises (a 'claim notice'), a person who is or has been a member of the company may be liable for costs incurred by the landlord and others in consequence of the claim notice. (See Note 6 below)

11. You are invited to become a member of the company. (See Note 7 below)

12. If you do not fully understand the purpose or implications of this notice you are advised to seek professional help.

SCHEDULE

The names of the members of the company are: [*state names of company members*]

The names of the company's directors are: [*state directors' names*]

[*If applicable*] The name of the company's secretary is: [*state company secretary's name*]

[*If applicable; see the second alternative in paragraph 9 above*] The following member[s] of the company [has][have] qualifications or experience in relation to the management of residential property: [*give details*]

Signed by authority of the company,
[*Signature of authorised member or officer*]

[*Insert date*]

NOTES

1. The notice inviting participation must be sent to each person who is at the time the notice is given a qualifying tenant of a flat in the premises but who is not already, and has not agreed to become, a member of the company. A qualifying tenant is defined in section 75 of the Commonhold and Leasehold Reform Act 2002 ('the 2002 Act').
2. The specified times must be periods of at least 2 hours on each of at least 3 days (including a Saturday or Sunday or both) within the 7 days beginning with the day following that on which the notice is given.
3. The ordering facility must be available throughout the 7 day period referred to in Note 2. The fee must not exceed the reasonable cost of providing the ordered copy.
4. An untransferred tenant covenant is a covenant in a tenant's lease that he must comply with, but which can be enforced by the company only by virtue of section 100 of the 2002 Act.
5. The functions relate to matters such as repairing obligations, administration and service charges, and information to be furnished to tenants. Details may be obtained from the RTM company.
6. If the claim notice is at any time withdrawn, deemed to be withdrawn or otherwise ceases to have effect, each person who is or has been a member of the company is liable (except in the circumstances mentioned at the end of this note) for reasonable costs incurred by—

(a) the landlord,
(b) any person who is party to a lease of the whole or any part of the premises otherwise than as landlord or tenant, or
(c) a manager appointed under Part 2 of the Landlord and Tenant Act 1987 to act in relation to the premises to which this notice relates, or any premises containing or contained in the premises to which this notice relates,

in consequence of the claim notice.
A current or former member of the company is liable both jointly with the company and every other person who is or has been a member of the company, and individually. However, a former member is not liable if he has assigned the lease by virtue of which he was a qualifying tenant to another person and that other person has become a member of the company.
7. All qualifying tenants of flats contained in the premises are entitled to be members. Landlords under leases of the whole or any part of the

premises are also entitled to be members, but only once the right to manage has been acquired by the company. An application for membership may be made in accordance with the company's articles of association which, if they do not accompany this notice, may be inspected as mentioned in paragraph 2 of the notice.

8. If the right to manage is acquired by the company, the company must report to any person who is landlord under a lease of the whole or any part of premises any failure to comply with any tenant covenant of the lease unless, within the period of three months beginning with the day on which the failure to comply comes to the attention of the company—

(a) the failure has been remedied,
(b) reasonable compensation has been paid in respect of the failure, or
(c) the landlord has notified the company that it need not report to him failures of the description of the failure concerned.

9. If the right to manage is acquired by the company, management functions of a person who is party to a lease of the whole or any part of the premises otherwise than as landlord or tenant will become functions of the company. The company will be responsible for the discharge of that person's duties under the lease and the exercise of his powers under the lease, with respect to services, repairs, maintenance, improvements, insurance and management. However, the company will not be responsible for matters concerning only a part of the premises consisting of a flat or other unit not subject to a lease held by a qualifying tenant, or relating to re-entry or forfeiture.

10. If the right to manage is acquired by the company, the company will be responsible for the exercise of the powers relating to the grant of approvals to a tenant under the lease, but will not be responsible for the exercise of those powers in relation to an approval concerning only a part of the premises consisting of a flat or other unit not subject to a lease held by a qualifying tenant.

Checklist 4.1: Notice of invitation to participate – contents

4.33 Contents of the notice of invitation to participate under regulations 3 and 8(1) of, and Schedule 1 to, the 2010 England Regulations and section 78(2), (4) and (5) of the CLRA 2002:

- Use the form prescribed in regulation 8(1) of the 2010 England Regulations found in Schedule 1.
- Comply with section 78(2) of the CLRA 2002 (see para 4.21).
- Include the 'additional content' prescribed by regulation 3 (this is contained in the prescribed form and is set out at para 4.26).
- Attach the prescribed notes to the form.
- Attach a copy of the Articles of Association or include the statement about inspection (see section 78(4) and (5)).
- The Schedule to the prescribed form requires that the NITP is required to be signed by an 'authorised member or officer' of the RTM company giving the notice.

PREPARATION AND SERVICE OF THE NOTICE OF INVITATION TO PARTICIPATE

Identifying relevant lessees for service

4.34 As a first step, the RTM company must complete the necessary due diligence to identify all names and addresses of the relevant recipients of the NITP. These will be those qualifying tenants of flats in the building who are not already members of the RTM company or who have not already agreed to be members. They can usually be identified by completing a search at the Land Registry. The definition of a qualifying tenant is contained at section 75 of the CLRA 2002. If held by joint tenants, each tenant must be served. Where the registered proprietor is deceased, 'the tenant' to be served will be the personal representatives.[11] The person to be served is the legal owner of the relevant flats at the time of the NITP except where the flat is let on an equitable lease and there is no legal lessee.[12]

4.35 The prescribed form assumes the identity of the qualifying tenant is known and requires that the name and address of the recipient be stated in the NITP.

---

11 *Assethold Limited v 7 Sunny Gardens Road RTM Company Limited* [2013] UKUT 509 (LC), [2013] 44 EG 99 (CS).

12 *Avon Freeholds Limited v Cresta Court E RTM Company Limited* [2024] UKUT 335 (LC), [2025] 1 WLR 1262.

Address for service

4.36 Section 111 of the CLRA 2002 deals with notices. It states as follows:

> (1) Any notice under this Chapter—
>
> (a) must be in writing, and
> (b) may be sent by post.
>
> (2) A company which is an RTM company in relation to premises may give a notice under this Chapter to a person who is landlord under a lease of the whole or any part of the premises at the address specified in subsection (3) (but subject to subsection (4)).
> (3) That address is—
>
> (a) the address last furnished to a member of the RTM company as the landlord's address for service in accordance with section 48 of the 1987 Act (notification of address for service of notices on landlord), or
> (b) if no such address has been so furnished, the address last furnished to such a member as the landlord's address in accordance with section 47 of the 1987 Act (landlord's name and address to be contained in demand for rent).
>
> (4) But the RTM company may not give a notice under this Chapter to a person at the address specified in subsection (3) if it has been notified by him of a different address in England and Wales at which he wishes to be given any such notice.
> (5) A company which is a RTM company in relation to premises may give a notice under this Chapter to a person who is the qualifying tenant of the flat contained in the premises at the flat unless it has been notified by the qualifying tenant of a different address in England and Wales at which he wishes to be given any such notice.

4.37 Section 111(5) of the CLRA 2002 provides that a tenant can be served with an NITP at the relevant flat save where the tenant has provided notification of an alternative address for service of notices under the CLRA 2002. In the case of *Avon Freeholds Limited v Regent Court RTM Company Limited*,[13] the Upper Tribunal (Lands Chamber) held that section 111(5) operates to confer a 'deemed' service of the NITP even in

---

13 *Avon Freeholds Limited v Regent Court RTM Company Limited* [2013] UKUT 213 (LC), [2013] L & TR 23.

circumstances where it can be demonstrated that the tenant did not actually receive the NITP. It held that section 111(5) is 'permissive rather than imperative'. This allowed for good service of the NITP at an alternative address. The Upper Tribunal determined that service at an address other than the flat was not fatal to the validity of the statutory process so long as service had been effected at the tenant's last known address, even if it could not be proven that notice had come to the tenant's attention. However, the authors advise to be wary of using an alternative address as this will take service outside the deemed service regime under the CLRA 2002. In turn, this will impose a burden on the RTM company of proving that the NITP has been received. It is advisable that the NITP (and, indeed, any statutory notice under the CLRA 2002) be served at the flat or at any address given in accordance with section 111(5) to avoid disputes relating to service.

4.38 If relying on service at an alternative address, it is important to first obtain notification of that alternative address in writing from the tenant and express confirmation that the address can be used for service of notices under the CLRA 2002.

Method of service

4.39 There is no prescribed method of service under the CLRA 2002. Section 111(1)(b) provides that any notice may be served by post. However, this is not a mandatory requirement. To avoid any disputes relating to validity of service, the authors suggest service of the NITP by hand at the lessee's flat and that a witness statement as to service be prepared. This can be used where there is a dispute as to the date and method of service. If serving by hand, the NITP will be deemed served on the day that it is delivered, even if served after business hours.

4.40 If serving by post, section 7 of the Interpretation Act 1978 will apply in respect of any notice under the CLRA 2002 and the relevant regulations. The notice will be deemed to have been given 'at the time at which the letter would have been delivered in the ordinary course of post'. Pursuant to section 7, service is deemed to be effective by correctly addressing, pre-paying and posting the document.

4.41 When calculating the date when deemed service will take place, it is important to bear in mind that first class post aims to deliver post on the next working day after posting and second class aims to deliver within 2–3 working days. If relying on service by post, it is crucial to ensure sufficient time is allowed for service when calculating relevant dates referred to in the notice. This is because section 79(2) of the CLRA 2002 requires that a minimum of 14 days' notice be given by service of the NITP before a claim notice can be served. The 14 days is calculated from the date that the last relevant recipient is deemed served. The CLRA 2002 contains no deeming provisions for service by recorded delivery or registered post. The authors consider it unwise to use this method because any evidence of non-service may displace the deemed service provision available under section 7 of the Interpretation Act 1978 when serving by ordinary post.

4.42 The position regarding service of the NITP by email is not clear. Interestingly, in the case of *Assethold v 110 Boulevard RTM Co*,[14] the Upper Tribunal (Lands Chamber) considered that service of a copy of the claim notice on each qualifying tenant pursuant to section 79(8) of the CLRA 2002 by email was valid. This was on the basis that there is nothing in the Act which requires the copy to be a hard copy and the Act contemplates that a claim notice can be given other than by post.

OMISSIONS OR MISTAKES IN THE NOTICE OF INVITATION TO PARTICIPATE

4.43 Challenging a claim in the counter-notice is discussed in more detail in Chapter 5. Non-compliance with section 78 of the CLRA 2002 or regulations may be relied upon by the landlord when serving a counter-notice challenging the right to acquire the right to manage.

4.44 Before examining the relevant case law on non-compliant notices, the statutory saving provisions which apply to NITPs are commented on.

---

14 *Assethold v 110 Boulevard RTM Company* [2017] UKUT 316 (LC), [2017] 4 WLR 181.

STATUTORY SAVING PROVISIONS: NOTICE OF INVITATION TO PARTICIPATE

4.45 Section 78(7) of the CLRA 2002 contains the statutory saving provision relating to NITPs. It states as follows:

> (7) A notice of invitation to participate is not invalidated by any inaccuracy in any of the particulars required by or by virtue of this section.

4.46 On that basis, section 78(7) of the CLRA 2002 may cure certain inaccuracies. However, the saving provision is not generous. It is limited to any inaccuracy in any of the particulars required by virtue of section 78 and only provides relief against the consequence of 'inaccuracies'. More substantial defects in the NITP may not be saved and may invalidate the NITP.

4.47 In the case of *Triplerose Limited v Mill House RTM Company Limited*,[15] the Upper Tribunal (Lands Chamber) held that a failure to attach the prescribed notes to the NITP could not be saved by section 78(7) of the CLRA 2002. This was a separate failure to comply with the requirements as to the form of the NITP rather than an inaccuracy in the particulars required by section 78. The NITP served did not comply with section 78 and was found to be invalid. Consequently, the subsequent claim notice could not be served and the right to manage therefore could not be acquired. The Upper Tribunal determined that the RTM company was prohibited by section 79(2) from then giving a claim notice to acquire the right to manage because the NITP was invalid.

4.48 The decision in *Triplerose Limited v Mill House RTM Company Limited* and the other cases discussed below pre-date the decision in *A1 Properties*. In the first decision post-dating *A1 Properties*, *Avon Freeholds Limited v Cresta Court E RTM Company Limited*,[16] the Court of Appeal held that where an NITP was not served on a qualifying tenant then, pursuant to section 79(2), no valid claim notice could be given.

---

15 *Triplerose Limited v Mill House RTM Company Limited* [2016] UKUT 80 (LC), [2016] L & TR 23.

16 *Avon Freeholds Limited v Cresta Court E RTM Company Limited* [2025] EWCA Civ 1016.

4.49 In the case of *Assethold Limited v 13–24 Romside Place RTM Company Limited*,[17] on appeal the Upper Tribunal (Lands Chamber) reversed the Leasehold Valuation Tribunal's decision that the RTM company was entitled to acquire the right to manage. The RTM company had correctly served the NITP but incorrectly stated the landlord's name. The LVT had determined that the error did not invalidate the claim notice subsequently served. The Upper Tribunal allowed the landlord's appeal. It considered that the NITP failed to comply with the requirements of section 78(2)(d) of the CLRA 2002 and regulations. Whilst section 78(7) provides that the NITP will not be invalidated by any inaccuracy in the particulars, the Upper Tribunal did not consider the identification of the wrong landlord to be a mistake that was an inaccuracy. It was considered a complete omission to provide the required particulars. Therefore, the NITP could not be saved by section 78(7) and was invalid. Where no valid NITP has been served, any subsequent claim notice is invalid. It seems likely that, following *A1 Properties*, the correct analysis is that the claim notice would be voidable, but only at the instance of the qualifying tenants.

4.50 The prescribed form of NITP requires that the name and address of the recipient be stated. In the case of *Carlton Homes Southsea RTM Company Limited v Sinclair Gardens Investments (Kensington) Limited*,[18] it was held that a failure to include the name and address of the qualifying tenant on whom the notice is served will invalidate the NITP. However, the authors consider the position is unclear. This case is only at First-tier Tribunal (Property Chamber) level and is not consistent with *Lay v Ackerman*.[19] The authors consider that the test for validity is whether a reasonable person in the position of the recipient when he or she received the notice could have been in any doubt that the notice was intended for

---

17 *Assethold Limited v 13–24 Romside Place RTM Company Limited* [2013] UKUT 603 (LC), [2013] 11 WLUK 825.

18 *Carlton Homes Southsea RTM Company Limited v Sinclair Gardens Investments (Kensington) Limited*, CH1/00MR/LRM/2016/0014, FTT (PC), 9 March 2017, unreported.

19 *Lay v Ackerman* [2004] EWCA Civ 184, [2004] HLR 40.

him or her as per *Mannai Investment Company Limited v Eagle Star Assurance*.[20] In any event, it seems likely that, following *A1 Properties*, the correct analysis is that the claim notice would be voidable, but only at the instance of the qualifying tenants.

SERVING FRESH NOTICES OF INVITATION TO PARTICIPATE

4.51 If a valid NITP is served but a defective claim notice is served, then does a fresh NITP need to be served prior to a second claim notice? In the case of *Gateway Property Holdings v 6–10 Montrose Gardens RTM Company Limited*,[21] the Upper Tribunal (Lands Chamber) considered that question. It was held that it is only necessary to serve a new NITP before serving a new claim notice if the nature of the claim has changed such that the existing NITP is no longer compliant with section 78 of the CLRA 2002. It was considered that an alternative interpretation would lead to unnecessary and costly duplication.

RIGHT TO OBTAIN INFORMATION

4.52 The RTM company has a right under section 82 of the CLRA 2002 to serve notice seeking information that may be relevant to the claim and the claim notice. The right to information is confined to the information required for the particulars to the claim notice and does not permit wider discovery. The CLRA 2002 does not prescribe the timing for service. It is likely to be most relevant prior to service of the claim notice as it seeks particulars relevant when drafting the claim notice. Commentators have said that it could be served as soon as the RTM company is incorporated, and the authors do not disagree.

4.53 Section 82(1) of the CLRA 2002 states as follows:

> (1) A company which is an RTM company in relation to any premises may give to any person a notice requiring him to provide the company with any information—

---

20 *Mannai Investment Company Limited v Eagle Star Assurance* [1997] AC 749 (HL).

21 *Gateway Property Holdings v 6–10 Montrose Gardens RTM Company Limited* [2011] UKUT 349 (LC), [2011] 9 WLUK 127.

(a) which is in his possession or control, and
(b) which the company reasonably requires for ascertaining the particulars required by or by virtue of section 80 to be included in a claim notice for claiming to acquire the right to manage the premises.

4.54 Section 82(2) of the CLRA 2002 states as follows:

> (2) Where the information is recorded in a document in the person's possession or control, the RTM company may give him a notice requiring him—
>
> (a) to permit any person authorised to act on behalf of the company at any reasonable time to inspect the document (or, if the information is recorded in the document in a form in which it is not readily intelligible, to give any such person access to it in a readily intelligible form), and
> (b) to supply the company with a copy of the document containing the information in a readily intelligible form … .

4.55 Section 82(3) of the CLRA 2002 states as follows:

> (3) A person to whom a notice is given must comply with it within the period of 28 days beginning with the day on which it is given.

4.56 The notice may be given to any person, but it is considered that this applies to the landlord or the landlord's managing agent. Interestingly, section 82(1) of the CLRA 2002 narrowly defines the information that can be sought by restricting it to information required for the particulars in a claim notice.

4.57 Section 82(2) of the CLRA 2002 allows for the RTM company to give notice requiring inspection of documents recording relevant information or to supply a copy of the documents. A person to whom a notice is given must comply within 28 days beginning on the day on which notice it is given in accordance with section 82(3). There is no prescribed form of notice under section 82. Enforcement of such obligations is by order of the county court pursuant to an application made under section 107(1) but prior to making such application, the applicant must serve a notice in default pursuant to section 107(2) giving 14 days' notice to make good the default. Interestingly, section 82 contains no provision for costs incurred by the recipient in complying with the notice. New section 82(4) of the CLRA 2002 states that the RTM company is liable for the reasonable costs incurred by a person complying with the notice under section 82.[22] Any question arising in relation to the amount of the costs payable by the RTM company is, absent agreement, to be determined by the appropriate tribunal.[23]

COMMENCING A CLAIM BY SERVING A CLAIM NOTICE

4.58 Section 79(1) of the CLRA 2002 states as follows:

> (1) A claim to acquire the right to manage any premises is made by giving notice of the claim (referred to in this Chapter as a 'claim notice') and in this Chapter the 'relevant date', in relation to any claim to acquire the right to manage, means the date on which notice of the claim is given.

4.59 Section 79(2) of the CLRA 2002 states as follows:

> (2) The claim notice may not be given unless each person required to be given a notice of invitation to participate has been given such a notice at least 14 days before.

4.60 A claim to acquire the right to manage is made by giving notice (the 'claim notice') pursuant to section 79(1) of the CLRA 2002. Only RTM companies may give the claim notice. Section 79(1) states that the 'relevant date' in relation to any claim means the date on which the claim notice is given. See further on service of the claim notice at paras 4.63–4.69.

4.61 The relevant date under section 79(1) of the CLRA 2002 is the date that the claim notice is given. If served by hand, this is the date of service. If served by post, it is necessary to calculate the deemed date of service.

---

22 Section 82(4) was inserted by the Leasehold and Freehold Reform Act 2024, ss 50(2)(b) and 124 (3); Leasehold and Freehold Reform Act 2024 (Commencement No 3) Regulations 2025 (SI 2025/131), reg 2(b).

23 See above.

As per *Moskovitz v 75 Worple Road RTM Company Limited*,[24] when serving by post, the claim notice is 'given' under section 79(1) on the date when it would be deemed delivered in the ordinary course of post. The CLRA 2002 makes a distinction in respect of the relevant date being the date the claim notice is given to the landlord under section 79(6) not the date when copies are served on the qualifying tenants under section 79(8).

4.62 Regulation 8(2) of the 2010 England Regulations states that the claim notice shall be in the form set out in Schedule 2.[25] As with the NITP, in order to serve a valid claim notice, the RTM company must use the prescribed form in Schedule 2. It must also contain the additional content of claim notice as prescribed by regulation 4 and, when serving, must contain the information provided in the notes to the prescribed form in Schedule 2. This is discussed further and in more detail at paras 4.83–4.87.

WHEN CAN THE CLAIM NOTICE BE SERVED?

4.63 Section 79(3)–(5) of the CLRA 2002 states as follows:

> (3) The claim notice must be given by a RTM company which complies with subsection (4) or (5).
> (4) If on the relevant date there are only two qualifying tenants of flats contained in the premises, both must be members of the RTM company.
> (5) In any other case, the membership of the RTM company must on the relevant date include a number of qualifying tenants of flats contained in the premises which is not less than one-half of the total number of flats so contained.

4.64 At the relevant date the RTM company must meet certain conditions in respect of membership of the RTM company.

4.65 If there are only two qualifying tenants of flats in the building, then both must be members of the RTM company in order to comply with section 79(4) of the CLRA 2002. In any other case, membership of the

---

24 *Moskovitz v 75 Worple Road RTM Company Limited* [2010] UKUT 393 (LC), [2011] 1 EGLR 95.

25 Regulations for Wales being the 2011 Wales Regulations or the equivalent.

RTM company must include not less than half of the total number of flats in the premises (section 79(3)–(5)).

4.66 To ensure that the statutory requirements are met, the RTM company must complete the register of members detailing the names of those who have agreed to become members. This must be completed by the relevant date.[26]

4.67 In accordance with section 79(2) of the CLRA 2002, the claim notice cannot be given until 14 days after service of the NITP. In the first decision post-dating *A1 Properties*, *Avon Freeholds Limited v Cresta Court E RTM Company Limited*,[27] the Court of Appeal held that where an NITP was not served on a qualifying tenant then, pursuant to section 79(2), no valid claim notice could be given. In *Triplerose v Mill House RTM Company Limited*[28] the Upper Tribunal held that service of the claim notice before the expiry of the 14-day period will render the claim notice invalid.

4.68 The 14-day period runs from the date of service on the last non-member of the RTM company who is a qualifying tenant. The RTM company should allow a sufficient delay between the date of service on the NITP before service of the claim notice to ensure that the 14-day period is provided and to ensure all non-members have been served. If all qualifying tenants are already members of the RTM company, then service of an NITP and compliance with section 79(2) of the CLRA 2002 are not required.

---

26 See the decision of the Lands Tribunal in *Southall Court (Residents) Limited v Buy Your Freehold Limited*, LRX/124/2007, LT, 23 July 2008, unreported.

27 *Avon Freeholds Limited v Cresta Court E RTM Company Limited* [2025] EWCA Civ 1016.

28 *Triplerose v Mill House RTM Company Limited* [2016] UKUT 80 (LC), [2016] L & TR 23.

4.69 When considering the date for deemed service of the statutory notices under the CLRA 2002, please note that the Civil Procedure Rules 1997[29] do not apply, nor do they apply to service provisions within the equivalent Tribunal rules.

TO WHOM MUST THE CLAIM NOTICE BE GIVEN?

4.70 Section 79(6) of the CLRA 2002 states as follows:

> (6) The claim notice must be given to each person who on the relevant date is—
>
> (a) landlord under a lease of the whole or any part of the premises,
> (b) party to such a lease otherwise than as landlord or tenant, or
> (c) a manager appointed under Part 2 of the Landlord and Tenant Act 1987 (c. 31) (referred to in this Part as the '1987 Act') to act in relation to the premises, as any premises containing or contained in the premises.

4.71 On that basis, section 79(6) of the CLRA 2002 contains a clear obligation that the RTM company must give the actual claim notice to the landlord. This is different to the requirements in section 79(8) and (9) as explained in paras 4.76 and 4.77.

4.72 The question of compliance with section 79(6) of the CLRA 2002 including who should be served with the claim notice and the consequences of non-compliance was considered on appeal to the Upper Tribunal (Lands Chamber) in the case of *Lexham House RTM Company Limited v European Investments and Development (Properties) Limited.*[30]

4.73 The freehold landlord in this case had granted a 999-year lease of the roof of the property, including the roof space over which lessees of the top floor flats held easements. This lease was held by an associated company of the freeholder. When serving the claim notice, the RTM company served the freeholder alone and not the associated company

---

29 The Civil Procedure Rules 1997 were introduced by the Civil Procedure Act 1997. The rules are listed in the Civil Procedure Rules 1998 (SI 1998/3132).

30 *Lexham House RTM Company Limited v European Investments and Development (Properties) Limited* [2019] UKUT 390 (LC), [2019] 12 WLUK 290.

which held the lease of the roof. The issue before the Upper Tribunal was whether the claim notice complied with section 79(6)(a) of the CLRA 2002, which requires that the claim notice be given to each person who is a landlord under a lease of the whole or any part of the premises.

4.74 The Upper Tribunal (Lands Chamber) found that the associated company was a landlord in respect of the top floor flats. Accordingly, the Upper Tribunal held that the associated company should have been served with the claim notice. The question then was the consequences of non-compliance.

4.75 The Upper Tribunal (Lands Chamber) considered that the associated company had no practical involvement in the property and did not need to be informed of the RTM company's existence and intentions under the CLRA 2002, because the associated company was in the common ownership and control of the freeholder who had been served. On that basis, the Upper Tribunal considered that the requirements under section 79(6) had been sufficiently complied with. This would seem to be in line with the approach Tribunals ought to adopt in accordance with the principles set out in *A1 Properties*.

4.76 Section 79(8) of the CLRA 2002 requires that a *copy* of the claim notice must be given to each person who, on the relevant date, is the qualifying tenant of a flat in the premises. The definition of a qualifying tenant is found at section 75. A copy of the claim notice may be given by email, rather than a hard copy.[31] In *Alleyn Court RTM Company Limited v Abou Hamdan*,[32] it was held that a copy of the claim notice could be given to the qualifying tenants at a date later than the relevant date. This would seem to align with the principles set out in *A1 Properties*.

4.77 Section 79(9) of the CLRA 2002 requires that where a manager has been appointed under Part 2 of the Landlord and Tenant Act 1987 (LTA

---

31 *Assethold Limited v 110 Boulevard RTM Company Limited* [2017] UKUT 316 (LC), [2017] 4 WLR 181.

32 *Alleyn Court RTM Company Limited v Abou Hamdan* [2012] UKUT 74 (LC), [2012] PLSCS 107.

1987), a copy of the claim notice must also be given to the tribunal or court by which he was appointed. This is important because the manager is an officer of the court or tribunal and, following the acquisition of the right to manage, an order will need to be made ending that person's appointment as manager.

Missing parties

4.78 Section 79(7) of the CLRA 2002 states as follows:

> (7) Subsection (6) does not require the claim notice to be given to a person who cannot be found or whose identity cannot be ascertained; but if this subsection means that the claim notice is not required to be given to anyone at all, section 85 applies.

4.79 On that basis, the claim notice need not be given to an individual who cannot be found or where their identity cannot be ascertained. However, if by virtue of section 79(7) of the CLRA 2002, a claim notice is not required to be given to anyone, section 85 then applies, whereby an application must be made to the tribunal for an order that the RTM company is to acquire the right to manage the premises (section 85(2)).

4.80 Section 85 of the CLRA 2002 relates to landlords who cannot be traced. It requires the RTM company to apply to the tribunal for an order that the RTM company is to acquire the right to manage the premises. Section 85 sets out the steps to be taken in these circumstances under the CLRA 2002.

4.81 Section 85 of the CLRA 2002 states as follows:

> (1) This section applies where a RTM company wishing to acquire the right to manage premises—
>
> (a) complies with subsection (4) or (5) of section 79, and
> (b) would not have been precluded from giving a valid notice under that section with respect to premises,
>
> but cannot find, or ascertain the identity of, any of the persons to whom the claim notice would be required to be given by subsection (6) of that section.
>
> (2) The RTM company may apply to the appropriate tribunal for an order that the company is to acquire the right to manage the premises.

(3) Such an order may be made only if the company has given notice of the application to each person who is the qualifying tenant of a flat contained in the premises.

(4) Before an order is made the company may be required to take such further steps by way of advertisement or otherwise as is deemed proper for the purpose of tracing the persons who are—

(a) landlords under leases of the whole or any part of the premises, or

(b) parties to such leases otherwise than as landlord or tenant.

(5) If any of those persons is traced—

(a) after an application for an order is made, but

(b) before the making of an order,

no further proceedings shall be taken with a view to the making of an order.

(6) Where that happens—

(a) the rights and obligations of all persons concerned shall be determined as if the company had, at the date of the application, duly given notice under section 79 of its claim to acquire the right to manage the premises, and

(b) the … tribunal may give such directions as it thinks fit as to the steps to be taken for giving effect to their rights and obligations, including directions modifying or dispensing with any of the requirements imposed by or by virtue of this Chapter.

(7) An application for an order may be withdrawn at any time before an order is made and, after it is withdrawn, subsection (6)(a) does not apply.

(8) But where any step is taken for the purpose of giving effect to subsection (6)(a) in the case of any application, the application shall not afterwards be withdrawn except—

(a) with the consent of the person or persons traced, or

(b) the permission of the … tribunal.

(9) And permission shall be given only where it appears just that it should be given by reason of matters coming to the knowledge of the RTM company in consequence of the tracing of the person or persons traced.

4.82 See *Re 59 Asbury Road RTM Company Limited*[33] and *289 Beckenham Road Company Limited v McGrath*[34] for examples of applications under section 85 of the CLRA 2002.

FORM AND CONTENT OF THE CLAIM NOTICE

4.83 The form and content of the claim notice are prescribed by section 80 of the CLRA 2002 and by Schedule 2 to the 2010 England Regulations, as amended by the Transfer of Tribunal Functions Order 2013 (SI 2013/1036). Schedule 2 contains the prescribed form of claim notice which must be accurately completed in full before service. The prescribed form contained at Schedule 2 (including additional content prescribed by regulation 4) must be used in accordance with regulation 8(2) and served with the information provided in the notes to the form set out in Schedule 2 (the prescribed notes) (see regulation 4(e)). The prescribed form of claim notice at Schedule 2 is set out at para 4.85.

4.84 Section 80 of the CLRA 2002 states as follows:

> (1) The claim notice must comply with the following requirements.
> (2) It must specify the premises and contain a statement of the grounds on which it is claimed that they are premises to which this Chapter applies.
> (3) It must state the full name of each person who is both—
>
> (a) the qualifying tenant of the flat contained in the premises, and
> (b) a member of the RTM company
>
> and the address of his flat.
> (4) And it must contain, in relation to each such person, such particulars of his lease as are sufficient to identify it, including—
>
> (a) the date on which it was entered into,
> (b) the term for which it was granted, and
> (c) the date of the commencement of the term.

---

33 *Re 59 Asbury Road RTM Company Limited*, LON/00AF/LRM/2004/0045, LVT, no date, unreported.

34 *289 Beckenham Road Company Limited v McGrath*, LON/00AF/LEE/2014/1, FTT (PC), no date, unreported.

(5) It must state the name and registered office of the RTM company.
(6) It must specify a date, not earlier than one month after the relevant date, by which each person who has given the notice on section 79(6) may respond to it by giving a counter notice under section 84.
(7) It must specify a date, at least three months after that specified under subsection (6), on which the RTM company intends to acquire the right to manage the premises.
(8) It must also contain such other particulars (if any) as may be required to be contained in claim notices by regulations made by the appropriate national authority.
(9) And it must comply with such requirements (if any) about the form of claim notices as may be prescribed by regulations so made.

Schedule 2: Form of claim notice

4.85

RIGHT TO MANAGE (PRESCRIBED PARTICULARS AND FORMS) (ENGLAND) REGULATIONS 2010/825

SCHEDULE 2
FORM OF CLAIM NOTICE

To [*name and address*] (See Note 1 below)

1. [*Name of RTM company*] ('the company'), of [*address of registered office*], and of which the registered number is [*number under Companies Act 2006*], in accordance with Chapter 1 of Part 2 of the Commonhold and Leasehold Reform Act 2002 ('the 2002 Act') claims to acquire the right to manage [*name of premises to which notice relates*] ('the premises').

2. The company claims that the premises are ones to which Chapter 1 of the 2002 Act applies on the grounds that [*state grounds*]. (See Note 2 below)

3. The full names of each person who is both—

(a) the qualifying tenant of a flat contained in the premises, and

(b) a member of the company,

and the address of that person's flat are set out in Part 1 of the Schedule below.

4. There are set out, in Part 2 of the Schedule, in relation to each person named in Part 1 of the Schedule—

(a) the date on which that person's lease was entered into,
(b) the term for which it was granted,
(c) the date of commencement of the term
(d) *such other particulars of the lease as are necessary to identify it.

**may be ignored if no other particulars need to be given.*

5. If you are—

(a) landlord under a lease of the whole or any part of the premises,
(b) party to such a lease otherwise than as landlord or tenant, or
(c) a manager appointed under Part 2 of the Landlord and Tenant Act 1987 to act in relation to the premises, or any premises containing or contained in the premises,

you may respond to this claim notice by giving a counter-notice under section 84 of the 2002 Act. A counter-notice must be in the form set out in Schedule 3 to the Right to Manage (Prescribed Particulars and Forms) (England) Regulations 2010. It must be given to the company, at the address in paragraph 1, not later than [*specify date not earlier than one month after the date on which the claim notice is given*]. If you do not fully understand the purpose or implications of this notice you are advised to seek professional help.

6. The company intends to acquire the right to manage the premises

on [*specify date, being at least three months after that specified in paragraph 5*].

7. If you are a person to whom paragraph 5 applies and—

(a) you do not dispute the company's entitlement to acquire the right to manage; and
(b) you are the manager party under a management contract subsisting immediately before the date specified in this notice,

you must, in accordance with section 92 (duties to give notice of contracts) of the 2002 Act, give a notice in relation to the contract to the person who is the contractor party in relation to the contract and to the company. (See Note 3 below).

8. From the date on which the company acquires the right to manage the premises, landlords under leases of the whole or any part of the premises are entitled to be members of the company (See Note 4 below).

9. This notice is not invalidated by any inaccuracy in any of the particulars required by section 80(2) to (7) of the 2002 Act or regulation 5 of the Right to Manage (Prescribed Particulars and Forms) (England) Regulations 2010. If you are of the opinion that any of the particulars contained in the claim notice are inaccurate you may notify the company of the particulars in question, indicating the respects in which you think that they are inaccurate.

SCHEDULE

PART 1

Full names and addresses of persons who are both qualifying tenants and members of the company
[*set out here the particulars required by paragraph 3 above*]

PART 2

Particulars of leases of persons named in Part 1
[*set out here the particulars required by paragraph 4 above*]

Signed by authority of the company,
[*Signature of authorised member or officer*]

[*Insert date*]

NOTES

1. A claim notice (a notice in the form set out in Schedule 2 to the Right to Manage (Prescribed Particulars and Forms) (England) Regulations 2010 of a claim to exercise the right to manage specified premises) must be given to each person who, on the date on which the notice is given, is—

(a) landlord under a lease of the whole or any part of the premises to which the notice relates,
(b) party to such a lease otherwise than as landlord or tenant, or
(c) a manager appointed under Part 2 of the Landlord and Tenant Act 1987 to act in relation to the premises, or any premises containing or contained in the premises.

But notice need not be given to such a person if he cannot be found, or if his identity cannot be ascertained. If that means that there is no one to whom the notice must be given, the company may apply to a [...]* tribunal for an order that the company is to acquire the right to manage the premises. In that case, the procedures specified in section 85 of the 2002 Act (landlords etc not traceable) will apply.
2. The relevant provisions are contained in section 72 of the 2002 Act (premises to which Chapter 1 applies). The company is advised to consider, in particular, Schedule 6 to the 2002 Act (premises excepted from Chapter 1).
3. The terms 'management contract', 'manager party' and 'contractor party' are defined in section 91(2) of the 2002 Act (notices relating to management contracts).
4. Landlords under leases of the whole or any part of the premises are entitled to be members of the company, but only once the right to manage has been acquired by the company. An application for

membership may be made in accordance with the company's articles of association, which may be inspected at the company's registered office, free of charge, at any reasonable time.

AMENDMENTS

* Words revoked by Transfer of Tribunal Functions Order 2013 (SI 2013/1036), Sch 2(1), para 43 (1 July 2013: revocation has effect subject to transitional provisions and savings specified in SI 2013/1036, art 6(3) and Sch 3).

Checklist 4.2: Claim notice – contents

4.86 Contents of the claim notice under section 80 of the CLRA 2002:

- Specify the premises and include a statement of the grounds on which it is claimed that they are premises to which the Chapter applies (section 80(2)).
- State the full name of each person who is both the qualifying tenant of a flat contained in the premises and a member of the RTM company and the address of the flat (section 80(3)).
- For each qualifying tenant identified under section 80(3), state the particulars of their lease of the flat as are sufficient to identify it including:

  - the date on which it was entered into,
  - the term for which it was granted, and
  - the commencement date of the term (section 80(4)).

- State the name and registered office of the RTM company (section 80(5)).
- Specify a date, not earlier than one month after the relevant date, by which each person who was given the notice under section 79(6) may respond to it by giving a counter-notice under section 84 (section 80(6)).
- Specify a date, at least 3 months after that specified under section 79(6), on which the RTM company intends to acquire the right contained to manage the premises (section 80(7)).
- Include such other particulars (if any) as may be required to be in claim notices by regulations made by the appropriate national

authority (section 80(8)). This includes the prescribed list of further particulars in regulation 4 of the 2010 England Regulations which must be included in the claim notice and is included in the wording of the prescribed form.

- Comply with such requirements (if any) about the form of claim notice as may be prescribed by regulations so made (section 80(9)) (use the prescribed form contained in Schedule 2 to the 2010 England Regulations, or equivalent, including prescribed notes).

Checklist 4.3: Claim notice – relevant recipients

4.87 Relevant recipients of the claim notice under section 79(6) of the CLRA 2002:

- All relevant landlords.
- Third parties (for example guarantors).
- A manager appointed under the LTA 1987.
- Relevant recipients of copies of the claim notice under section 79(8) and (9) of the CLRA 2002.
- All qualifying tenants in the premises (copy only required).
- Where a manager has been appointed under the LTA 1987, the tribunal or court which appointed the manager (copy only required).

PREMISES AND APPURTENANT PROPERTY

4.88 The claim notice must comply with section 80(2) of the CLRA 2002 by clearly specifying the premises claimed and a statement of the grounds on which it is claimed that it is premises to which the CLRA 2002 applies. This is to ensure that it is clear to recipients the extent of the premises claimed.

4.89 Likewise, whilst the claim notice must give details of the qualifying premises, it is not necessary for it to state that there is any property appurtenant to the building or part of the building over which the right to manage is claimed. If there is reference to appurtenant property, it is not necessary to state what that property is. The CLRA 2002 and regulations only require that the premises be named. In fact, there is authority that there is no requirement for appurtenant property to be referred to in the claim notice at all, whether by plan or otherwise.[35]

4.90 In the Supreme Court decision in the case of *Firstport Property Services Limited v Settlers Court RTM Company Limited*,[36] on appeal from the Upper Tribunal (Lands Chamber),[37] the court had to decide to what extent an RTM company in respect of a single building on a wider estate acquires the right to manage wider estate facilities shared with leaseholders of other blocks on the estate. The Supreme Court held that an RTM company acquires the right to manage only the relevant building together with nearby property over which the leaseholders of the relevant building have exclusive rights. This decision overruled the earlier Court of Appeal authority on this question in the case of *Gala Unity Ariadne Road RTM Company Limited*.[38]

4.91 The Supreme Court decision makes clear that the CLRA 2002 confers rights to manage the block and not the wider estate. The CLRA 2002 makes no provision for how to deal effectively with management of shared facilities and relevant disputes arising in respect of services, which indicated the RTM company was not intended to get management functions over the wider estate. The earlier decision in *Gala Unity* had led to absurd results, so the Supreme Court's decision brings clarity on this point, namely that in these circumstances the RTM company will manage the relevant building/block and functions relating to land which exclusively serves that block/building, for example, a private garden or car park. It will not exercise management functions over any other land.

---

[35] See *Miltonland Limited v Platinum House (Harrow) RTM Company Limited* [2015] UKUT 236 (LC), [2016] L & TR 9, as subsequently followed in *Q Studios (Stoke) RTM Company Limited v Premier Ground Rents No 6 Limited and Another* [2020] UKUT 197 (LC), [2021] L & TR 9.

[36] *Firstport Property Services Limited v Settlers Court RTM Company Limited* [2022] UKSC 1, [2022] 1 WLR 519.

[37] *Firstport Property Services Limited v Settlers Court RTM Company Limited* [2019] UKUT 243 (LC), [2019] 8 WLUK 77.

[38] *Gala Unity Ariadne Road RTM Company Limited* [2012] EWCA Civ 1372, [2013] 1 WLR 988.

MULTIPLE PREMISES

4.92 In the case of *Triplerose v Ninety Broomfield Road RTM Company Limited*,[39] the Court of Appeal held that a single RTM company cannot exercise a right to manage over more than one set of premises. It considered that the right applies only to a single self-contained building or part of a building and it was not open to an RTM company to acquire the right to manage more than one self-contained building or part of a building.

4.93 For further commentary on inaccuracies in the claim notice, see the discussion at paras 4.116–4.129.

COUNTER-NOTICE

Deadline for service of the counter-notice

4.94 As per section 80(6) of the CLRA 2002, the claim notice must specify a date for the landlord's counter-notice, which must be not less than one month after service of the claim notice. In the case of *Moskowitz v 75 Worple Road RTM Company*,[40] the Upper Tribunal (Lands Chamber) held that the claim notice was invalid as the date specified for service of the counter-notice was less than one month after service of the claim notice. Following *A1 Properties*, there seems a good argument that a failure of this sort might be within the doctrine of substantial compliance, so that in a case where, for example, the landlord still served a counter-notice, then the short notice in the claim form might be overlooked.

4.95 The well-established corresponding date rule has been held to apply to section 80(7) of the CLRA 2002[41] and almost certainly applies to section 80(6). The rule is that where notice is counted in months, the period of notice ends on the day of the month bearing the same number as that on which the notice was given. As per section 80(6), the date stated must be not less than one month 'after' service of the claim form.

---

39 *Triplerose v Ninety Broomfield Road RTM Company Limited* [2015] EWCA Civ 282, [2016] 1 WLR 275.

40 *Moskowitz v 75 Worple Road RTM Company* [2010] UKUT 393 (LC), [2011] 1 EGLR 95.

41 *Windermere Court Kenley RTM Company Limited v Sinclair Gardens Investments (Kensington) Limited* [2014] UKUT 420 (LC), [2014] 9 WLUK 408.

Therefore, if the notice was given on 30 September, the date stated for service of the counter-notice may not be prior to 31 October.

Calculating the date for the counter-notice

4.96 The claim notice must also specify the acquisition date, being the date on which the RTM company proposes to take over management of the premises (section 80(7) of the CLRA 2002). This must be at least 3 months after the date for the landlord's counter-notice. For further comments on the commencement date for acquisition, see paras 4.135–4.139. The corresponding date rule applies.[42]

SERVICE OF THE CLAIM NOTICE

4.97 Section 111(1)(b) of the CLRA 2002 allows for service by post. This is not a mandatory method. The authors suggest service by hand and post, retaining evidence in case of a dispute.

Service of the claim notice on intermediate landlords

4.98 Section 79(6) of the CLRA 2002 states as follows:

> (6) The claim notice must be given to each person who on the relevant date is—
>
> (a) landlord under a lease of the whole or any part of the premises,
> (b) party to such a lease otherwise than as landlord or tenant, or
> (c) a manager appointed under Part 2 of the Landlord and Tenant Act 1987 (c. 31) (referred to in this Part as the '1987 Act') to act in relation to the premises, or any premises containing or contained in the premises.

4.99 In *A1 Properties (Sunderland) Limited v Tudor Studios RTM Company Limited*,[43] the Supreme Court held that a failure to serve a claim notice on an intermediate landlord as required by section 79(6)(a) of the

42 *Windermere Court Kenley RTM Company Limited v Sinclair Gardens Investments (Kensington) Limited* [2014] UKUT 420 (LC), [2014] 9 WLUK 408.

43 *A1 Properties (Sunderland) Limited v Tudor Studios RTM Company Limited* [2024] UKSC 27, [2025] AC 1075.

CLRA 2002 did not automatically invalidate the notice. Such a failure *might* make the claim notice voidable by the unserved intermediate landlord (per Lord Briggs at [91]–[92]):

> 91. ... the question to be addressed is whether a relevant party has been deprived of a significant opportunity to have their opposition to the making of an order to transfer the right to manage considered, having regard to (a) what objections they could have raised and would have wished to raise and (b) whether, despite the procedural omission, they in fact had the opportunity to have their objections considered in the course of the process leading to the making of the order to transfer the right to manage. If there was no substantive objection which they could have raised or would have wished to raise, they have lost nothing of significance so far as the regime is concerned and the inference is that Parliament intended that the transfer of the right to manage should be effective notwithstanding the omission. If their objection has in fact been considered in the process, even though the claim notice was not served at the proper time, again they have lost nothing of significance so far as the regime is concerned and the inference as to Parliament's intention is the same.
>
> 92. In both cases, the focus is on the position of the party directly affected by the procedural omission. The omission does not give other persons who are not so affected (for example, other landlords who have been properly served with a claim notice) a right to object to the making of a transfer order if the party who is so affected has not sought to complain about this.

4.100 The right to challenge the validity of the notice on grounds of non-service may also be lost by waiver.

Service of the claim notice on agents

4.101 In the case of *32 Southend Crescent RTM Company Limited v Vergara Properties Limited*,[44] a claim notice was addressed to the managing agent and not the landlord. The Tribunal considered whether a valid claim notice had been served in compliance with section 80 of the CLRA 2002. It considered that section 79(6)(b) is intended to allow service of a claim notice to be effected on a non-contractual party to a lease acting on a landlord's behalf and therefore the section allowed for valid service by this route. It is considered that the relevant question is whether the agent in question had authority to receive the claim notice.

---

44 *32 Southend Crescent RTM Company Limited v Vergara Properties Limited*, LON/00AL/LOA/2005/0002, no date, unreported.

4.102 Likewise, in *Plintal SA v 36–48A Edgewood Drive RTM Company Limited*,[45] the Lands Tribunal held that the claim notice had been validly given under section 79 of the CLRA 2002 so long as it could be shown to have been received. In that case the claim notices were given to the landlord's agents in the United Kingdom and this was good service even though the registered office was in Panama.

Service on third parties

4.103 This is a further obligation under section 79(6)(b) of the CLRA 2002, which applies, for example, to a management company or surety. This should not be overlooked to ensure compliance. Likewise, as per section 79(6)(c), any manager appointed under Part 2 of the LTA 1987 must be served.

Address for counter-notice stated in the claim notice

4.104 In the Upper Tribunal (Lands Chamber) case of *Triplerose Limited v Mill House RTM Company*,[46] it was held that there was nothing in the statutory regime to prohibit the RTM company from specifying an alternative address for service to the company's registered office and, therefore, inserting the address of the landlord's solicitors did not invalidate the claim notice. Section 80(5) of the CLRA 2002 requires that the contents of the claim notice must state the name and registered office of the RTM company. However, this section does not require the counter-notice to be served at this address, and section 84 (which deals with counter-notices) does not require that the counter-notice be served at the RTM company's registered office.

Address for service on landlords

4.105 An RTM company may serve notices on a landlord at the address last given to a member of the company as that landlord's address for service in accordance with section 48 of the LTA 1987 or, if no such address has been given, the address on rent or service charge demands (section 111(2)–(3) of the CLRA 2002), but the RTM company may not

---

[45] *Plintal SA v 36–48A Edgewood Drive RTM Company Limited*, LRX/16/2007, LT, 5 March 2008, unreported.

[46] *Triplerose Limited v Mill House RTM Company* [2016] UKUT 80 (LC), [2016] L & TR 23.

give a notice at such an address if it has 'been notified by him of a different address in England and Wales at which he wishes to be given any such notice' (section 111(4)). Two cases have explored what amounts to sufficient notification under section 111(4). In the case of *Gateway Property Holdings Limited v Ross Wharf RTM Company Limited*,[47] an earlier RTM claim (claim 1) and a counter-notice had been served which stated that future communications in respect of the claim should be sent to the landlord at the landlord's solicitor's address. Claim 1 was subsequently withdrawn. Thereafter, the landlord served service charge demands containing notices under sections 47 and 48 of the LTA 1987, giving the landlord's address for service of notices as its registered office.

4.106 A second claim to acquire the right to manage the premises was commenced (claim 2). The claim notice was served at the landlord company's registered office, being the address specified in the section 47 and section 48 notices. The landlord sought to argue that the second claim notice should have been given to the landlord at the solicitors' address stated in the counter-notice relating to claim 1.

4.107 The Upper Tribunal (Lands Chamber) rejected that argument. It considered that the claim 2 notice was validly given. The solicitors' address related to claim 1 only and notices had subsequently been given under sections 47 and 48 of the LTA 1987 informing the tenants that the address for service was the landlord's registered office. Service of the claim notice at the landlord's registered office had been identified without qualification or restriction, and reliance on that address was not restricted by section 111 of the CLRA 2002 because no different address had been identified by the landlord to the RTM company as its address for future claims under the CLRA 2002.

4.108 In the case of *Assethold Limited v 429 New Cross Road RTM Company Limited*,[48] there were again two claim notices. The RTM company served the first claim notice and then served a withdrawal notice simultaneous with a second claim notice. Both claim notices were served on the appellant's offices. A counter-notice to the first claim notice had

---

[47] *Gateway Property Holdings Limited v Ross Wharf RTM Company Limited* [2016] UKUT 97 (LC), [2016] L & TR 15.

[48] *Assethold Limited v 429 New Cross Road RTM Company Limited* [2024] UKUT 113 (LC), [2024] 5 WLUK 302.

specified the appellants' solicitors' address as an address at which 'future communications concerning the subject matter of the [claim] notice' should be served.

4.109 That wording was sufficient to mandate that address pursuant to section 111(4) of the CLRA 2002, and accordingly the notice of withdrawal of the first claim notice was not served at the correct address. This decision pre-dates *A1 Properties* and proceeds, wrongly, on the basis that 'substantial compliance' is irrelevant.

WHO CAN SIGN THE CLAIM NOTICE?

4.110 Section 79(3) of the CLRA 2002 states as follows:

> (3) The claim notice must be given by a RTM company which complies with subsection (4) and (5).

4.111 The statutory requirements in the CLRA 2002 do not require the claim notice to be signed by the RTM company itself. Likewise, the 2010 England Regulations contain no such requirement. The prescribed form contains a requirement for a signature, but this only requires that the claim notice be signed 'by authority' of the RTM company, and it was noted by the Court of Appeal in *Elim Court RTM Company Limited v Avon Freeholds Limited*[49] that there is no explicit requirement for the claim notice to be signed by anyone in particular.

4.112 In the *Elim* appeals, the Upper Tribunal (Lands Chamber) and subsequently the Court of Appeal considered the question of who can sign the claim notice and, on the facts in the case, whether it was effectively signed in accordance with the CLRA 2002. The landlord challenged the validity of the claim notice on the basis that it was not signed in accordance with the statutory requirements for execution by a company under section 44 of the Companies Act 2006. (See the facts of the case, as recited at para 4.12.)

4.113 The Upper Tribunal (Lands Chamber) considered the requirements in section 44(2) of the Companies Act 2006 where the claim notice had

---

49 *Elim Court RTM Company Limited v Avon Freeholds Limited* [2017] EWCA Civ 89, [2018] QB 571.

been signed using the single signature of one of the company directors. It considered whether the signature was given in the individual's personal capacity or as that of the secretarial company of which the signatory was the director. It considered that section 44(2) had not been satisfied in order to have been validly signed on behalf of the secretarial company. However, the director had signed with his own name and had authority to sign claim notices on behalf of the RTM company (as director of each). On that basis, the requirement under the CLRA 2002 that a claim notice must be signed by someone who has the authority of the company and is an authorised member or officer had been satisfied and the claim notice was valid. The Court of Appeal agreed.

4.114 In the case of *Pineview v 83 Crampton Street RTM Company Limited*,[50] the Upper Tribunal (Lands Chamber) determined that a claim notice was not invalidated on the basis that it was signed by the RTM company's solicitor or authorised agent. Likewise, in the case of *Assethold Limited v 14 Stansfield Road RTM Company Limited*,[51] the Upper Tribunal held that it was sufficient for the signatory simply to have the authority of the RTM company to sign the claim notice. He or she did not need to be a member or officer of the RTM company.

WHEN IS THE CLAIM NOTICE GIVEN?

4.115 As explained at paras 4.60–4.61, section 79(1) states that the relevant date in relation to any claim means the date on which the claim notice is given. If served by hand, this is straightforward to calculate. However, if served by post, the claim notice will be treated as 'given' on the date when the notice would be determined in the ordinary course of post. See the Upper Tribunal (Lands Chamber) decision in *Moskowitz v 75 Worple Road RTM Company*.[52]

---

50 *Pineview v 83 Crampton Street RTM Company Limited* [2013] UKUT 598 (LC), [2014] 1 EGLR 65.

51 *Assethold Limited v 14 Stansfield Road RTM Company Limited* [2012] UKUT 262 (LC), [2014] 43 EG 115 (CS).

52 *Moskowitz v 75 Worple Road RTM Company* [2010] UKUT 393 (LC), [2011] 1 EGLR 95.

4.116 Calculating when the claim notice will be given is very important in order to calculate accurately the appropriate deadline for the counter-notice to be inserted in the claim notice.

INACCURACIES IN THE CLAIM NOTICE

4.117 Section 81(1) of the CLRA 2002 contains the saving provision that relates to claim notices. It states as follows:

> (1) A claim notice is not invalidated by any inaccuracy in any of the particulars required by or by virtue of section 80.

4.118 Section 81(2) of the CLRA 2002 states as follows:

> (2) Where any of the members of the RTM company whose names are stated in the claim notice was not the qualifying tenant of a flat contained in the premises on the relevant date, the claim notice is not invalidated on that account, so long as a sufficient number of qualifying tenants of flats contained in the premises were members of the company on that date; and for this purpose a 'sufficient number' is a number (greater than one) which is not less than one-half of the total number of flats contained in the premises on that date.

4.119 Section 81(3) of the CLRA 2002 states as follows:

> (3) Where any premises have been specified in a claim notice, no subsequent claim notice which specifies—
>
> (a) the premises, or
> (b) any premises containing or contained in the premises,
>
> may be given so long as the earlier claim notice continues in force.

4.120 This was illustrated in the case of *Brixton Hill RTM Company v Springquote Limited*.[53]

4.121 Section 81(4) of the CLRA 2002 states as follows:

---

[53] *Brixton Hill RTM Company Limited v Springquote Limited*, LON/00AY/LRM/2013/00013, no date, unreported.

(4) Where a claim notice is given by an RTM company it continues in force from the relevant date until the right to manage is acquired by the company unless it has previously—

(a) been withdrawn or deemed to be withdrawn by virtue of any provision of this Chapter, or
(b) ceased to have effect by reason of any other provision of this Chapter.

4.122 The saving provision in section 81(1) of the CLRA 2002 provides that a claim notice is not invalidated by any inaccuracy in the particulars required in section 80 or regulations. 'Particulars' means all the matters listed in section 80(2)–(7). However, a failure to comply with the mandatory requirements in section 79 and section 80 or regulations will likely invalidate the claim notice.

4.123 The current approach of the courts and tribunals relating to the validity of notices is examined at paras 4.9–4.16 and must be equally borne in mind in the context of claim notices. Earlier decisions relating specifically to claim notices to illustrate particular issues on validity that may arise are summarised in paras 4.124–4.131. However, decisions which pre-date *A1 Properties* must be treated with care as they may not be consistent with the guidelines set in that case.

4.124 The case of *Ellithom RTM Company Limited v Landpoint Limited*[54] is an example of the saving provisions being applied. It was submitted that the claim notice was defective because it should have read that the premises claimed 'consist of a self-contained part of a building' rather than 'consist of a self-contained building'. The Leasehold Valuation Tribunal (as it was then) determined section 81(1) of the CLRA 2002 applied so as not to invalidate the claim notice by virtue of an inaccuracy in any of the particulars required by section 80. As a result, even if the claim notice was defective, it was still valid as it was saved by section 81(1).

4.125 In the case of *Assethold Limited v 15 Yonge Park RTM Company Limited*,[55] the Upper Tribunal (Lands Chamber) considered section 81(1)

---

[54] *Ellithom RTM Company Limited v Landpoint Limited*, CHI/29 UN/LOA/2004/0002, LVT, no date, unreported.

[55] *Assethold Limited v 15 Yonge Park RTM Company Limited* [2011] UKUT 379 (LC), [2011] 9 WLUK 546.

of the CLRA 2002. It held that the section could not render valid a claim notice which stated an entirely wrong address for the RTM company's registered office. This was a breach of the statutory requirements. It emphasised the narrow interpretation of 'inaccuracy' referred to in section 81(1), whereby an inaccuracy was intended to deal with, for example, typographical errors, spelling mistakes, etc. In a further case of *Assethold Limited v 14 Stansfield Road RTM Co*,[56] the Upper Tribunal made the distinction between the failure to provide the required particulars and an inaccuracy in the statement of the particulars. It will only be in the case of the latter that a claim notice may be saved from invalidity by virtue of section 81(1). It held that all the information required by section 80(2)–(7) was 'particulars' for the purposes of section 81(1). *Assethold Limited v 15 Yonge Park RTM Company Limited*[57] applied and *Moskovitz v 75 Worple Road RTM Company Limited*[58] was not followed on this point. The claim notice used differed from the one required in the regulations and this raised an argument on validity. The inaccuracy was limited. It amounted to a reference to the earlier Right to Manage (Prescribed Particulars and Forms) (England) Regulations 2003 (SI 2003/1988) instead of the 2010 England Regulations, and the Companies Act 1985 instead of the Companies Act 2006. The Upper Tribunal held there was no material difference between the form used and the required form, and the error was an inaccuracy for the purpose of section 81(1).

4.126 In the case of *Brixton Hill RTM Company v Springquote Limited*,[59] the First-tier Tribunal (Property Chamber) determined that the omission of two tenants from the claim notice had the effect of invalidating the claim notice, where section 80(3) of the CLRA 2002 requires that the claim notice must state the full name of each person who is both a qualifying tenant of a flat and a member of the RTM company. The saving provisions could not rescue this mistake.

4.127 One must be careful to distinguish between a failure to provide one of the particulars required by the CLRA 2002 or comply with the statutory

---

56 *Assethold Limited v 14 Stansfield Road RTM Company* [2012] UKUT 262 (LC), [2014] 43 EG 115 (CS).

57 *Assethold Limited v 15 Yonge Park RTM Company Limited* [2011] UKUT 379 (LC), [2011] 9 WLUK 546.

58 *Moskovitz v 75 Worple Road RTM Company Limited* [2010] UKUT 393 (LC), [2011] 1 EGLR 95.

59 *Brixton Hill RTM Company Limited v Springquote Limited*, LON/00AY/LRM/2013/00013, FTT (PC), no date, unreported.

requirements in respect of the form of notice and including information or a statement in the required particulars that is inaccurate. If the main substance of the information required to be provided has been given, an inaccuracy in the material is unlikely to render the claim notice invalid, but it is likely that if, reading the claim notice as a whole, there has been a total failure to provide a required piece of information, that failure will not be a mere 'inaccuracy' and therefore could render the claim notice void.

4.128 The case of *Marina Court (Paignton) RTM Company Limited v Gibbs*[60] determined that a failure to provide the names of the tenants who were members of the RTM company (section 80(3) of the CLRA 2002) would invalidate the claim notice.

4.129 In the case of *Miltonland Limited v Platinum House (Harrow) RTM Company Limited*,[61] the claim notice wrongly included a claim over land that could not form part of the RTM claim. The Upper Tribunal (Lands Chamber) held this was not an inaccuracy in the particulars required and could not be saved by section 81(1) of the CLRA 2002 as the claim wrongly included land that could not be subject to the right to manage. However, the case also held that a reference to land by mistake was an inaccuracy that could be saved by section 81(1). The case also held that it is not necessary to specify appurtenant property.

Failure to include the prescribed notes

4.130 In the case of *18 Langdale Road RTM Company Limited v Assethold Limited*,[62] failure to include note 1 in relation to a missing landlord was held not to invalidate the notice. The information within that note would rarely be needed and its omission was unlikely to cause any prejudice.

---

60 *Marina Court (Paignton) RTM Company Limited v Gibbs*, CH1/00HN/LRM/2004/0003, LVT, no date, unreported.

61 *Miltonland Limited v Platinum House (Harrow) RTM Company Limited* [2015] UKUT 236 (LC), [2016] L & TR 9.

62 *18 Langdale Road RTM Company Limited v Assethold Limited* [2022] UKUT 215 (LC), [2023] L & TR 1.

4.131 In the case of *Triplerose Limited v Mill House RTM Company Limited*,[63] which related to a failure to attach the notes to the NITP, this was held to invalidate the NITP. The approach in this decision suggests that a failure to likewise attach the prescribed notes to the claim notice may invalidate it, but the proper approach following *A1 Properties* would be to consider whether there had been substantial compliance and whether any prejudice had been caused.

CONSEQUENCE OF SERVICE OF THE CLAIM NOTICE

4.132 Unless a valid counter-notice is served challenging the validity of the claim notice, the RTM company will be acquired on the date specified in the claim notice being the acquisition date. The CLRA 2002 does not allow concurrent claims in respect of the same building. Where the right to manage has been claimed in respect of a building pursuant to a claim notice that remains in force, no subsequent claim notice may be given in respect of the building. Likewise, once a claim notice has been served, it remains in force until the acquisition date unless it is withdrawn or deemed withdrawn or ceases to have effect (see section 81(4)). A claim notice ceases to have effect if it is determined by the tribunal that the RTM company was not entitled to acquire the right to manage at the appropriate date (see section 84(6)). Such a determination becomes final at the end of the period for bringing an appeal (or further appeal) if no such appeal is brought. If it is appealed against, a determination becomes final when the appeal (or any future appeal) is disposed of. As to when an appeal is disposed of, this means where it is determined under the period for bringing an appeal or any further appeal has ended or in circumstances where the appeal is discontinued or otherwise ceases to have effect (see section 84(7) and (8)). Section 81(3) provides that no subsequent claim notice can be served in respect of the premises whilst a valid claim notice continues in force.

---

63 *Triplerose Limited v Mill House RTM Company Limited* [2016] UKUT 80 (LC), [2016] L & TR 23.

IS IT NECESSARY TO WITHDRAW AN INVALID CLAIM NOTICE?

4.133 In the case of *Avon Freeholds v Regent Court RTM Company*,[64] it was common ground that the first claim notice was invalid. The issue before the Upper Tribunal (Lands Chamber) was: did the first claim notice prevent a subsequent claim notice from being served? It was held that it did not. As the first claim notice was invalid, it had no legal effect and therefore it did not need to be withdrawn prior to a second claim notice being effected.

4.134 Section 86 of the CLRA 2002 states that a notice of withdrawal must be given to the landlord and each qualifying tenant of a flat contained in the premises. In the case of *Eastern Pyramid Group Corp SA v Spire House RTM Company Limited*,[65] the notice of withdrawal was not given to each qualifying tenant as it should have been, but the Court of Appeal considered that this failure did not invalidate the subsequent fresh claim notice served.

COMMENCEMENT DATE FOR ACQUISITION

4.135 The claim notice must clearly state a date under section 80(7) of the CLRA 2002 for commencement of the right to manage. Section 80(7) states in respect of the claim notice as follows:

> (7) It must specify a date, at least three months after that specified under subsection (6), on which the RTM company intends to acquire the right to manage the premises.

4.136 The date in section 80(6) of the CLRA 2002 is a reference to the date for service of the counter-notice, whereby it must state a date not earlier than one month after the claim notice is given for service of the counter-notice in accordance with section 84. Counter-notices under the CLRA 2002 are discussed in Chapter 5. The date for service of the counter-notice is calculated from the date when service of the claim notice

---

64 *Avon Freeholds v Regent Court RTM Company* [2013] UKUT 213 (LC), [2013] L & TR 23.

65 *Eastern Pyramid Group Corp SA v Spire House RTM Company Limited* [2021] EWCA Civ 1658, [2022] 1 WLR 503.

is effected on the last person required to be served under the CLRA 2002. The authors suggest that when calculating the date to insert in the claim notice, care is taken to calculate the time required to complete service on all relevant recipients, and it is sensible to add some additional time by way of a buffer in case there are delays in completing service. Specifying a date of less than one month in the claim notice will invalidate it. Likewise, failure to comply with section 80(7) will invalidate the claim notice. When calculating the acquisition date, the Upper Tribunal (Lands Chamber) in the case of *Windermere Court Kenley RTM Company Limited v Sinclair Gardens Investments (Kensington) Limited*[66] held that the 'corresponding date rule' applied to the date specified under section 87.

4.137 As discussed in Chapter 5, in circumstances where no counter-notice is served disputing the right to manage by the deadline inserted in the claim notice, section 90(2) of the CLRA 2002 states that this will be the date when the right to manage is acquired and management responsibilities are transferred to the RTM company.

4.138 In the case of *3 Kings Road Westcliffe Essex RTM Company Limited v Westleigh Properties Limited*,[67] the claim notice failed to state a date for the commencement of management and accordingly was held to be an invalid claim.

4.139 The CLRA 2002 ensures there is a minimum of 4 months between service of the claim notice and the acquisition date, and so long as the minimum 4 months' notice is given, there is nothing to stop the RTM company stating a longer period to ensure it has sufficient time to make the necessary arrangements to take over management and ensure management commences conveniently in the service charge calendar or after relevant works have been completed.

---

66 *Windermere Court Kenley RTM Company Limited v Sinclair Gardens Investments (Kensington) Limited* [2014] UKUT 420 (LC), [2014] 9 WLUK 408.

67 *3 Kings Road Westcliffe Essex RTM Company Limited v Westleigh Properties Limited*, CAM/00KF/LRM/2005/0001, LVT, no date, unreported.

Chapter 5

Procedure Following Service of the Claim Notice

SUMMARY

5.1 This chapter examines the procedural steps following service of the claim notice in advance of the right to manage being acquired. The chapter focuses on the provisions in sections 83–94 of the Commonhold and Leasehold Reform Act 2002 (CLRA 2002). Service of a valid claim notice under section 79 gives rise to a series of important practical consequences for both the RTM company and the landlord. These include a right to obtain information, a right to access the premises and a statutory requirement on the landlord, manager or third party to serve 'contractor notices' and 'contract notices' in respect of existing management contracts in the premises. There is also a duty to provide information. Likewise, those in receipt of the claim notice must elect whether to serve a counter-notice. These steps are considered in turn.

5.2 Whilst the claim notice remains in force, section 81(3) of the CLRA 2002 states that no further claim notices relating to the premises or any part of the premises may be served. Likewise, the claim notice continues in force from the 'relevant date' (section 79(1)), being the date on which the claim notice is given, until the right to manage is acquired by the RTM company unless it is withdrawn or is deemed withdrawn or ceases to have effect (section 81(4)).

RIGHT OF ACCESS

5.3 The provision relating to rights of access is contained at section 83 of the CLRA 2002. This states as follows:

> (1) Where a RTM company has given a claim notice in relation to any premises, each of the persons specified in subsection (2) has a right of access to any part of the premises if that is reasonable in connection with any matter arising out of the claim to acquire the right to manage.
>
> (2) The persons referred to in subsection (1) are—
>
> (a) any person authorised to act on behalf of the RTM company,
> (b) any person who is landlord under a lease of the whole or any part of the premises and any person authorised to act on behalf of any such person,
> (c) any person who is party to such a lease otherwise than as landlord or tenant and any person authorised to act on behalf of any such person, and
> (d) any manager appointed under Part 2 of the 1987 Act to act in relation to the premises, or any premises containing or contained in the premises, and any person authorised to act on behalf of any such manager.
>
> (3) The right conferred by this section is exercisable, at any reasonable time, on giving not less than ten days' notice—
>
> (a) to the occupier of any premises to which access is sought, or
> (b) if those premises are unoccupied, to the person entitled to occupy them.

5.4 Following service of the claim notice, the RTM company has a right of access to any part of the premises on giving not less than 10 days' notice so long as access is reasonably required in relation to any aspect of the claim to acquire the right to manage. This is likely to be important to the RTM company in order to inspect the state of repair and condition of the premises including any plant or machinery (for example lifts, communal boilers).

5.5 If there is a dispute as to access, a party may apply to the 'appropriate tribunal' for an order that access to the premises be given by making an application for an order under section 107(1) of the CLRA 2002. This states as follows:

> (1) The appropriate tribunal may, on the application of any person interested, make an order requiring a person who has failed to comply with a requirement imposed on him by, under or by virtue of any provision of this Chapter to make good the default within such time as is specified in the order.

5.6 'Appropriate tribunal' is defined in section 112(1) of the CLRA 2002 as follows:

> (a) in relation to premises in England, the First-tier Tribunal or, where determined by Tribunal Procedure Rules, the Upper Tribunal; and
> (b) in relation to premises in Wales, a leasehold valuation tribunal;

5.7 Prior to 3 March 2025 the application was required to be made to the county court. After that date the application must be made to the 'appropriate tribunal' and, if necessary, an application made to the county court for enforcement (section 107(3) of the CLRA 2002).

5.8 The right of access only applies to access that is for a 'reasonable' purpose. It is considered that access to residential parts of the premises (for example a flat) is likely to be justifiable only if good reason can be shown and if no viable alternative exists.

5.9 Section 83(3)(a) of the CLRA 2002 states that the right of access is exercisable at any reasonable time on giving not less than 10 days' notice to 'the occupier' of any premises or if those premises are unoccupied, to the person entitled to occupy them. 'Occupier' would include sub-tenants and other categories of occupiers, not just the long lessee of the flat. An example would include a tenant occupying the flat under an assured shorthold tenancy.

5.10 An application under section 107(1) of the CLRA 2002 may be made by 'any person interested' (see further comments in para 5.13). The order should require the person who has failed to allow access to do so within the timeframe contained in the order.

5.11 The application for an order should be made against the person who has been served with notice under section 83(3)(a) or (b) of the CLRA 2002, i.e. either the occupier as per section 83(3)(a) or, if the property is unoccupied, the person entitled to occupy, most likely the long leaseholder (section 83(3)(b)).

5.12 If faced with an occupier who refuses or fails to respond or comply, it may be prudent to also then serve notice under section 83(3)(b) of the CLRA 2002, for example, on the long leaseholder thus enabling the sender to subsequently seek an order as against both the occupier and the person entitled to occupy.

5.13 The application under section 107 of the CLRA 2002 can be made by an interested party. Section 83 limits who the 'interested party' is for the purposes of section 107. Whilst 'interested party' is broad in the context of section 107, in the context of a breach of section 83(3), it is confined to the RTM company that served the notice under section 83(3)(a) or (b).

5.14 Before issuing the application, the applicant must serve the person in default with a notice giving him or her 14 days to make good the default (section 107(2) of the CLRA 2002).

CONTRACTOR NOTICES AND CONTRACT NOTICES

5.15 This section begins by looking at the wording in the statutory definitions contained in sections 91 and 92 of the CLRA 2002 relating to management contracts and duties to give notice of contracts. It then considers the operative terms in the relevant sections.

5.16 Sections 91 and 92 of the CLRA 2002 contain obligations on the existing manager of the premises ('the manager party'). First, to serve 'contractor notices' on the relevant contractor parties where there are existing management contracts in place at the premises, and, second, there is an obligation to serve corresponding 'contract notices' on the RTM company informing the RTM company of the management contract(s) in place. Section 91 contains the defined terms and definitions relating to a management contract. Section 92 sets out the duties to give notice of contracts.

5.17 The purpose behind the service of contractor notices and contract notices is to require the manager party to give notice to both relevant contractor parties (with whom there is an existing contract relating to the premises) and the RTM company who will be taking over the management of the premises in due course. This ensures that contractor parties are aware that a claim to acquire the right to manage has been made. The aim is to facilitate relevant discussions and to make the RTM company aware of all existing management contracts relating to the premises in advance of the acquisition date. The acquisition date is the date when the right to manage is acquired in accordance with section 90 of the CLRA 2002. For a detailed discussion of the definition and meaning of acquisition date, see Chapter 7.

5.18 The contractor parties will need to consider and decide whether the existing contract(s) will be adopted by the RTM company and, if not, commence arrangements to terminate the existing contract(s) (subject to the terms of the contract(s)). The RTM company will also need to consider which contract(s) it wishes to adopt. Both the contractors and the RTM company need to carefully consider their respective positions in advance of the acquisition date to facilitate a smooth and efficient handover of management responsibilities.

Notices relating to management contracts

5.19 Section 91(1) and (2) of the CLRA 2002 states as follows:

> (1) Section 92 applies where—
>
> (a) the right to manage premises is to be acquired by a RTM company (otherwise than by virtue of an order under section 85), and
> (b) there are one or more existing management contracts relating to the premises.
>
> (2) A management contract is a contract between—
>
> (a) an existing manager of the premises (referred to in this Chapter as the 'manager party'), and
> (b) another person (so referred to as the 'contractor party')
>
> under which the contractor party agrees to provide services, or do any other thing, in connection with any matter relating to a function which will be a function of the RTM company once it acquires the right to manage.

Meaning of 'management contract'

5.20 The term 'management contract' relates to management agreements in general terms plus all contracts for services or to do 'any other thing' relating to a function which will become a function of the RTM company on the acquisition date, namely 'management functions' as defined in section 96(5) of the CLRA 2002. For a detailed discussion of the meaning of management functions, see Chapter 8.

5.21 The CLRA 2002 gives a discrete definition to an 'existing management contract' (see para 5.22). This describes a management contract that subsists on the determination date or a contract that is entered into between the determination date (1) and the acquisition date (2).

Meaning of 'existing management contract'

5.22 'Existing management contract' is defined in section 91(3) of the CLRA 2002, which states as follows:

> (3) And in this Chapter 'existing management contract' means a management contract which—
>
> (a) is subsisting immediately before the determination date, or
> (b) is entered into during the period beginning with the determination date and ending with the acquisition date.

Meaning of 'existing manager'

5.23 'Existing manager' is defined in section 91(4) of the CLRA 2002, which states as follows:

> (4) An existing manager of the premises is any person who is—
>
> (a) landlord under a lease relating to the whole or any part of the premises,
> (b) party to such a lease otherwise than as a landlord or tenant, or
> (c) a manager appointed under Part 2 of the 1987 Act to act in relation to the premises, or any premises containing or contained in the premises.

Meaning of 'determination date'

5.24 'Determination date' is defined in section 91(5) of the CLRA 2002, which states as follows:

> (5) In this Chapter 'determination date' means—
>
> (a) where there is no dispute about entitlement, the date specified in the claim notice under section 80(6),
> (b) where the right to manage the premises is acquired by the company by virtue of a determination under section 84(5)(a), the date when the determination becomes final, and
> (c) where the right to manage the premises is acquired by the company by virtue of subsection (5)(b) of section 84, the day

on which the person (or the last person) by whom a counter-notice containing a statement such as is mentioned in subsection (2)(b) of that section was given agrees in writing that the company was on the relevant date entitled to acquire the right to manage the premises.

Duties to give notice of contracts

5.25 Once the management contract(s) have been identified, section 92 of the CLRA 2002 imposes duties to give notice of contracts. Different notices apply depending on the recipient. The 'manager party' pursuant to the 'existing management contracts' must serve notices in relation to the contract. The 'manager party' means an existing manager, i.e. the landlord or a third-party manager or a manager appointed under Part 2 of the Landlord and Tenant Act 1987 (LTA 1987) (section 91(4) of the CLRA 2002). Section 92(1) of the CLRA 2002 requires service of a contractor notice on the contractor party and a contract notice on the RTM company in respect of each existing management contract. Section 92(2) sets out the timing of service of such notices.

Who must give notice and what type of notice is required?

5.26 Section 92(1) of the CLRA 2002 states as follows:

> (1) The person who is the manager party in relation to an existing management contract must give a notice in relation to the contract—
>
> (a) to the person who is the contractor party in relation to the contract (a 'contractor notice'), and
> (b) to the RTM company (a 'contract notice').

Timing

5.27 In terms of timing for service of contractor and contract notices, section 92(2) of the CLRA 2002 states as follows:

> (2) A contractor notice and a contract notice must be given—
>
> (a) in the case of a contract subsisting immediately before the determination date, on that date or as soon after that date as is reasonably practicable, and

(b) in the case of a contract entered into during the period beginning with the determination date and ending with the acquisition date, on the date on which it is entered into or as soon after that date as is reasonably practicable.

5.28 The obligation to serve contractor notices and contract notices only arises after a claim notice is served. This is because the obligation arises after the 'determination date' as defined by section 91(5) of the CLRA 2002.

5.29 As set out in section 91(5) of the CLRA 2002 the determination date is:

(a) where there is no dispute about entitlement, the date specified in the claim notice under section 80(6),
(b) where the right to manage the premises is acquired by the company by virtue of a determination under section 84(5)(a), the date when the determination becomes final, and
(c) where the right to manage the premises is acquired by the company by virtue of subsection (5)(b) of section 84, the day on which the person (or the last person) by whom a counter-notice containing a statement such as is mentioned in subsection (2)(b) of that section was given agrees in writing that the company was on the relevant date entitled to acquire the right to manage the premises.

5.30 The contractor and contract notices must be served either on the determination date or as soon as is reasonably practicable after that date, as per section 92(2)(a) of the CLRA 2002. In circumstances where new contracts are entered into after the determination date, notices must be served on the date the contract is entered into or as soon as reasonably practicable thereafter, as per section 92(2)(b).

5.31 The CLRA 2002 only requires service of contractor notices and contract notices on or after the determination date. However, this does not allow much time for the RTM company to obtain details of the relevant management contracts relating to the premises in advance of the right to manage being acquired.

Contents of the contractor notice

5.32 Section 92(3) of the CLRA 2002 states that a contractor notice must:

(a) give details sufficient to identify the contract in relation to which it is given,
(b) state that the right to manage the premises is to be acquired by a RTM company,
(c) state the name and registered office of the RTM company,
(d) specify the acquisition date, and
(e) contain such other particulars (if any) as may be required to be contained in contractor notices by regulations made by the appropriate national authority,

and must also comply with such requirements (if any) about the form of contractor notices as may be prescribed in regulations so made.

5.33 Section 92(3)(e) of the CLRA 2002 and regulation 6 of the Right to Manage (Prescribed Particulars and Forms) (England) Regulations 2010 (SI 2010/825) (2010 England Regulations) set out additional content to the contractor notice. This is detailed at paras 5.34–5.39. The relevant regulations that apply to property in Wales are the Right to Manage (Prescribed Particulars and Forms) (Wales) Regulations 2011 (SI 2011/2684) (2011 Wales Regulations). See Appendix 1 for the 2010 England Regulations and Appendix 2 for the 2011 Wales Regulations.

Regulation 6 of the 2010 England Regulations: additional content for contractor notice

5.34 Regulation 6 of the 2010 England Regulations contains additional content to be included in the contractor notice. It essentially requires the inclusion of a statement which advises the contractor party that it should contact the RTM company if it wishes to continue to provide the services to the RTM company.

5.35 Regulation 6 of the 2010 England Regulations states as follows:

> 6. A contractor notice shall contain (in addition to the particulars referred to in paragraphs (a) to (d) of section 92(3) (duties to give notice of contracts) of the 2002 Act) the statement that, should the person to whom the notice is given wish to provide to the RTM company services which, as the contractor party, it has provided to the manager party under the contract, it is advised to contact the RTM company at the address given in the notice.

5.36 There is no prescribed form of contractor notice for properties in England. A suggested form is set out at para 5.40.

Regulation 6 of the 2011 Wales Regulations: additional content for contractor notice

5.37 The position in Wales is different as the 2011 Wales Regulations (regulation 8(4)) require that contractor notices must be in the form set out in Schedule 4 to the 2011 Wales Regulations (see Appendix 2).

5.38 Regulation 6(1) of the 2011 Wales Regulations contains additional content to be included in the contractor notice. It states as follows:

> 6.—(1) A contractor notice must contain (in addition to the particulars referred to in paragraphs (a) to (d) of section 92(3) (duties to give notice of contracts) of the 2002 Act) the statement that, should the person to whom the notice is given wish to provide to the RTM company services which, as the contractor party, it has provided to the manager party under the contract, it is advised to contact the RTM company at the address given in the notice; …

5.39 Regulation 6(2) of the 2011 Wales Regulations requires additional information be provided in the notes to the form. The notes are set out in Schedule 4 and must be attached to the contractor notice when served.

Form of contractor notice (property in England)

5.40

FORM OF CONTRACTOR NOTICE (PROPERTY IN ENGLAND)

[*date*]

To: [*name and address of contractor party*]

Contract [*provide sufficient details to identify the contract*] (the Contract)

I/We [*name and address*] as the [landlord OR as managing agent for and on behalf of the landlord] of premises known as [provide sufficient details to identify the premises] and as the manager party under the Contract hereby give you notice in relation to the Contract that:

> 1 The right to manage the premises to which the Contract relates is to be acquired by a RTM company
> 2 The name and registered office of the RTM company are [*give name and address*]
> 3 The date on which the RTM company is to acquire or acquired the right to manage the premises is [*date*]
> 4 Should you wish to provide to the RTM company services which you have provided to me/us under the Contract, you are advised to contact the RTM company at the address given in this notice
>
> Signed:
>
> [*Signature by or on behalf of the person/entity giving the notice.*]

Checklist 5.1: Contractor notice – contents

5.41 Contents of the contractor notice under section 92(3)(e) of the CLRA 2002 and regulation 6 of the 2010 England Regulations and regulations 6 and 8(4) of, and Schedule 4 to, the 2011 Wales Regulations:

- Provide sufficient information to identify the contract that the notice relates to.
- Clearly state that the right to manage the premises is to be acquired by the RTM company.
- State the name of the RTM company and its registered office.
- Specify the acquisition date.
- In Wales, use the prescribed form.
- Include a statement advising the contractor party that if it wishes to continue providing services to the RTM company, it should contact the RTM company.

EXISTING MANAGEMENT SUB-CONTRACT(S)

5.42 As set out at paras 5.43–5.46, there are additional provisions contained at section 92(4)–(6) of the CLRA 2002 in relation to sub-contracts and the service of further contractor and contract notices down the chain.

Where there is an existing management sub-contract(s), section 92(4) requires the contractor, on receipt of the contractor notice, to send a copy of the contractor notice to the sub-contractor and give the RTM company a contract notice in relation to the existing management sub-contract.

5.43 Section 92(4) of the CLRA 2002 states as follows:

> (4) Where a person who receives a contractor notice (including one who receives a copy by virtue of this subsection) is party to an existing management sub-contract with another person (the 'sub-contractor party'), the person who received the notice must—
>
> (a) send a copy of the contractor notice to the sub-contractor party, and
>
> (b) give to the RTM company a contract notice in relation to the existing management sub-contract.

Meaning of existing management sub-contract

5.44 Section 92(5) of the CLRA 2002 provides the definition for an existing management sub-contract. It states as follows:

> (5) An existing management sub-contract is a contract under which the sub-contractor party agrees to provide services, or to do any other thing, in connection with any matter relating to a function which will be a function of the RTM company once it acquires the right to manage and which—
>
> (a) is subsisting immediately before the determination date, or
>
> (b) is entered into during the period beginning with the determination date and ending on the acquisition date.

5.45 See para 5.54 for an example of a form of contract notice under section 94(2) of the CLRA 2002 to be given by the contractor party to the RTM company where there is an existing management sub-contract.

5.46 Further requirements in respect of timing are contained in section 92(6) of the CLRA 2002. This prescribes the timeframes for completion of steps relating to sub-contracts and the service of contractor notices and contract notices on sub-contractor parties. In respect of sub-contracts, the contractor party must serve: (a) the copy contractor notice; and (b) the contract notice relating to the sub-contract on the date the contractor notice is received or as soon as possible thereafter (section 92(6)(a)). In relation to any sub-contracts entered into after the determination date, the contractor and contract notice must be served on the date the sub-contract was entered into or, again, as soon as practicable thereafter (section 92(6)(b)).

Contents of the contract notice

5.47 Section 92(7) of the CLRA 2002 states as follows:

> (7) A contract notice must—
>
> (a) give particulars of the contract in relation to which it is given and of the person who is the contractor party, or sub-contractor party, in relation to that contract, and
> (b) contain such other particulars (if any) as may be required to be contained in contract notices by regulations made by the appropriate national authority,
>
> and must also comply with such requirements (if any) about the form of contract notices as may be prescribed by such regulations so made.

Regulation 7 of the 2010 England Regulations: additional content for contract notice

5.48 Regulation 7 contains additional content to be included in the contract notice. This is in addition to the content required by section 92(7) of the CLRA 2002. The regulation states as follows:

> 7. A contract notice shall contain (in addition to the particulars referred to in section 92(7)(a) of the 2002 Act)—
>
> (a) the address of the person who is the contractor party, or sub-contractor party[1] under the contract of which particulars are given in the notice; and
> (b) a statement that, should the RTM company wish to avail itself of the services which the contractor party, or sub-contractor party, has provided to the manager party under that contract, it is advised to contact the contractor party or sub-contractor party, at the address given in the notice.

---

1 As to 'sub-contractor party', see CLRA 2002, s 92(4).

5.49 There is no prescribed form of contract notice for properties in England but there is prescribed content as required by the 2010 England Regulations. An example form of contract notice is set out at para 5.53.

Regulation 7 of the 2011 Wales Regulations: additional content for contract notice

5.50 The position in Wales is different as the 2011 Wales Regulations (regulation 8(5)) require that contract notices must be in the form set out in Schedule 5 to the 2011 Wales Regulations.

5.51 Regulation 7 contains additional content to be included in the contract notice. Regulation 7(c) of the 2011 Wales Regulations requires the inclusion of the information provided in the notes to the form set out in Schedule 5 (see Appendix 2).

5.52 Accordingly, the contract notice must give sufficient details of the contract to identify it and give particulars of the relevant contractor party or sub-contractor party in respect of that contract (section 92(7)(a) of the CLRA 2002). The notice must also state the address of the relevant contractor party (or sub-contractor as applicable) (section 92(7)(b) and regulation 7 of the relevant England or Wales Regulations) and contain a statement that should the RTM company wish to retain the contractor (or sub-contractor) party, it should contact that party.

Form of contract notice relating to an existing management contract (property in England)

5.53

FORM OF CONTRACT NOTICE RELATING TO AN EXISTING MANAGEMENT CONTRACT (PROPERTY IN ENGLAND)

[*date*]

To: [*name and address of RTM company*]

Premises [*address of premises*] (the Premises)

I/We [*name and address*] as [the landlord of the Premises OR as managing agent for and on behalf of the landlord] and as the manager party under an existing management contract in relation to the Premises (the Contract) hereby give you notice that:

1 The Contract is [*give particulars, of the relevant contract, e.g. a contract for the repair and maintenance of the lift at the Premises and state the date and parties to the contract*].
2 The name and address of the person who is the contractor party in relation to the Contract is [*name and address*].
3 Should you wish to avail yourself of the services which the contractor party has provided to me/us under the Contract, you are advised to contact the contractor party at the address given in this notice.

[Signed:
[*signature by or on behalf of the person/entity giving the notice.*]

Form of contract notice for existing management sub-contracts

5.54

FORM OF CONTRACT NOTICE RELATING TO AN EXISTING MANAGEMENT SUB-CONTRACT (PROPERTY IN ENGLAND)

[*date*]

To: [*name and address of RTM company*]

Premises [*address of premises*] (the Premises)

Contract [*give particulars of the relevant contract between the manager party and the contractor party*] (the Contract)

I/We [*name and address*] as the contractor party to the Contract hereby give you notice that:

1. There is an existing management sub-contract in relation to the Premises (the Sub-contract). The Sub-contract is [*give*

particulars, e.g. a contract for the repair and maintenance of the lift at the Premises].

2. The name and address of the person who is the sub-contractor party in relation to the Sub-contract is [*name and address*].
3. Should you wish to avail yourself of the services which the sub-contractor party has provided to the manager party under the Sub-contract, you are advised to contact the sub-contractor party at the address given in this notice.

Signed:
[*signature by or on behalf of the contractor party.*]

Checklist 5.2: Contract notice – contents

5.55 Contents of the contract notice under section 92(7) of the CLRA 2002 and regulation 7 of the 2010 England Regulations and regulation 7 of, and Schedule 5 to, the 2011 Wales Regulations:

- Provide sufficient information to identify the contract that the notice relates to.
- Give particulars of the contractor party (or where being served by the contractor party, the sub-contractor party) in relation to that contract.
- State the address of the contractor party (or the sub-contractor party where notice is being given by the contractor party).
- Include a statement that if the RTM company wishes to avail itself of the services of the contractor party (or the sub-contractor party as applicable), it should contact that party.
- In Wales, use the prescribed form.

ERRORS RELATING TO CONTRACTOR AND CONTRACT NOTICES

5.56 The authors refer to the general approach of the courts and tribunals to the validity of statutory notices, as set out in Chapter 4 and in this chapter at paras 5.106–5.107. As at the date of writing, the authors are not aware of any cases considering the validity of contract and contractor notices. However, it should be noted that there are no statutory saving provisions relating to these forms of notices.

What happens to existing contracts?

5.57 Whilst the CLRA 2002 makes provisions for service of contractor and contract notices to make both contractors and the RTM company aware of the existing contracts in place, it does not address what happens to those existing contracts when the right to manage is acquired. Do the contracts continue in the name of the RTM company (in place of the landlord) by way of a statutory transfer or are they frustrated by the CLRA 2002? The fact that regulation 6 of the 2010 England Regulations requires a contractor notice to contain a statement advising the person to whom the notice is given to contact the RTM company if it wishes to continue to provide services to the RTM company, suggests that there is no automatic transfer. That provision is mirrored by regulation 7, which requires a contract notice to contain a similar advisory statement to the RTM company supporting the conclusion that there is no automatic transfer.

5.58 In the absence of any statutory continuation, what happens to the contracts will depend on the position under the general common law. The authors consider that the exercise of the right to manage would frustrate existing contracts. Generally, a frustrating event has a number of features, namely, it is one which occurs after the contract is entered into; it is so fundamental as to strike to the root of the contract and beyond what was contemplated by the parties when they entered into the contract; and it is not the fault of either contracting party and renders further performance impossible. Since the RTM company will become responsible for the management of the building on the acquisition date and from that point the landlord will no longer be able to fulfil his or her part of the contract, it is considered that the common purpose underlying the contract can no longer be fulfilled and that the contract will be frustrated. The effect of frustration is that each party is prospectively released from its obligations under the contract.

5.59 The purpose of the contractor and contract notices under sections 91 and 92 of the CLRA 2002 is to give both the contractor parties and the RTM company the opportunity to make decisions as to how to proceed.

Duty to provide information

5.60 Where the right to manage is to be acquired, section 93 of the CLRA 2002 permits the RTM company to serve notice on the landlord, any management company and managers appointed under Part 2 of the LTA 1987 requiring the provision of information which is in their possession or control and which the RTM company reasonably requires in connection with the exercise of the right to manage. There is no prescribed form and the right can be exercised using a simple notice which the recipient must answer within 28 days. See the example notice at para 5.61.

Form of Information Notice pursuant to section 93 of the Commonhold and Leasehold Reform Act 2002

5.61

FORM OF INFORMATION NOTICE PURSUANT TO SECTION 93 OF THE COMMONHOLD AND LEASEHOLD REFORM ACT 2002 (THE 'ACT')

[*insert date*]

To: [*insert name and address*]

[*Name of RTM Company*] (the 'Company'), a private company limited by guarantee, of [*address of registered office*] and of which the registered number is [*insert company number under Companies Act 2006*] hereby give notice pursuant to section 93 of the Act, requiring the provision of information which is in your possession or control in relation to the premises known as [*insert full address of premises to be acquired*] relating to the following:

1. [*set out specific information sought*]

2. [ ]

5.62 Section 93(2) of the CLRA 2002 allows for inspection of information recorded in a document in the recipient's possession or control. A document means anything in which information is recorded (section 112(1)). This will therefore include electronic files.

5.63 It would seem from the opening words of section 93(1) of the CLRA 2002, i.e. 'where the right to manage premises is to be acquired by a RTM company', that an information notice may only be served prior to acquisition of the right to manage. Such a notice may not require a person to do anything under section 93 before the acquisition date (section 93(3)). However, subject to that restriction, section 93(4) goes on to state that a person who is required by a notice to do anything under this section must do so within the period of 28 days beginning with the day on which the notice is given.

5.64 The provision of information is a key step in the process. It is an opportunity for the RTM company to gain relevant information relating to existing management arrangements for the premises. In the case of default, section 107 of the CLRA 2002 allows for enforcement of the obligation to provide information by an application to the appropriate tribunal, followed if necessary by an application to the county court.

THE COUNTER-NOTICE

5.65 Section 84 of the CLRA 2002 relates to counter-notices. The service of a counter-notice is not mandatory under the CLRA 2002. This is seen from the wording in the section, which states that recipients of claim notices 'may' give a counter-notice. This is in contrast to the statutory wording in the enfranchisement legislation (Leasehold Reform, Housing and Urban Development Act 1993 (LRHUDA 1993)), which states that the landlord 'shall' serve a counter-notice.

5.66 Section 84(1) of the CLRA 2002 states as follows:

> (1) A person who is given a claim notice by a RTM company under section 79(6) may give a notice (referred to in this Chapter as a 'counter-notice') to the company no later than the date specified in the claim notice under section 80(6).

5.67 However, whilst service of the counter-notice is optional, if no counter-notice challenging the claim is served by the date specified in the claim notice then the RTM company will automatically acquire the right to manage on the acquisition date.

5.68 Likewise, a significant consequence of a counter-notice which denies entitlement being served is to postpone the date on which the right to manage is acquired, as discussed further at para 5.84.

Who can serve a counter-notice?

5.69 It is worth noting that section 84(1) of the CLRA 2002 provides for any recipient of a claim notice to serve a counter-notice. This right is not limited to the landlord of the building. Therefore, this provision allows third parties to leases (for example management companies and, separately, managers appointed pursuant to Part 2 of the LTA 1987) to also serve counter-notices. Whilst section 79(8) of the CLRA 2002 requires the RTM company to serve a copy of the claim notice on all qualifying tenants, the qualifying tenants have no right to serve a counter-notice, including those who may not be members of the RTM company and may therefore wish to otherwise oppose the right to manage being acquired.

Statement in the counter-notice

5.70 As per counter-notices under the LRHUDA 1993, it is similarly a fundamental requirement in order for a counter-notice under the CLRA 2002 to be valid that it either admits or denies that the RTM company is entitled to acquire the right to manage. If the counter-notice is ambiguous, it is likely to be treated as invalid.[2]

5.71 Section 84(2) of the CLRA 2002 states that:

> (2) A counter-notice is a notice containing a statement either—
>
> > (a) admitting the RTM company was on the relevant date entitled to acquire the right to manage the premises specified in the claim notice, or

---

2 See *Burman v Mount Cook Land Limited* [2001] EWCA Civ 1712, [2002] Ch 256, a case on the LRHUDA 1993.

(b) alleging that, by reason of a specified provision of this Chapter, the RTM company was on that day not so entitled,

and containing such other particulars (if any) as may be required to be contained in counter-notices, and complying with such requirements (if any) about the form of counter-notices, as may be prescribed by regulations made by the appropriate national authority.

Timeframe for service of the counter-notice

5.72 The claim notice will specify the date by which any counter-notice must be served. Section 80(6) of the CLRA 2002 states that the claim notice must specify a date not less than one month after the giving of the notice under section 79(6) for each person to respond by service of a counter-notice. The time available to consider whether or not the RTM company is entitled to acquire the right to manage is therefore limited.

5.73 Arguably, there is no requirement to serve a counter-notice if the recipient is admitting the right to acquire the right to manage. If no counter-notice is served, the right to manage will simply be acquired on the acquisition date stated in the claim notice. However, as noted at para 5.67, if the recipient wishes to dispute the right then a counter-notice opposing the right must be served on or before the deadline stated in the claim notice.

Extension of time for service of the counter-notice

5.74 There is no provision in the CLRA 2002 to extend time for service of the counter-notice, either by agreement between the parties or by order of the tribunal or the court. However, in the case of *A1 Properties (Sunderland) Limited v Tudor Studios RTM Company Limited*,[3] Lord Briggs contemplated at [88] that a party who had not been served with a claim notice might challenge the acquisition of the right to manage by seeking a declaration of rights in the High Court if there had been no proceedings in the tribunal, or by seeking judicial review if there had been a decision in the tribunal, and presumably this would be the case where that party, ignorant of the claim, had not served a counter-notice.

3 *A1 Properties (Sunderland) Limited v Tudor Studios RTM Company Limited* [2024] UKSC 27, [2025] AC 1075.

Late service of the counter-notice

5.75 The statutory deadline for service of the counter-notice is strict under the CLRA 2002 and it is considered that a late counter-notice will be invalid and of no effect. In the case of *Alleyn Court RTM Company Limited v Abou Hamdan*,[4] where no counter-notice was served by the landlord, the Upper Tribunal (Lands Chamber) relied on section 90(2) of the CLRA 2002, which states that where there is no challenge or dispute about entitlement, the acquisition date (section 90) is the date specified in the claim notice. On that basis the Upper Tribunal appeared to consider, *obiter*, that a valid counter-notice is essential to dispute an RTM company's entitlement, and in the absence of a valid counter-notice, the right could not be challenged and the right to manage is automatic on the acquisition date. Section 90(2) states that where there is no dispute about entitlement, the acquisition date is the date specified in the claim notice under section 80(7).

5.76 Likewise, section 90(3) of the CLRA 2002 states as follows:

> (3) For the purposes of this Chapter, there is no dispute about entitlement if—
>
> (a) no counter-notice is given under section 84, or
> (b) the counter-notice given under that section, or (where more than one is so given) each of them, contains a statement such as is mentioned in subsection (2)(a) of that section.

5.77 Where a counter-notice has been given late, there is no need for the RTM company to apply for a determination as to entitlement by the tribunal.

Form and content of the counter-notice

5.78 The 2010 England Regulations contain the prescribed form of counter-notice at Schedule 3. This prescribed form (including all of the notes) must be used in order to serve a valid counter-notice under the CLRA 2002. This is as per regulation 8(3) of the 2010 Regulations in respect of the form itself, and regulation 5(c) in respect of the notes. As above, in respect

---

4 *Alleyn Court RTM Company Limited v Abou Hamdan* [2012] UKUT 74 (LC), [2012] PLSCS 107.

of properties in Wales, the equivalent regulations are the 2011 Wales Regulations. The relevant prescribed form of counter-notice is also at Schedule 3 to the 2011 Wales Regulations. See Appendix 1 for the 2010 England Regulations and Appendix 2 for the 2011 Wales Regulations.

Regulation 5 of, and Schedule 3 to, the 2010 England Regulations: additional content for counter-notice

5.79 In respect of properties in England, regulation 5 of, and Schedule 3 to, the 2010 England Regulations set out a requirement for additional content for a counter-notice whereby the counter-notice must also contain the following statements:

> 5. A counter-notice shall contain (in addition to the statement referred to in paragraph (a) or (b) of section 84(2) (counter-notices) of the 2002 Act)—
>
> (a) a statement that, where the RTM company has been given one or more counter-notices containing such a statement as is mentioned in paragraph (b) of section 84(2) of the 2002 Act, the company may apply to a tribunal for a determination that, on the date on which the notice of claim was given, the company was entitled to acquire the right to manage the premises specified in the claim notice;
>
> (b) a statement that, where the RTM company has been given one or more counter-notices containing such a statement as is mentioned in paragraph (b) of section 84(2) of the 2002 Act, the company does not acquire the right to manage the specified premises in the claim notice unless—
>
> (i) on an application to a tribunal, it is finally determined that the company was entitled to acquire the right to manage the premises; or
>
> (ii) the person by whom the counter-notice was given agrees, or the persons by whom the counter-notices were given agree, in writing that the company was so entitled; and
>
> (c) the information provided in the notes to the form set out in Schedule 3 to these Regulations.

5.80 There is also a requirement to attach the notes at Schedule 3 of the 2010 England Regulations on service of the counter-notice.

Regulation 5 of, and Schedule 3 to, the 2011 Wales Regulations: additional content for counter-notice

5.81 In respect of properties in Wales, the requirement for additional content is contained in regulation 5 of the 2011 Wales Regulations. The prescribed form of counter-notice is contained at Schedule 3 and must be the form used in accordance with regulation 8(3). There is a requirement to serve the notes as set out in Schedule 3.

Counter-notice disputing entitlement

5.82 If a counter-notice disputing the claim is served, the RTM company has 2 months from service of the counter-notice to apply to the tribunal for a declaration as to entitlement pursuant to section 84(3) of the CLRA 2002. For a more detailed discussion relating to the tribunal procedure under section 84(3) following service of a counter-notice denying the right to manage, see Chapter 6. The relevant provisions are in section 84(3)–(6), which are set out at paras 5.87–5.90.

5.83 The service of a counter-notice disputing the RTM company's entitlement to acquire the right to manage the premises triggers the RTM company's right under section 84(3) of the CLRA 2002 to make an application to the tribunal seeking a determination as to entitlement. Section 84(4) states that the application must be made no later than 2 months beginning with the day on which the counter-notice was given.

5.84 A dispute as to entitlement will delay the acquisition of the right to manage until such time as there is a determination of the company's entitlement or agreement is reached with the person by whom the counter-notice was given that they agree (in writing) that the company is entitled. This is as per section 84(5)(a) and (b) of the CLRA 2002 (set out at para 5.88). Section 84(6) states that if, following the application under section 84(3), it is finally determined that the RTM company was not entitled to acquire the right to manage the premises, the claim-notice ceases to have effect.

5.85 A tribunal determination becomes final at the end of the period for bringing an appeal or on the disposal of an appeal. An appeal is disposed of if it is determined and the period for bringing any further appeal has ended or if it is abandoned or ceases to have effect. For further detail, see section 84(7) and (8) of the CLRA 2002.

5.86 Section 84(3) of the CLRA 2002 states as follows:

> (3) Where the RTM company has been given one or more counter-notices containing a statement such as is mentioned in subsection 2(b), the company may apply to the appropriate tribunal for a determination that it was on the relevant date entitled to acquire the right to manage the premises.

5.87 Section 84(4) of the CLRA 2002 states as follows:

> (4) An application under subsection (3) must be made not later than the end of the period of two months beginning with the day on which the counter-notice (or, where more than one, the last of the counter-notices) was given.

5.88 Section 84(5) of the CLRA 2002 states as follows:

> (5) Where the RTM company has been given one or more counter-notices containing a statement such as is mentioned in subsection (2)(b), the RTM company does not acquire the right to manage the premises unless—
>
> (a) on an application under subsection (3) it is finally determined that the company was on the relevant date entitled to acquire the right to manage the premises, or
> (b) the person by whom the counter-notice was given agrees, or the persons by whom the counter-notices were given agree, in writing, that the company was so entitled.

5.89 Section 84(6) of the CLRA 2002 states as follows:

> (6) If on an application under subsection (3) it is finally determined that the company was not on the relevant date entitled to acquire the right to manage the premises, a claim ceases to have effect.

Grounds for disputing entitlement to the right to manage

5.90 There are two grounds on which to resist the right to manage, namely:

(1) the premises do not qualify for right to manage pursuant to the CLRA 2002;
(2) the RTM company is not entitled to acquire the right to manage.

In respect of the second ground, one should carefully consider whether there are defects in the constitution of the RTM company (see Chapter 2) or whether the membership criteria required under the CLRA 2002 has been met (see Chapter 3) and whether all procedural steps pursuant to the CLRA 2002 have been completed prior to service of the claim notice (see Chapter 4).

5.91 Section 84(2)(b) of the CLRA 2002 requires that a counter-notice not admitting the claim must specify, by reference to the provisions of the CLRA 2002, why the RTM company is not entitled to acquire the right to manage on the relevant date.[5] The grounds identified in the counter-notice may be supplemented by additional grounds in a subsequent tribunal application.[6]

5.92 Where the RTM company has been served with a counter-notice containing the statement at section 84(2)(b) of the CLRA 2002, it may apply to the tribunal for a determination as to entitlement.

Validity of claim notice itself

5.93 Separately to considering the validity of the claim itself and the grounds summarised above, the recipient of the claim notice should consider whether the claim notice served is valid (see Chapter 4).

Challenging the acquisition of the right to manage in the absence of service of a counter-notice

5.94 In the case of *Alleyn Court RTM Company Limited v Abou Hamdan*,[7] where no counter-notice was served by the landlord, the Upper Tribunal (Lands Chamber) relied on section 90(2) of the CLRA 2002, which states that where there is no challenge or dispute about entitlement, the acquisition date (section 90) is the date specified in the claim notice. On that basis, the tribunal appeared to consider, *obiter*, that a valid counter-notice is essential to dispute an RTM company's entitlement and,

---

5 See *St Stephens Mansions RTM Company Limited v Fairhold NW Limited* [2014] UKUT 541 (LC), [2015] EGLR 15.

6 See *Fairhold (Yorkshire) Limited v Trinity Wharf (SE16) RTM Company Limited* [2013] UKUT 502 (LC), [2014] L & TR 6, which was subsequently followed in *Albion Residential Limited v Albion Residential Residents RTM Company Limited* [2014] UKUT 6 (LC), [2014] 1 WLUK 141.

7 *Alleyn Court RTM Company Limited v Abou Hamdan* [2012] UKUT 74 (LC), [2012] PLSCS 107.

in the absence of a valid counter-notice, the right could not be challenged and the right to manage is automatic on the acquisition date.

5.95 However, subsequently in the case of *Avon Freehold Limited v Regent Court RTM Company Limited*,[8] the Upper Tribunal (Lands Chamber) doubted whether the decision in *Alleyn Court* was correct. It stated that Parliament could not have intended that the right to manage be acquired on the basis of an invalid claim notice. It considered that section 90 of the CLRA 2002 could be construed on the basis that there is both a valid claim notice and either no counter-notice has been served or a counter-notice admitting the claim has been served. That is consistent with the case of *A1 Properties (Sunderland) Limited v Tudor Studios RTM Company Limited*,[9] where Lord Briggs contemplated at [88] that a party who had not been served with a claim notice might challenge the acquisition of the right to manage by seeking a declaration of rights in the High Court if there had been no proceedings in the tribunal, or by seeking judicial review if there had been a decision in the tribunal, and presumably this would be the case where that party, ignorant of the claim, had not served a counter-notice.

5.96 Likewise, *Alleyn Court* was considered and not followed by the Upper Tribunal (Lands Chamber) in the case of *St Stephens Mansions RTM Company Limited v Fairhold NW Limited*.[10] Deputy President Martin Roger QC considered that unless the premises are premises to which the CLRA 2002 applies, no statutory right applies at all. In other words, he made a distinction that if the premises are not premises to which the right to manage applies, i.e. they do not qualify, then the absence of a counter-notice disputing entitlement should not result in the right to manage being acquired. Accordingly, the Upper Tribunal drew a distinction between cases where no statutory right arises because the premises do not qualify and those cases with less fundamental defects, for example, a failure to comply with the procedural steps under the statute. In the latter situation, a counter-notice should be served.

---

8 *Avon Freehold Limited v Regent Court RTM Company Limited* [2013] UKUT 213 (LC), [2013] L & TR 23.

9 *A1 Properties (Sunderland) Limited v Tudor Studios RTM Company Limited* [2024] UKSC 27, [2025] AC 1075.

10 *St Stephens Mansions RTM Company Limited v Fairhold NW Limited* [2014] UKUT 541 (LC), [2015] EGLR 15.

5.97 The authors consider it is good practice that if a recipient of a claim notice wishes to pursue an argument that the claim notice is invalid, it should always serve a counter-notice opposing the acquisition on grounds mentioned (if applicable) and without prejudice to the contention that because the claim notice is invalid, it is not required to serve a counter-notice at all. Thereafter, if the RTM company continues to rely on the claim notice, the recipient can consider applying to the tribunal for a declaration as to validity.

Schedule 3: Form of counter-notice

5.98

RIGHT TO MANAGE (PRESCRIBED PARTICULARS AND FORMS) (ENGLAND) REGULATIONS 2010/825

SCHEDULE 3
FORM OF COUNTER-NOTICE

To [*name and address*] (See Note 1 below)

1. *I admit that, on [*insert date on which claim notice was given*], [*insert name of company by which claim notice was given*] ('the company') was entitled to acquire the right to manage the premises specified in the claim notice.

*I allege that, by reason of [*specify provision of Chapter 1 of Part 2 of the Commonhold and Leasehold Reform Act 2002 relied on*], on [*insert date on which claim notice was given*], [*insert name of company by which claim notice was given*] ('the company') was not entitled to acquire the right to manage the premises specified in the claim notice.

**Delete one of these statements, as the circumstances require.*

2. If the company has been given one or more counter-notices containing such a statement as is mentioned in paragraph (b) of subsection (2) of section 84 of the Commonhold and Leasehold Reform Act 2002, the company may apply to a [...]* tribunal for

a determination that, on the date on which notice of the claim was given, the company was entitled to acquire the right to manage the premises specified in the claim notice (See Note 2 below).

3. If the company has been given one or more counter-notices containing such a statement as is mentioned in paragraph (b) of subsection (2) of section 84 of the Commonhold and Leasehold Reform Act 2002, the company does not acquire the right to manage those premises unless—

(a) on an application to a […]* tribunal, it is finally determined that the company was entitled to acquire the right to manage the premises; or
(b) the person by whom the counter-notice was given agrees, or the persons by whom the counter-notices were given agree, in writing that the company was so entitled. (See Note 3 below)

Signed:
[*Signature of person on whom claim notice served, or of agent of such person. Where an agent signs, insert also 'Duly authorised agent of [insert name of person on whom claim notice served]'*]

Address:
[*Give the address to which future communications relating to the subject-matter of the notice should be sent*]

Date:
[*Insert date*]

OR

Signed by authority of the company on whose behalf this notice is given [*Signature of authorised member or officer and statement of position in company*]

Address:
[*Give the address to which future communications relating to the subject-matter of the notice should be sent*]

Date:
[*Insert date*]

NOTES

1. The counter-notice is to be given to the company that gave the claim notice. The company's name and address are given in that notice.
2. An application to a […]* tribunal must be made within the period of two months beginning with the day on which the counter-notice (or, where more than one, the last of the counter-notices) was given.
3. For the time at which an application is finally determined, see section 84(7) and (8) of the Commonhold and Leasehold Reform Act 2002.

AMENDMENTS

* Words revoked by Transfer of Tribunal Functions Order 2013 (SI 2013/1036), Sch 2(1), para 44 (1 July 2013: revocation has effect subject to transitional provisions and savings specified in SI 2013/1036, art 6(3) and Sch 3).

Checklist 5.3: Counter-notice – contents

5.99 Contents of the counter-notice under regulations 5(a) and (b) and 8 of, and Schedule 3 to, the 2010 England Regulations and regulation 5(c) of, and Schedule 3 to, the 2011 Wales Regulations:

- Regulation 8(3) of the 2010 England Regulations requires that the counter-notice be in the prescribed form as set out in Schedule 3 to the 2010 England Regulations.
- Address the counter-notice to the company that gave the claim notice. Use the company name and address given in the claim notice (see note 1 of the prescribed form).

- The notice must either admit or deny that the RTM company is entitled to acquire the right to manage the premises. This is a fundamental requirement for a valid counter-notice. Any ambiguity is likely to make the counter-notice invalid.[11]
- If denying the right 'by reason of a specified provision of this Chapter', the counter-notice must identify and refer to the relevant section of the CLRA 2002 or the 2010 England Regulations which is relied upon (or the 2011 Wales Regulations, as applicable).
- Include additional content to the counter-notice in accordance with regulation 5(a) and (b) of the 2010 England Regulations (or the 2011 Wales Regulations, as applicable).
- When serving the prescribed form, ensure that all information in the attached notes to the prescribed form is also served (regulation 5(c) of the 2010 England Regulations). (In Wales, regulation 5(c) of the 2011 Wales Regulations requires the inclusion of information provided in the notes in the form set out in Schedule 3.)

Case law relating to the validity of counter-notices

5.100 Reference should be made to the discussion of the general principles applicable to notices post-*A1 Properties (Sunderland) Limited v Tudor Studios RTM Company Limited*[12] in Chapter 4. The same principled approach should be adopted in relation to the validity of counter-notices.

5.101 In the Welsh case of *St Stephens Mansions RTM Company Limited v Fairhold NW Limited*,[13] on appeal, the Upper Tribunal (Lands Chamber) held that the error in the counter-notice which wrongly stated the name of the RTM company was minor and obvious. In particular, it had been sent under cover of a letter which correctly identified the relevant RTM company. The principles in the case of *Mannai Investment Company Limited v Eagle Star Assurance*[14] were applied, namely, that any 'reasonable' person receiving the counter-notice would have understood

---

11 See *Burman v Mount Cook Land Limited* [2001] EWCA Civ 1712, [2002] Ch 256.

12 *A1 Properties (Sunderland) Limited v Tudor Studios RTM Company Limited* [2024] UKSC 27, [2025] AC 1075.

13 *St Stephens Mansions RTM Company Limited v Fairhold NW Limited* [2014] UKUT 541 (LC), [2015] EGLR 15.

14 *Mannai Investment Company Limited v Eagle Star Assurance* [1997] AC 749 (HL).

that it was intended to refer to the relevant RTM company. It was held that the counter-notice did comply with section 84(2)(b) of the CLRA 2002 and that the failure to correctly identify the name of the RTM company was not fatal in this particular case. That is consistent with the approach in *A1 Properties*.

Who can serve a counter-notice?

5.102 In the case of *Alleyn Court RTM Company Limited v Abou Hamdan*,[15] the Upper Tribunal (Lands Chamber) considered whether the landlord's mortgagee could serve a counter-notice.

5.103 The respondent was a mortgagee in possession of the head lease of the block. The appellant RTM company served notice on the freeholder, the head lessees and the respondent under section 79 of the CLRA 2002 but did not serve copies on any of the qualifying tenants in the block as required. It then served a second claim notice in identical form on all relevant parties. The mortgagee served counter-notices in respect of both the first and second notice of claim as 'duly authorised agent' for the landlord disputing the right to manage.

5.104 The Upper Tribunal (Lands Chamber) held that the particular terms of the mortgage deed appointing the mortgagee allowed the mortgagee to serve the counter-notice on behalf of the mortgagor/freeholder.

Service of the counter-notice

5.105 This is governed by section 111 of the CLRA 2002. See the comments in Chapter 4 which apply to service of notices generally under the CLRA 2002.

Costs

5.106 A point not to be overlooked is that if an RTM company is required to make an application to the tribunal for a determination as to whether it is entitled to acquire the right to manage, there is a possible risk on costs for the RTM company.

---

15 *Alleyn Court RTM Company Limited v Abou Hamdan* [2012] UKUT 74 (LC), [2012] PLSCS 107.

5.107 As from 3 March 2025, section 50 of the Leasehold and Freehold Reform Act 2024 substitutes sections 87A and 87B of the CLRA 2002 for the old rules on costs in section 88.

5.108 Section 87A of the CLRA 2002 sets out the general rule that RTM companies and RTM company members are not liable for the costs incurred by another person because of an RTM claim. It contains a provision that prevents arrangements to the contrary or the recovery of costs by other means. There is a proviso to the effect that section 87A does not affect agreements to pay or contribute to costs made between RTM company members, and between RTM company members with an RTM company.

5.109 Section 87B of the CLRA 2002 allows the tribunal to order an RTM company to pay the reasonable costs of specified people that arise from an RTM claim being made. An order can only be made if the claim notice is withdrawn or ceases to have effect and the RTM company has acted unreasonably. Where an order is made, members of the RTM company are jointly and severally liable, and former members may also be liable in specified circumstances.

Chapter 6

Applications to the Tribunal, Withdrawal and Costs

SUMMARY

6.1 This chapter deals with the procedure where an application to the 'appropriate tribunal' is to be made.

6.2 Section 112(1) of the Commonhold and Leasehold Reform Act 2002 (CLRA 2002) defines the 'appropriate tribunal' as follows:

> (a) in relation to premises in England, the First-tier Tribunal or, where determined by Tribunal Procedure Rules, the Upper Tribunal; and
> (b) in relation to premises in Wales, a leasehold valuation tribunal.

6.3 In most instances, an application relating to the right to manage of premises in England will be made to the First-tier Tribunal (Property Chamber). Applications relating to premises in Wales are to the Leasehold Valuation Tribunal (LVT). Unless the context admits otherwise, references in this chapter to 'the tribunal' are to the 'appropriate tribunal' within the meaning of the CLRA 2002.

6.4 Specifically, this chapter examines the circumstances in which applications may be made, and the form and content they should take. The procedure once the application has been made is also outlined, with particular emphasis on the First-tier Tribunal (Property Chamber), given it is the forum in which most RTM applications are dealt with.

6.5 The circumstances in which an RTM company may need to apply to the tribunal under the CLRA 2002 are as follows:

(a) under section 84(3), where the RTM company has been given one or more counter-notices in which it is alleged that, by reason of a specified provision within Chapter 1, the company was not entitled to acquire the right to manage on the date it gave its claim notice;
(b) under section 85(2), where the person to whom the claim notice would be required to be given in accordance with section 79(6) cannot be found (i.e. the recipient is 'missing');
(c) under section 94(3), where there is a dispute as to the amount of any accrued uncommitted service charges; or
(d) under section 99(5), where a person to whom notice is given under section 98(4) objects to the grant of an approval before the time when the RTM company would first be entitled to grant it, applies to the appropriate tribunal for a determination of the terms on which to grant any such approval; or,
(e) under section 107, where a person who has failed to comply with a requirement imposed on him by, under or by virtue of Chapter 1 of Part 2, to make good the default within such time as is specified in the order.

SECTION 84(3) OF THE CLRA 2002 – APPLICATIONS FOLLOWING A CHALLENGE TO THE ENTITLEMENT TO THE RIGHT TO MANAGE

6.6 An RTM company which has been given one or more counter-notices in which it is alleged the RTM company was not entitled to acquire the right to manage on 'the relevant date', must apply to the tribunal for a determination that it was on the relevant date entitled to acquire the right to manage the premises (section 84(3) of the CLRA 2002).

When an application can (and should) be made

6.7 The effect of a counter-notice alleging that the RTM company was not entitled to acquire the right to manage is that the RTM company may apply to the appropriate tribunal for a decision, which will determine whether it is entitled to acquire the right to manage. A statutory process is, therefore, begun. It is open to the RTM company either to go on with the process by making an application to a tribunal, or to refrain from doing so (and, as shall be seen, ultimately result in the process ceasing).

6.8 Plainly, if the RTM company is serious about continuing with the acquisition, an application should be made. This is so even if the counter-notice appears to be invalid or late. In circumstances where the counter-notice appears to be invalid or late, it might be tempting for the RTM company to refrain from making an application under section 84(3) of the CLRA 2002 on the basis that it considers the counter-notice can be ignored. There are nevertheless several good reasons why this course should not be adopted and, instead, the RTM company should proceed to make an application:

(a) First, if an application is not made, and it subsequently transpires that the counter-notice was valid or in time, failure to apply to the tribunal under section 84(3) in the meantime would cause the RTM claim to be deemed withdrawn.
(b) Second, if a section 84(3) application is made, then the tribunal can rule on the question of validity of the notice in that application.[1] If it rules that the counter-notice is valid, then it can and will go on to deal with the merits of the RTM claim itself.
(c) Third, it avoids the unsatisfactory situations which can arise where a landlord nevertheless disputes the acquisition of the right to manage on jurisdictional grounds. A section 84(3) application provides the forum in which jurisdictional issues can be addressed, rather than the parties being left with having to fight out the issue in court in the context of a claim for a declaration. But, again, if the RTM company loses the jurisdictional dispute and has not made an application under section 84(3) in the meantime, the failure to apply would cause the right to manage claim to be deemed withdrawn. (See further Chapter 5.)

6.9 The application must be made within 2 months of the date on which the counter-notice was given. Where more than one counter-notice has been given, the application must be made within 2 months from the date on which the last notice was given (section 84(4) of the CLRA 2002). In practice, the RTM company will not know how many counter-notices it may receive until the one-month period for giving the counter-notice has expired (see sections 80(6) and 84(1)). The RTM company should therefore work on the assumption that it has 2 months from the date the

---

1 *Assethold Limited v 14 Stansfield Road RTM Company Limited* [2012] UKUT 262 (LC), [2012] 43 EG 115 (CS).

first counter-notice is received unless and until any further counter-notice is given.

6.10 The deadline for the application is important due to the consequences that flow from failure to make an application in time. The use of the word 'must' in section 84(4) of the CLRA 2002 indicates that it is mandatory that an application be made within the specified time. Further, there is no power to extend the time limit for making such an application to the tribunal under the CLRA 2002 or the respective procedure rules for the tribunal.

6.11 Failure to make an application within the specified time results in the claim notice being deemed withdrawn at the end of the 2-month period for making the application (section 87(1) and (2) of the CLRA 2002). In other words, if the application is not made in time, the RTM company will be deemed to have withdrawn its notice on the date 2 months from the date on which the only (or, where there were multiple, last) counter-notice(s) was given.

6.12 Section 87(1) of the CLRA 2002 is not engaged if, before the 2-month period expires, the person(s) by whom the counter-notice or counter-notices were given, has agreed in writing that the RTM company was on the relevant date entitled to acquire the right to manage the premises (section 87(3)). In practice, it is important to note that not only does that agreement need to be in place before the 2-month period for making an application expires, but also that the agreement should be in writing.

Effect of the application and the issues which may be raised

6.13 Section 84(5) of the CLRA 2002 provides as follows:

> (5) Where the RTM company has been given one or more counter-notices containing a statement such as is mentioned in subsection (2)(b), the RTM company does not acquire the right to manage the premises unless—
>
> (a) on an application under subsection (3) it is finally determined that the company was on the relevant date entitled to acquire the right to manage the premises, or
> (b) the person by whom the counter-notice was given agrees, or the persons by whom the counter-notices were given agree, in writing that the company was so entitled.

6.14 This provision sets out the most significant effect of service of a counter-notice challenging the RTM company's entitlement to the right to manage on the relevant date. The effect of this provision is that the RTM company does not acquire the right to manage until either the application under section 84(3) of the CLRA 2002 is finally determined, or all persons who gave a counter-notice agree in writing that the RTM company is so entitled.

6.15 It is evidently intended that the effect of section 84(5)(b) of the CLRA 2002 is that, if the parties reach agreement, there is no need to appear before the tribunal to obtain a formal determination in the application before the RTM company acquires the right to manage. However, the drafting of section 84(5)(b) is somewhat imperfect in one main respect. It is not clear on what date the RTM company acquires the right to manage in circumstances where there is an agreement. Is it the date on which the agreement is reached? Is it the date given in the claim notice under section 80(7)? Given it is possible that agreement may be reached after the date for acquisition of the right to manage specified in the claim notice under section 80(7) and given the lack of specification as to either date acting as default position, the authors consider it unlikely that either of those dates apply. This leaves two possibilities: either as part of the compromise or agreement the parties agree the date upon which the right to manage will be acquired; or, absent such agreement, the RTM company (or, indeed, the landlord) may wish to proceed to an unopposed final hearing or determination on paper in order for the tribunal to determine the date on which the right to manage will be acquired. This is the procedure that was adopted in the case of *BCL (RTM) Company Limited v Barrington Developments Limited*.[2] The authors consider a 'cleaner' and likely less costly approach would be for the agreement to provide for the date upon which the parties consider the right to manage will be acquired.

6.16 Neither section 84 of the CLRA 2002 nor the regulations make expressly clear whether, at any hearing before the tribunal under section 84(3), the landlord (or the other giver of a counter-notice) is limited to arguing the grounds relied upon in the counter-notice. That being so, RTM companies have sought to take a point over the scope of what the landlord can argue. In the early days of the CLRA 2002, the

2 *BCL (RTM) Company Limited v Barrington Developments Limited*, LON/00AP/LRM/2004/0002, LVT, 23 June 2004, unreported.

Leasehold Valuation Tribunal held that the landlord was limited to the grounds relied on in the counter-notice.[3] That decision seemed rather harsh given the statutory requirements for counter-notices in section 84(2), regulation 5 of the Right to Manage (Prescribed Particulars and Forms) (England) Regulations 2010 (SI 2010/825) and the content of the form set out in Schedule 3.

6.17 In the case of *Fairhold (Yorkshire) Limited v Trinity Wharf (SE16) RTM Company Limited*,[4] the Upper Tribunal (Lands Chamber) has dealt head-on with the issue of whether, in opposing an application under section 84(3) of the CLRA 2002, a landlord was limited to arguing only the grounds raised in its counter-notice. In that case, the respondent RTM company argued that it was incumbent on the appellant landlord to raise in the counter-notice every matter it wanted the tribunal to decide. The then President, Sir Keith Lindblom, squarely rejected this proposition and explained why (at [34]):

> In the first place, there is no statutory requirement to that effect. Section 84 does not provide that if an application is made by the RTM company under s.84(3) a counter-notice is to be treated by the leasehold valuation tribunal as delimiting its jurisdiction. Section 84(3) effectively defines the scope of a tribunal's jurisdiction as being to determine whether the RTM company was 'on the relevant date entitled to acquire the right to manage the premises'. That is its statutory remit. There is no provision in s.84, or elsewhere in the 2002 Act, whose effect is to confine that jurisdiction to the contents of the counter-notice that has prompted the RTM company to apply for a determination of its entitlement to acquire the right to manage.

He went on to express the view that it is perfectly legitimate for a landlord who is opposing the claim to acquire a right to manage its premises to take points about whether the procedures prescribed in the CLRA 2002 and the regulations have been correctly followed, whether or not it has been raised in the counter-notice. Although, he did make the point, which practitioners should note, that it is always desirable to raise matters at the earliest opportunity and such points 'should, if possible, be raised in the counter-notice given under s.84'. As practitioners, it is always worth heeding such warnings.

---

3 *Dawlin RTM Limited v Oakhill Park Estate (Hampstead) Limited*, LON/00AG/LEE/2005/00012, LVT, 21 September 2005, unreported.

4 *Fairhold (Yorkshire) Limited v Trinity Wharf (SE16) RTM Company Limited* [2013] UKUT 502 (LC), [2014] L & TR 6.

6.18 The decision in *Fairhold* was followed shortly after by the case of *Albion Residential Limited v Albion Riverside Residents RTM Company Limited.*[5] In *Albion*, Martin Rodger QC focussed on the principle that statutory rights should not and could not be acquired based off an invalid claim notice. The Upper Tribunal (Lands Chamber) held (at [44]):

> We do not accept that inaction on the part of the recipient of an invalid claim notice can result in the acquisition (and deprivation) of rights in circumstances which do not come within those to which Chapter 1 of Part 2 of the 2002 Act applies. If a claim notice is invalid because it relates to a building which is not self-contained, or because it is given by leaseholders who are too few in number or who are not qualifying tenants, or if for any other reason the qualifying conditions set out in section 72 are not satisfied, none of the provisions in the remaining sections of Chapter 1 have any application. The satisfaction of the qualifying conditions is essential to the jurisdiction of the LVT to make a determination of entitlement under section 84(3). Where an issue going to the jurisdiction of a first instance tribunal is raised in proceedings before it, or where the same tribunal itself identifies such an issue, it is entitled to investigate it and to determine it subject to the safeguards identified by the tribunal in [36] of *Fairhold.*

6.19 The safeguards referred to in *Fairhold* are that its procedure is fair throughout and, therefore, that the parties are given a reasonable opportunity to present any relevant evidence or submissions.

6.20 That said, there are two things to note about the decisions in *Fairhold* and *Albion*: first, they are not authority for the proposition that every failure to take a point in the notice will be forgiven such that the landlords are entitled to argue their case afresh regardless of their counter-notice; and, second, practitioners should not condone a failure to comply with statutory requirements, and such a failure may have costs consequences.

6.21 If, on an application under section 84(3) of the CLRA 2002, it is finally determined that the RTM company was not entitled to acquire the right to manage the premises, then the claim notice ceases to have effect.

---

5 *Albion Residential Limited v Albion Riverside Residents RTM Company Limited* [2014] UKUT 6 (LC), [2014] 1 WLUK 141.

6.22 If the right to manage is acquired, it will be acquired on one of three dates (see section 90 of the CLRA 2002):

(a) (if there is no challenge): the date specified in the claim notice under section 80(7); or
(b) (if there is a challenge which is pursued): 3 months after the determination of the appropriate tribunal in favour of the RTM company becomes 'final' (see section 90(4)); or
(c) (if there is a challenge which is then dropped, by agreement in writing by all persons who have served a counter-notice): 3 months from the date of that agreement (see section 90(5)).

THE APPLICATION TO THE TRIBUNAL

Form and content

6.23 The relevant application form to be used when making an application to the tribunal is Form 'RTM Application Relating to (No Fault) Right to Manage' under section 84(3).[6]

6.24 In the First-tier Tribunal (Property Chamber), rule 26 of the Tribunal Procedure (First-tier Tribunal) (Property Chamber) Rules 2013 (SI 2013/1169) makes provision for starting proceedings, and specifies the information required in an application to the First-tier Tribunal. This rule is supplemented by paragraph 6 of, and Schedule 6 to, the Practice Directions for the Property Chamber, First-tier Tribunal Areas in the Property Chamber (9 September 2013), which list various matters which must be included in an application to the tribunal.

6.25 An applicant must start proceedings before the tribunal by sending or delivering a notice of application to the tribunal (rule 26(1) of the Tribunal Procedure (First-tier Tribunal) (Property Chamber) Rules 2013). Such application must be signed and dated and, unless a practice direction makes different provision (which it does not currently), details of the applicant, the respondent, the nature of the claim and the matters listed in rule 26(2) must be included. The application must be accompanied by the

6 The relevant form for right to manage applications to the LVT in Wales is Application Form (RTM 1).

particulars and document specified in an applicable practice direction (see the reference to paragraph 6 and Schedule 6 at para 6.24) (rule 26(3)).

6.26 Accordingly, an application under section 84(3) of the CLRA 2002 should provide:

(a) the name and address for service of the RTM company;
(b) the name and address of the freeholder, any intermediate landlord and any manager;
(c) a copy of the memorandum and articles of association of the RTM company.
(d) a copy of the claim notice and a copy of the counter-notice received.

6.27 Further, the application must be accompanied by the documents specified in the applicable rules. An application which is not accompanied by sufficient information and documentation to enable the application to be determined will not be a valid application.[7]

6.28 The practical effect of this latter rule is that it will be difficult for applications to be filed by fax where there are a great many documents, although, of course, making the application by such method will remain permissible and possible.

Calculating time

6.29 In the case of *Gateway Property Holdings Limited v 6–10 Montrose Gardens RTM Company Limited*,[8] it was held that the 2-month period under section 84(4) begins with the day on which the counter-notice was given (in that case, 3 August 2010), and so the time for making the application expires at 23:59 on the date 2 months later (in that case, 2 October 2010). However, the Upper Tribunal (Lands Chamber) did not seem entirely confident on this point and concluded that, if it was wrong about 2 October 2010 being the final date for making the application, then the latest date must have been 3 October 2010. On the facts in that case, the point made no difference.

---

7 See Form Leasehold 8: Applications relating to Right to Manage.

8 *Gateway Property Holdings Limited v 6–10 Montrose Gardens RTM Company Limited* [2011] UKUT 349 (LC), [2011] 9 WLUK 127.

6.30 The authors are of the view that this Upper Tribunal was wrong to doubt itself. As determined by the Court of Appeal in the case of *Zoan v Rouamba*,[9] where something must be done within a period described as 'beginning with' a specified day, then that day is included in the calculation of the period. This can be distinguished with cases where the period runs 'from' or 'after' a specified day, in which case the specified day is to be excluded from the calculation of the period. As the period under section 84(4) of the CLRA 2002 is the 'period of two months beginning with the day on which the counter-notice', it should therefore include the date on which the counter-notice was given.

'Making' the application to the tribunal

6.31 Given the importance of time limits under section 84 of the CLRA 2002, it is important to understand what is required to 'make' an application. In *Gateway*, although the point was not directly considered, the Upper Tribunal (Lands Chamber) suggested that a fax received by the Leasehold Valuation Tribunal with the application would be sufficient to 'make' the application such as to stop time running.

6.32 The question was considered by HHJ Behrens in the case of *Salehabady v Eyre Estate Trustees*.[10] In that case it was held that – albeit in the context of enfranchisement – an application to the tribunal had been made 'by the posting of a correctly addressed (and sufficiently stamped) notice of application to the FTT'. This reasoning was based on the fact that under rule 26(1) of the Tribunal Procedure (First-tier Tribunal) (Property Chamber) Rules 2013, an 'applicant must start proceedings before the Tribunal by sending or delivering to the Tribunal a notice of application'. Thus, the Upper Tribunal (Lands Chamber) held, what was required was a unilateral act by the applicant. This is so even if the application notice is delayed in the post or does not arrive. Provided it is posted to the First-tier Tribunal (Property Chamber), proceedings have been started.

---

9 *Zoan v Rouamba* [2000] 1 WLR 1509.

10 *Salehabady v Eyre Estate Trustees* [2017] UKUT 60 (LC), [2017] L & TR 22.

Withdrawing an application

6.33 It is not clear on the face of section 84 of the CLRA 2002 if and how an application may be withdrawn. This is important as the liability for costs incurred as a party to proceedings before the tribunal only arises, however, if the tribunal dismisses the application.

6.34 However, in accordance with rule 22(3) of the Tribunal Procedure (First-tier Tribunal) (Property Chamber) Rules 2013, it is now clear that a notice of withdrawal must be given and the First-tier Tribunal (Property Chamber) must consent to the withdrawal before it takes effect.[11] It is notable that in the case of *R (O Twelve Baytree Limited) v Leasehold Valuation Tribunal and Others*,[12] the court held that, even in cases where the RTM company no longer wished to pursue its application for the right to manage, there may be rare cases in which the First-tier Tribunal considers it appropriate to determine the substantive points raised by the application.

WITHDRAWAL OF A CLAIM NOTICE

6.35 In accordance with section 86 of the CLRA 2002, a claim notice may be withdrawn by the RTM company at any time before it actually acquires the right to manage. That means the RTM company may withdraw its claim notice at any time before the following dates:

(a) (if there is no challenge): the date specified in the claim notice; or
(b) (if there is a challenge which is pursued): 3 months after the determination of the appropriate tribunal in favour of the RTM company becomes 'final'; or
(c) (if there is a challenge which is then dropped, by agreement in writing by all persons who have served a counter-notice): 3 months from the date of that agreement.

6.36 Where it seeks to withdraw the claim notice, the RTM company must give a 'notice of withdrawal' to the persons specified in section 86(2) of the CLRA 2002. These are broadly the same as the parties on whom the

---

11 *R (O Twelve Baytree Limited) v Leasehold Valuation Tribunal and Others* [2014] EWHC 1229 (Admin), [2015] 1 WLR 276 at [44]–[45].

12 Ibid.

claim notice had to be served, except there is no requirement to serve the appropriate tribunal which appointed any manager under Part II of the Landlord and Tenant Act 1987 (LTA 1987).

6.37 It has been held to be sufficient to serve a covering letter with a fresh claim notice which states, 'Following receipt of your counter-notice the decision has been made to re[-]serve the Notice of Claim and to restart the process from this stage relying on the existing Notices of Participation'.[13] In the case of *Eastern Pyramid Group Corporation SA v Spire House RTM Company Limited*,[14] the Upper Tribunal (Lands Chamber), in a point not pursued on appeal, adopted the reasonable recipient test in construing whether the covering letter was a sufficient notice of withdrawal.[15]

6.38 There is no saving provision where there is a failure to serve one of the parties to be served; however, the authors consider that following the Supreme Court's decision in the case of *A1 Properties (Sunderland) Limited v Tudor Studios RTM Company Limited*[16] (see Chapter 5), the correct approach is to ask whether it was a purpose of the legislature that failure to serve one of the required parties invalidates the notice of withdrawal. The focus will be on: (a) the purpose served by the requirement as assessed in light of a detailed analysis of the particular statute; and (b) the specific facts of the case, having regard to whether any (and what) prejudice might be caused or whether any injustice might arise if the validity of the statutory process is affirmed notwithstanding the breach of the procedural requirement. In *A1 Properties*, the failure to serve a claim notice on all required parties did not invalidate the claim. As a result, it is probable that in many cases failure to serve a notice of withdrawal on all required parties will not necessarily invalidate the withdrawal. Although it is noted that this is a fact-specific enquiry.

---

[13] *Eastern Pyramid Group Corporation SA v Spire House RTM Company Limited* [2021] EWCA Civ 1658, [2022] 1 WLR 503.

[14] *Eastern Pyramid Group Corporation SA v Spire House RTM Company Limited* [2020] UKUT 199 (LC), [2020] 6 WLUK 555.

[15] *Mannai Investment Company Limited v Eagle Star Life Assurance Company Limited* [1997] AC 749 (HL).

[16] *A1 Properties (Sunderland) Limited v Tudor Studios RTM Company Limited* [2024] UKSC 27, [2025] AC 1075.

6.39 It is important to note that under section 111 of the CLRA 2002 any notice, including a notice of withdrawal: (a) must be in writing; and (b) may be sent by post. Moreover, if an RTM company has been notified of an address at which a landlord wishes to be served with notices, it cannot rely on an address provided under section 47 or section 48 of the LTA 1987. Hence, in the case of *Assethold v 429 New Cross Road RTM Company Limited*,[17] where an address for service of notices in relation Chapter 1 of Part II of the CLRA 2002 was specified in the landlord's counternotice, the RTM company was wrong to serve a notice of withdrawal on the address specified in the last service charge demand. Notably, this case was decided without reference to the law as it now stands in *A1 Properties*, and it remains to be seen if, under the law as now clarified, such a failure will still render the notice of withdrawal invalid.

Deemed withdrawal

6.40 There are a number of situations under the CLRA 2002 where the claim notice is deemed to have been withdrawn:

(a) under section 87(1)(a), where a counter-notice is served denying the right to acquire the right to manage but the RTM company fails to apply to the tribunal in time;
(b) under section 87(1)(b), where the tribunal application is withdrawn; and
(c) where the tribunal finds that the RTM company was not entitled to acquire the right to manage.

6.41 Under section 87(4) of the CLRA 2002, there are the following further situations where the claim notice will be deemed withdrawn:

(a) where the RTM company is wound up or placed into administration;
(b) where receivers or managers of property of the RTM company are appointed;
(c) if a company voluntary arrangement is approved in respect of the RTM company; and
(d) if the RTM company is struck off the Companies Register under sections 1000, 1001, 1002 or 1003 of the Companies Act 2006.

---

[17] *Assethold v 429 New Cross Road RTM Company Limited* [2024] UKUT 113 (LC), [2024] 5 WLUK 302.

6.42 The authors consider the situations contained within section 87(4) of the CLRA 2002 are unlikely to arise in practice given the RTM company will likely have been incorporated in close proximity to the service of the claim notice.

6.43 As for the situation which may arise under section 87(1)(a) of the CLRA 2002, it ought to be avoidable. Practitioners acting for the RTM company should be alive to deadlines, and should diarise carefully the latest date on which it would be possible to apply to the tribunal. Without such reminders, the deadline could easily be missed and a dissatisfied client or, worse, in the event of a causative loss, negligence claim could ensue.

COSTS OF THE APPLICATION TO ACQUIRE THE RIGHT TO MANAGE

6.44 The costs of the application to acquire the right to manage in particular circumstances were previously addressed by sections 88 and 89 of the CLRA 2002. As of 3 March 2025, these provisions have now been repealed and replaced by sections 87A and 87B.[18]

6.45 Under the old regime, it was presumed that an RTM company would be liable for costs incurred as a consequence of a claim notice. However, the new section 87A of the CLRA 2002 reverses this presumption such that RTM companies are not liable for the costs incurred by another person because of an RTM claim (section 87A(1)) unless certain exceptions are met. As a result, it is now unlikely that a landlord can recover any costs in an uncontentious right to manage case.

6.46 One exception is that a court or tribunal relying on another power makes an order rendering the RTM company liable. Section 87B of the CLRA 2002 gives the appropriate tribunal the power to award costs if various cumulative conditions are met. Section 87B(2) provides as follows:

18 Amended by Leasehold and Freehold Reform Act 2024, section 50(3).

(a) the claim notice—

(i) is at any time withdrawn or deemed to be withdrawn by virtue of any provision of this Chapter, or
(ii) at any time ceases to have effect by reason of any other provision of this Chapter;

(b) the RTM company acts unreasonably in—

(i) giving the claim notice, or
(ii) not withdrawing it, causing it to be deemed withdrawn, or causing it to cease to have effect sooner;

(c) the applicant is—

(i) a landlord under a lease of the whole or any part of the premises,
(ii) party to such a lease otherwise than as landlord or tenant, or
(iii) a manager appointed under Part 2 of the 1987 Act to act in relation to the premises, or any premises containing or contained in the premises;

(d) the costs are incurred before the claim notice is withdrawn, is deemed withdrawn, or ceases to have effect;
(e) the costs are incurred other than in connection with proceedings before a court or tribunal;
(f) the costs are reasonably incurred.

6.47 If the tribunal makes an order under section 87B of the CLRA 2002, then the members of the RTM company are joint and severally liable for those costs (section 87B(3)) unless their lease has been assigned and the assignee has become a member of the RTM company (section 87B(4)).

6.48 There is an anti-avoidance provision rendering any lease, transfer, or contract void to the extent that it provides for costs recovery in such cases (section 87A(2) of the CLRA 2002). However, this does not affect any agreements made between RTM company members or between an RTM company and its members.

6.49 There is no express power to award costs in favour of the RTM company if the landlord unsuccessfully resists the application for the right to manage.

Costs in the First-tier Tribunal (Property Chamber)

6.50 Practitioners should bear in mind that, in addition to the statutory provisions on costs, under the Tribunal Procedure (First-tier Tribunal) (Property Chamber) Rules 2013, the First-tier Tribunal (Property Chamber) possesses the following powers to award costs:

(a) under rule 13(2) to order reimbursement of fees by one party to another;
(b) under rule 13(1)(a) to make wasted costs orders against representatives; and
(c) under rule 13(1)(b) to award costs payable by one party to another where that party has acted unreasonably in bringing, defending or conducting proceedings.

6.51 The test under the latter provision has been considered by the Upper Tribunal (Lands Chamber) in the case of *Willow Court Management Company (1985) Limited v Alexander*.[19] A detailed consideration of that case is beyond the scope of this text, but the test can be summarised as follows:

(a) the First-tier Tribunal (Property Chamber) must first assess (as a value judgement and not as the exercise of discretion) whether the conduct complained of is sufficient to meet the objective standard of conduct threshold;
(b) second, it must consider whether, in the exercise of its discretion, and taking account of all relevant factors, it is appropriate to make a costs award; and
(c) third, it must, as a further exercise of discretion, consider the form and quantum of the costs award.

---

[19] *Willow Court Management Company (1985) Limited v Alexander* [2016] UKUT 290 (LC), [2016] L & TR 34 (recently approved in *Lea v GP Ilfracombe Management Company Limited* [2024] EWCA Civ 1241, [2024] PLSCS 185).

Chapter 7

Acquisition and Handover

SUMMARY

7.1 This chapter covers those parts of the Commonhold and Leasehold Reform Act 2002 (CLRA 2002) which provide a code for the exercise of the right to manage by the RTM company. First, it considers sections 90–94, which make provision for the acquisition of the right; and, second, it examines:

(a) the registration of the right to manage and the consequences of registration;
(b) the transfer of management responsibility;
(c) the duty to provide information;
(d) the duty to pay accrued uncommitted service charges; and
(e) the consequences of breach of covenants on acquisition.

MANNER OF ACQUISITION

7.2 The right to manage is not something acquired by bilateral (or multilateral) agreement but is a statutory right. As a result, provided a valid claim notice has been served, then the RTM company is 'deemed' to have acquired the right to manage. This has a number of important consequences. First, it guarantees uniformity and predictability for leaseholders; the rights that they acquire are not dependent on complex agreements with landlords.

7.3 Second, this 'deeming' restricts the landlord's powers to object; they are not entitled to object arbitrarily. A landlord cannot object for reasons of self-interest, but only on the basis of whether or not statutory criteria are met. In practice, landlords will often raise objections with the ulterior motive of protecting their own interests; however, the statutory scheme severely restricts this ability.

7.4 Third, it prevents financial interests from coming into play. A landlord cannot negotiate a price for the right to manage; if the criteria are met, they must hand over the right. This final factor is the key that separates the right to manage from the enfranchisement process which, in cases of large developments with commercial premises, can be prohibitively expensive for lessees to acquire. How and when this handover occurs is the focus of this chapter.

7.5 Lastly, it is worth noting that as a result of this statutory transfer that the RTM company should not in a material sense be considered to be an 'agent' of the landlord; its authority has not been delegated but transferred.

7.6 In the circumstances set out in the quotation below, where no tribunal determination is involved, the effect of Part 2 of Chapter 1 of the CLRA 2002 is that there is deemed to be no dispute.[1] The effect of this deeming is summarised in the joint judgment of Lord Briggs and Lord Sales at [88] of the decision in the case of *A1 Properties (Sunderland) Limited v Tudor Studios RTM Company Limited*[2] as follows:

> There is no jurisdiction in the tribunal to revisit and undo a transfer of the right to manage which has purportedly occurred as a result of the operation of section 90 or a determination of the tribunal, so the way in which a challenge would be brought would be by proceedings in the High Court simply seeking a declaration of rights (in the former situation) or seeking judicial review of the order of the tribunal and a declaration (in the latter).

ACQUISITION DATE

7.7 The acquisition date is of fundamental importance to the exercise of the right to manage under the CLRA 2002; it is on this date that the

---

1 *A1 Properties (Sunderland) Limited v Tudor Studios RTM Company Limited* [2024] UKSC 27, [2025] AC 1075 at [71], [74], [80] and [81].

2 Ibid, at [88].

management functions under the leases of a qualifying premises formally transfer to the RTM company under sections 96–98.

7.8 It will be recalled that a claim notice is required to specify a date on which the RTM company intends to acquire the right to manage the premises (see further Chapter 2).[3] This date must be not less than 3 months after the date of service of the claim notice. The intention, on the face of the claim notice, is that this is the acquisition date. However, whether it in fact takes effect as such will depend on the service and/or contents of any counter-notice(s):

(a) If no counter-notice is served, then the acquisition date is the date specified in the claim notice.[4]
(b) If a counter-notice is served admitting that the RTM company was on the relevant date entitled to acquire the right to manage, then the acquisition date is again the date specified in the claim notice.[5]
(c) Where the right to manage is acquired following a determination by the First-tier Tribunal (Property Chamber) as to the RTM company's entitlement, then the acquisition date is the date falling 3 months after the determination becomes final.[6]
(d) Where a counter-notice is served not admitting the right to manage, but the person(s) by whom the counter-notice(s) were served later agree the entitlement in writing, the acquisition date is 3 months after the agreement.[7]
(e) Where a landlord cannot be traced and an application is made to the First-tier Tribunal (Property Chamber) under section 85 of the CLRA 2002, the acquisition date is specified by the First-tier Tribunal in its order.[8]

7.9 The First-tier Tribunal (Property Chamber)'s order will become 'final' for the purposes of section 90(4) of the CLRA 2002 either: (a) at

---

3 CLRA 2002, s 80(7).

4 CLRA 2002, s 90(2) and (3)(a).

5 CLRA 2002, s 90(2) and s(3)(b).

6 CLRA 2002, s 90(4).

7 CLRA 2002, s 90(5). It is a question of fact when the agreement in writing is given, see for example *Assethold Limited v Piano Works Building RTM Company Limited* [2024] UKUT 399 (LC), [2025] L & TR 10 at [24].

8 CLRA 2002, s 90(6).

the end of the time specified for bringing an appeal; or (b) when any appeal (or further appeal) is finally determined and the period for a further appeal has ended or that appeal is otherwise abandoned or ceases to be of effect.[9] Hence, where the First-tier Tribunal makes a determination in favour of the RTM company, the following time line applies:

(a) 28 days[10] (or 21 days in Wales)[11] from the date on which the decision is sent out to make an application for permission to appeal;
(b) if permission to appeal is applied for and refused, 14 days from the date on which the First-tier Tribunal (or Leasehold Valuation Tribunal) refuses the appeal to renew the application for permission to the Upper Tribunal (Lands Chamber);[12]
(c) if the Upper Tribunal refuses permission, this is when the decision becomes final. Alternatively, if permission is given (provided procedural requirements are complied with),[13] final disposal comes 28 days after the Upper Tribunal disposes of the application;
(d) thereafter, there are 28 days to file an appellant's notice to the Court of Appeal;[14]
(e) lastly, there are a further 28 days to file an appellant's notice to the Supreme Court.[15]

7.10 The period of 3 months given in section 90 of the CLRA 2002 is indicative of the time which Parliament considered was appropriate to allow for arrangements to be made for the handover of responsibilities from the landlord to the RTM company.[16]

---

9 CLRA 2002, s 84(7) and (8).

10 Tribunal Procedure (First-tier Tribunal) (Property Chamber) Rules 2013 (SI 2013/1169), r 52(2).

11 Leasehold Valuation Tribunal (Procedure) (Wales) Regulations 2004 (SI 2004/681), reg 20(a).

12 Tribunal Procedure (Upper Tribunal) (Lands Chamber) Rules 2010 (SI 2010/2600), r 21(2).

13 For example the Tribunal Procedure (Upper Tribunal) (Lands Chamber) Rules 2010, rr 23 and 24.

14 Civil Procedure Rules, PD 52D, para 3.3. This is an exception to the usual rule that provides just 21 days to file an appellant's notice to the Court of Appeal under Civil Procedure Rules, r 52.12(2)(b).

15 UK Supreme Court Practice Directions, PD 1.16.

16 *A1 Properties (Sunderland) Limited v Tudor Studios RTM Company Limited* [2024] UKSC 27, [2025] AC 1075 at [105].

7.11 In order for the acquisition to in fact take place on the date specified in section 90 of the CLRA 2002, a valid claim notice under section 90 must have been served (or in the circumstances envisaged in section 90(3)(b), a valid counter-notice under section 84). As Sir Keith Lindblom commented in the case of *Avon Freeholds Limited v Regent Court RTM Company Limited*:[17]

> Parliament cannot have intended that a right to manage could be acquired on the basis of notices that were inherently unlawful, or that there should be no remedy to prevent that result.

REGISTRATION OF THE RIGHT TO MANAGE

7.12 While the right to manage itself does not confer ownership or proprietary rights in the land, its recognition has practical implications for third parties, especially in relation to dealings affecting the premises and the leases under it. Accordingly, the right to manage should be registered with HM Land Registry (HMLR) to ensure transparency and to protect the RTM company's position. Unfortunately, it is not possible to register a claim notice, as set out in HMLR, Practice guide 27: the leasehold reform legislation, Section 7 (updated 22 April 2025).

7.13 The right to register the right to manage was introduced in 2008 by what is now rule 79A of the Land Registration Rules (SI 2003/1417). Once the right to manage has been acquired, the RTM company may apply to HMLR on Form AP1 for an entry to be made to record the acquisition of the right to manage.

7.14 An application must be accompanied by evidence to prove: (a) that the applicant is an RTM company; (b) that the right to manage relates to the registered estate; (c) that the registered proprietor of the estate is a landlord under a lease; and (d) that the right to manage has been acquired and remains exercisable. Generally, such evidence may be made by way

---

17 *Avon Freeholds Limited v Regent Court RTM Company Limited* [2013] UKUT 213 (LC), [2013] L & TR 23 at [75]. The distinction between notices being voidable rather than void, introduced in *A1 Properties (Sunderland) Limited v Tudor Studios RTM Company Limited* [2024] UKSC 27, [2025] AC 1075, makes the position less clear.

of a certificate given by a conveyancer or the RTM company.[18] However, in practice, HMLR will also require a copy of the claim notice.[19]

7.15 It should be noted that an entry on the register does not guarantee that the right to manage remains exercisable.

7.16 One other key relevance of the register is that one of the functions transferred to the RTM company under section 98(7) of the CLRA 2002 is the power to grant approvals required by virtue of any restriction entered on the register. This is dealt with further in Chapter 8.

7.17 It should be noted that HMLR takes the view that the right to manage is not an adverse right affecting the landlord's title to the estate. As a result, an agreed or unilateral notice (in the case of a registered estate) or registration of a caution against first registration (in the case of an unregistered estate) are not considered to be appropriate.[20] Hence, it may be said that failure to register the right to manage will not affect the validity of the process. This is supported by the Law Commission, which took the view that the existence of a notice on the register should not force a landlord's successor in title to accept that the right to manage has been validly acquired.[21]

TRANSFER OF THE MANAGEMENT RESPONSIBILITY

7.18 On the acquisition date, the RTM company acquires the landlord's 'management functions' under the leases. It is important to recall that this does not amount to the RTM company becoming the landlord or acquiring the landlord's title. Importantly, the management functions are transferred

---

18 See HMLR, Practice guide 27: the leasehold reform legislation (updated 22 April 2025), Section 7.

19 See Law Commission, *Leasehold home ownership: exercising the right to manage: Consultation Paper* (Consultation Paper 243), January 2019, §7.182.

20 HMLR, Practice guide 27: the leasehold reform legislation (updated 22 April 2025).

21 Law Commission, *Leasehold home ownership: exercising the right to manage: Consultation Paper* (Consultation Paper 243), January 2019, §7.185.

both from the landlord[22] and from any third-party to a lease (for example a management company).[23]

Transferred management functions

7.19 The transferred 'management functions' under the leases are those functions relating to services, repairs, maintenance, improvements, insurance and management. The word 'functions' includes obligations, duties and powers.[24] This definition is problematic, not least as it includes a degree of circularity with management functions being defined as including functions in relation to management. There are also special provisions in relation to approvals; these are addressed in Chapter 8.

7.20 It is important to note that the rights and duties acquired by the RTM company are not modified from those exercised by the landlord in any way, nor are any new rights or duties created which were not previously exercisable by the landlord. In addition, the fact that these rights are now exercisable by an RTM company as opposed to a landlord or management company does not affect the construction of the lease.[25] However, the 'lease' is to be construed broadly, and may include obligations in a settlement agreement collateral to a lease.[26]

7.21 Once the management functions are transferred to the RTM company, the landlord (or other third party) then loses the right to carry out those functions, regardless of whether the function is mandatory or discretionary, unless the RTM company agrees for them to do so.[27] The Supreme Court, in the case of *FirstPort Property Services Limited v Settlers Court RTM Company Limited*,[28] gave the example of a tenants'

---

22 CLRA 2002, s 96(2).

23 CLRA 2002, s 96(3).

24 *Francia Properties Limited v Aristou* [2017] L & TR 5 at [63].

25 *Wilson v Lesley Place (RTM) Company Limited* [2010] UKUT 342 (LC), [2011] L & TR 11 at [13].

26 See for example *AHM Block 5 RTM Company Limited v Crystal Water Limited*, Central London County Court, 28 July 2016, unreported, Recorder Cohen QC, cited in Tanfield Chambers, *Service Charges and Management: Law and Practice* (Sweet & Maxwell, 5th edn, 2021), para 27-06.

27 CLRA 2002, s 97(2).

28 *FirstPort Property Services Limited v Settlers Court RTM Company Limited* [2022] UKSC 1, [2022] 1 WLR 519.

car park for use by both tenants and third parties. In such a case it would make 'obvious sense' to agree for the landlord or management company to continue to manage the car park as a whole.[29]

Untransferred tenant's covenants

7.22 The CLRA 2002 expressly provides for the power to enforce 'untransferred tenant's covenants', being covenants which fall to be complied with by a tenant under the lease, and a tenant covenant is otherwise unenforceable by the RTM company.[30] An RTM company is entitled to enforce such covenants (see further Chapter 8).[31] This entitlement is not to the preclusion of the other parties entitled to enforce the said covenants. Where there is a power under a lease to enter any part of the premises to determine whether a tenant is complying with any untransferred tenant covenant, that power of entry is also exercisable by the RTM company.[32]

7.23 Indeed, section 101 of the CLRA 2002 compels the RTM company to monitor and report any breaches of tenant's covenants to the landlord. When an RTM company becomes aware of a breach, it must report this to the landlord within 3 months, unless: (a) the failure has been remedied; (b) reasonable compensation has been paid in respect of the failure; or (c) the landlord has notified the RTM company that it need not report to him or her failures of that type.

7.24 The exception to the RTM company's powers of enforcement is the power of re-entry or forfeiture which remains in the hands of the landlord.[33] That said, the RTM company can still apply to the First-tier Tribunal (Property Chamber) for a determination that a tenant is in breach of a covenant under his or her lease pursuant to section 168 of the CLRA 2002.[34] Once the RTM company has secured the determination of the

---

29 *FirstPort Property Services Limited v Settlers Court RTM Company Limited* [2022] UKSC 1, [2022] 1 WLR 519 at [42].

30 CLRA 2002, s 100(2).

31 CLRA 2002, s 100(2).

32 CLRA 2002, s 100(5).

33 CLRA 2002, s 100(3).

34 *Eastpoint Block A RTM Company Limited v Otubaga* [2023] EWCA Civ 879, [2023] 1 WLR 3896.

First-tier Tribunal that a breach has indeed been committed, the way is clear for the landlord to serve a section 146 notice and, if the breach remains unremedied, to begin proceedings for forfeiture.[35] However, it is worth noting that as the RTM company cannot exercise rights of forfeiture, it is unlikely that the costs of section 168 proceedings can be recovered by the RTM company via an administration charge, which only provides for costs relating to forfeiture proceedings.[36]

Limitations on management functions

7.25 Not all functions, rights and responsibilities under the leases are transferred when the right to manage is acquired.[37] The limitations can be summarised as:

(a) functions relating only to premises not held by qualifying tenants;
(b) functions relating to forfeiture;
(c) functions relating to retained parts;
(d) functions relating to shared estate facilities.

7.26 The first limitation relates to premises not held by qualifying tenants. Where the management function relates only to premises not held by qualifying tenants then it is not transferred to the management company. For example, if there is a management function in relation to maintaining a car park, and the car park is held by a third party, then management of this may not transfer to the RTM company. However, where the management function overlaps with the functions in relation to parts held by qualifying tenants, then it is transferred. For example, if the car park is an underground car park, the repair of the structure of the car park may overlap with the repair of the structure of the parts managed by the RTM company. In such circumstances, it is the RTM company which is responsible for the management (including repair).

---

35 *Eastpoint Block A RTM Company Limited v Otubaga* [2023] EWCA Civ 879, [2023] 1 WLR 3896 at [29].

36 A typical clause may read the costs 'of and occasioned by the preparation and service of a notice served under section 146 of the Law of Property Act 1925'.

37 The enforcement of these 'untransferred' functions are dealt with further in Chapter 8.

7.27 The second limitation relates to re-entry or forfeiture of leases.[38] This is expressly reserved by the CLRA 2002 as being outside the RTM company's powers. Notably, as discussed in para 7.24, the RTM company can still apply to the First-tier Tribunal (Property Chamber) for a determination that a tenant is in breach of a covenant under his or her lease pursuant to section 168.[39]

7.28 Third, as a result of the RTM company not acquiring title, it does not acquire the retained parts of the property. These remain in the hands of the landlord to dispose of as he or she pleases. Plainly, this means that a landlord is entitled to grant leases out of his or her retained parts.[40] It has not yet been conclusively established if this means that where the new lease is a qualifying lease, the RTM company acquires the management functions under that lease. In the authors' view, a plain reading of section 96(4) of the CLRA 2002 means that if there is a lease of premises of which the right to manage has been acquired, then unless an exception applies (i.e. that it relates to parts not held by a qualifying tenant), the management functions are transferred.

7.29 The case of *Francia Properties Limited v Aristou*[41] concerned the landlord's proposal to construct a new flat on the roof space of a building that was subject to the right to manage. The roof space had been retained by the landlord. It was argued by the tenants that prohibition on landlords doing anything which the RTM company is required or empowered to do under the lease by section 97(2) of the CLRA 2002 meant that the landlord could not proceed. The planned works required the removal of the current roof, the construction of a new flat and the reinstallation of the roof above. The RTM company had obligations to manage the roof. The judge held that while the RTM company's management of the roof would be affected during and by the building work, there was no express prohibition under the CLRA 2002.[42] The purpose of the CLRA 2002 was not to replace enfranchisement rights under pre-existing legislation,[43] and so it would

[38] CLRA 2002, ss 96(6)(b) and 100(3).

[39] *Eastpoint Block A RTM Company Limited v Otubaga* [2023] EWCA Civ 879, [2023] 1 WLR 3896.

[40] *Francia Properties Limited v Aristou* [2017] L & TR 5 at [65].

[41] Ibid.

[42] Ibid, at [76].

[43] Ibid, at [58]–[59].

appear unfair to deprive a landlord of valuable property rights without compensation.

7.30 The balance that was struck in this case was to permit the landlord to carry out development works 'providing it has taken all reasonable steps to minimise the disturbance to the management functions of the RTM both during and after the works'.[44] There are two important points to note about this decision. First, it is a county court decision and therefore non-binding. Second, it is caveated by the word 'reasonable'. As the judge went on to hold:

> There may come a point when the development scheme is so significant in its effects on the RTM that it cannot be said that the landlord has taken all reasonable steps. For example, the replacement of a pitched roof with a flat roof that is likely to cost enormous sums to maintain. Likewise, the example discussed above in relation to the provision of bins. But that would have to be resolved on a case-by-case basis.[45]

7.31 The final limitation relates to shared estate facilities. Previously, it had been held by the Court of Appeal that where the right to manage was acquired by one block on an estate, and there were shared estate facilities, that the right to manage 'appurtenant property' included the right to manage the shared facilities.[46] This decision was overruled by the Supreme Court in the case of *FirstPort Property Services Limited v Settlers Court RTM Company Limited*.[47] There were insuperable practical problems with an RTM company managing shared facilities while the landlord or third-party manager has the right and obligation to manage those facilities under the potentially very large number of leases of flats outside the RTM company's block. Hence, the management functions conferred in relation to appurtenant property are limited to only that appurtenant property in the exclusive use of that building's occupants.

---

44 *Francia Properties Limited v Aristou* [2017] L & TR 5 at [77].

45 Ibid, at [79].

46 *Gala Unity Limited v Ariadne Road RTM Company Limited* [2012] EWCA Civ 1372, [2013] 1 WLR 988.

47 *FirstPort Property Services Limited v Settlers Court RTM Company Limited* [2022] UKSC 1, [2022] 1 WLR 519.

Effect on an employee

7.32 At common law, the transfer of the business of a company will generally terminate the contracts of employment held by that company.[48] However, the rights of employees are now partially protected by the Transfer of Undertakings (Protection of Employment) Regulations 2006 (SI 2006/246) (TUPE). The role and effect of TUPE in specific circumstances is a matter of employment law, and as such falls outside the scope of this work. Notwithstanding, it is worth briefly setting out the relevant legal landscape.

7.33 Rights under TUPE can arise where:

(a) there is an 'employee': an employee is an 'individual who works for another person whether under a contract of service or apprenticeship or otherwise but does not include anyone who provides services under a contract for services'.[49] Whether a particular contract is a contract of employment or a contract for services is a complex area of employment law;
(b) there is a 'relevant transfer': a relevant transfer occurs when there is a 'transfer of undertaking, business' to another person 'where there is a transfer of an economic entity which retains its identity'.[50] Whether an economic entity 'retains its identity' will depend on a number of factors, including the type of business concerned, what assets are transferred, and which employees and customers are retained.

7.34 Subject to some conditions and exceptions, an employee under a contract which meets these criteria will not have his or her contract automatically terminated, rather the contract will be treated as if originally made between the RTM company and the employee.[51] This includes any rights in the employment contract to live in on-site accommodation.[52] This has further consequences regarding the requirement to provide information and consultation between the outgoing employer, the RTM

---

48 *Re Foster Clark Limited's Indenture Trusts* [1966] 1 WLR 125.

49 TUPE, reg 2.

50 TUPE, reg 3(1)(a).

51 TUPE, reg 4(1).

52 TUPE, reg 4(2)(a).

company and the employee.[53] Although it should be noted that an employee can object and the contract will not transfer.[54]

7.35 Generally speaking, these protections are less likely to apply in cases where the landlord has contracted-out services to a managing agent who then sources individual contractors on an ad hoc basis. At the other end of the spectrum are cases such as resident caretakers, employed directly by the outgoing landlord, third-party management company or manager. In such circumstances, the relevant parties are advised to seek specialist advice in employment law.[55]

7.36 It is worth noting that the role of TUPE in the RTM process was considered by the Law Commission in its most recent review of the right to manage. The Law Commission also concluded that TUPE may apply and also advised that 'RTM companies should take legal advice if they are unsure whether the TUPE Regulations apply in their individual circumstances'.[56]

THE DUTY TO PROVIDE INFORMATION

7.37 Similar to the requirement to give notice of management contracts, a landlord, or third-party management company, or manager is under a duty to provide any information within its possession or control that is required by the RTM company in connection with the exercise of the right to manage. The obligation is triggered by the service of a written request, and the response must be received within 28 days.[57] If the relevant information is recorded in a document, the RTM company can require that an authorised representative inspect it and that a copy be supplied.

7.38 Typical documents may include: leases, deeds of variation, plans, regulatory compliance certificates, historic accounts, historic building reports, etc.

---

53 See for example TUPE, regs 11, 13 and 13A.

54 TUPE, reg 4(7).

55 Notably, this is also the advice given by the Law Commission, see para 7.36.

56 Law Commission, *Leasehold home ownership: exercising the right to manage* (Law Com No 393), 21 July 2020, §11.102.

57 CLRA 2002, s 93(1).

7.39 However, the obligation does not become enforceable until the acquisition date. It is therefore common to serve a request 28 days prior to the acquisition date, thereby requiring the information to be handed over on the acquisition date.[58] Otherwise, the RTM company can apply to the tribunal to enforce the obligation.[59]

THE DUTY TO PAY ACCRUED UNCOMMITTED SERVICE CHARGES

7.40 It is unlikely that the acquisition date will line up with the service charge financial year under the leases. It is also common for leases to provide for a reserve fund which may be held by the landlord or third-party management company or manager. On the acquisition date, the relevant party is obliged to hand over 'accrued uncommitted service charges' to the RTM company.[60]

7.41 These accrued uncommitted charges are defined as any sums paid over by way of service charges (including sums held on account, reserve funds, and sinking funds),[61] as well as any investments which represent such service charges and any income which has accrued on them (such as interest).

7.42 However, section 94(2) of the CLRA 2002 then excludes such amount as is required to meet the costs incurred before the acquisition date. Broadly, these are the costs that the landlord (or third-party management company or manager) has committed and expended prior to the acquisition date in pursuance of their own obligations. For a cost to be 'incurred', it is generally the position that the payer need not have actually paid the cost, but merely is liable to do so.[62] This is supported by the use of the un-prefixed word 'committed', which implies an obligation to pay a sum.

---

58 CLRA 2002, s 93(3) and (4).

59 CLRA 2002, s 107.

60 CLRA 2002, s 94(1).

61 CLRA 2002, s 94(2)(a) and Landlord and Tenant Act 1985 (LTA 1985), s 18.

62 See for example *OM Property Management v Burr* [2013] EWCA Civ 479, [2013] 1 WLR 3071, albeit this decision focussed on the meaning of the same words in LTA 1985, s 20B.

7.43 This reasoning appears in the case of *Sutton London Borough Council v Theowal Limited, Aspects RTM Company Limited*,[63] which concerned an insurance liability that arose prior to the acquisition date but which was billed late. There it was held that the relevant date was the date on which the liability arose.

7.44 In the case of *OM Limited v New River Head RTM Company Limited*,[64] it was held that the words of section 94(1) of the CLRA 2002 are 'deliberately limited' and the section does not require an investigation into the landlord's or manager's historic accounting practice, nor does it require a determination of what the landlord ought to have collected but failed to collect. Nor does it require a determination of what the landlord should have but now does not have (although this may be subject to separate restitutionary proceedings if there has been a breach of trust). Nor does it require any investigation as to whether the amount held is justifiable or reasonable. The same logic applies in relation to what sums are 'uncommitted'. It does not matter whether the amounts that have been committed are reasonable, etc. All that matters – for the purposes of section 94 – is whether they have been committed.

7.45 The duty under section 94 of the CLRA 2002 only applies to sums held on the acquisition date, and not to sums subsequently paid or received,[65] although again any sums subsequently paid to the previous managing party are likely to be recoverable under a restitutionary claim.

7.46 If there is a dispute as to the amount payable, then either party may apply to the appropriate tribunal for a determination of the amount falling due under section 94 of the CLRA 2002.[66] As discussed in para 7.44, the tribunal does not have jurisdiction to determine questions of reasonableness, but it does have jurisdiction to, for example, order the repayment of sums where there has been an error of accounting.[67]

---

[63] *Sutton London Borough Council v Theowal Limited, Aspects RTM Company Limited*, 3CL10101, County Court (Central London), 27 July 2014, decision of HHJ Deborah Taylor, unreported.

[64] *OM Limited v New River Head RTM Company Limited* [2010] UKUT 394 (LC), [2011] 1 EGLR 97 at [23].

[65] *Wilson v Lesley Place (Maidstone) Limited RTM Company Limited* [2010] UKUT 139 (LC), [2010] 5 WLUK 272.

[66] CLRA 2002, s 94(3).

[67] *Gateway Property Holdings Limited v Westwood (Colchester) RTM Company Limited* [2016] UKUT 489 (LC), [2016] 11 WLUK 82.

CONSEQUENCES OF HISTORIC BREACH OF COVENANTS ON ACQUISITION

Breaches by leaseholders

7.47 As regards most continuing breaches of covenant, the RTM company can apply to the First-tier Tribunal (Property Chamber) for a determination that a tenant is in breach of a covenant under his or her lease pursuant to section 168 of the CLRA 2002.[68]

7.48 The decision in the case of *Eastpoint Block A RTM Company Limited v Otubaga*[69] was not based on any factual findings (the decision being appealed was a strike out of the original case prior to trial) and so did not address whether an RTM company may also apply for a determination of breach in relation to a once-and-for-all breach that took place prior to the acquisition date. However, the judgment of Andrews LJ makes it clear that the effect of section 104 of the CLRA 2002 is 'to confer on the RTM company a right which it would not otherwise have (because it is not a landlord) to make an application that the landlord could make under section 168(4)'.[70] There is no suggestion that this is limited to continuing breaches. Rather the right is to be exercised 'in the same manner' as the landlord.[71] As a result, it may be arguable that the RTM company can apply to the First-tier Tribunal (Property Chamber) for a determination that a tenant is in breach of a covenant pursuant to section 168 even if that breach occurred prior to the acquisition date.[72]

7.49 A separate issue arises in relation to service charge arrears. As set out at para 7.40, the RTM company is only entitled to have transferred the sums 'held by' the landlord, management company, or manager on the acquisition date. The CLRA 2002 gives the RTM company no power, still less a right, to take over a tenant's claim for the recovery of overpaid service charges.[73] There is nothing in the CLRA 2002 which obliges the

---

[68] *Eastpoint Block A RTM Company Limited v Otubaga* [2023] EWCA Civ 879, [2023] 1 WLR 3896.

[69] Ibid.

[70] Ibid, at [44].

[71] Ibid, at [36].

[72] Ibid.

[73] Ibid, at [28].

landlord to pursue the recovery of any arrears by leaseholders,[74] and indeed once the landlord does recover any service charge arrears, these should, unless the landlord has unmet service charge expenses, be handed over to the RTM company (or else the landlord may be subject to a restitutionary claim) so there is no financial incentive for the landlord to recover the arrears. In such circumstances, the RTM company must seek to co-operate with the landlord in order to be able to utilise the landlord's ultimate remedy of the threat of forfeiture to enforce the lessee's covenant to pay.

Service charges incurred before the right to manage was acquired

7.50 The RTM company cannot sue for service charges incurred before the right to manage was acquired. They remain payable to the landlord. Section 97(4) of the CLRA 2002 provides that any function or obligation owed by a tenant to a landlord or to a third party under a lease will, instead, be owed to the RTM company if it relates to any of the management functions taken on by the company. However, this is subject to section 97(5), which states as follows:

> (5) But subsection (4) does not require or permit the payment to the RTM company of so much of any service charges payable by a tenant under a lease of the whole or any part of the premises as is required to meet costs incurred before the right to manage was acquired by the RTM company in connection with matters for which the service charges are payable.

7.51 Where the transfer of management occurs in the middle of a service charge year, it is not clear how the landlord is to recover the cost of service charges incurred before the right to manage was acquired by the RTM company if they have not already been deducted from service charge reserves. Usually, the lease provides for a closing account and a balancing charge, but the account will be taken and the balancing demand sent out by the RTM company.

---

[74] A suggestion that landlords be required to use reasonable endeavours to pursue arrears was rejected by the Law Commission: Law Commission, *Leasehold home ownership: exercising the right to manage* (Law Com No 393), 21 July 2020, §10.184.

Chapter 8

Exercise of the Right to Manage

SUMMARY

8.1 On the acquisition date (see Chapter 7), there is a statutory transfer of management functions from the landlord (or third party) to the RTM company. In respect of management functions, there is both a transfer of the functions of management under section 96(2) of the Commonhold and Leasehold Reform Act 2002 (CLRA 2002) from the landlord (or third party) to the RTM company and a transfer of the benefit of the corresponding obligations owed by the tenant to the landlord under the lease to the RTM company under section 97(4). It is this latter transfer which makes the service charge payable by the tenant to the RTM after the acquisition date. The benefits of other covenants are not subject to this statutory transfer, and these are referred to as 'untransferred tenant covenants'.

8.2 Such untransferred covenants are enforceable both by the landlord and the RTM company (section 100(2) of the CLRA 2002), and the RTM company must monitor and report breaches of those covenants to the landlord (section 101). Covenants in the lease requiring the tenants to seek the approval of the landlord occupy a middle ground. They are not transferred by virtue of section 96(2) and section 97(4), but the CLRA 2002 creates a special procedure whereby under section 98 the approval function is transferred to the RTM company, but the RTM company cannot give approval without first notifying the landlord. If the landlord objects there is a reference to the First-tier Tribunal (Property Chamber).

TRANSFER OF MANAGEMENT FUNCTIONS

8.3 Section 96 of the CLRA 2002 provides for the transfer of 'management functions', as follows:

> (1) This section and section 97 apply in relation to management functions relating to the whole or any part of the premises.
> (2) Management functions which a person who is landlord under a lease of the whole or any part of the premises has under the lease are instead functions of the RTM company.
> (3) And where a person is party to a lease of the whole or any part of the premises otherwise than as landlord or tenant, management functions of his under the lease are also instead functions of the RTM company.
> (4) Accordingly, any provisions of the lease making provision about the relationship of—
>
> (a) a person who is landlord under the lease, and
> (b) a person who is party to the lease otherwise than as landlord or tenant,
>
> in relation to such functions do not have effect.
> (5) 'Management functions' are functions with respect to services, repairs, maintenance, improvements, insurance and management.
> (6) But this section does not apply in relation to—
>
> (a) functions with respect to a matter concerning only a part of the premises consisting of a flat or other unit not held under a lease by a qualifying tenant, or
> (b) functions relating to re-entry or forfeiture.
>
> (7) An order amending subsection (5) or (6) may be made by the appropriate national authority.

8.4 Section 97 of the CLRA 2002 supplements section 96, as follows:

> (1) Any obligation owed by the RTM company by virtue of section 96 to a tenant under a lease of the whole or any part of the premises is also owed to each person who is landlord under the lease.
> (2) A person who is—
>
> (a) landlord under a lease of the whole or any part of the premises,
> (b) party to such a lease otherwise than as landlord or tenant, or

(c) a manager appointed under Part 2 of the 1987 Act to act in relation to the premises, or any premises containing or contained in the premises,

is not entitled to do anything which the RTM company is required or empowered to do under the lease by virtue of section 96, except in accordance with an agreement made by him and the RTM company.

(3) But subsection (2) does not prevent any person from insuring the whole or any part of the premises at his own expense.

(4) So far as any function of a tenant under a lease of the whole or any part of the premises—

(a) relates to the exercise of any function under the lease which is a function of the RTM company by virtue of section 96, and

(b) is exercisable in relation to a person who is landlord under the lease or party to the lease otherwise than as landlord or tenant,

it is instead exercisable in relation to the RTM company.

(5) But subsection (4) does not require or permit the payment to the RTM company of so much of any service charges payable by a tenant under a lease of the whole or any part of the premises as is required to meet costs incurred before the right to manage was acquired by the RTM company in connection with matters for which the service charges are payable.

'function'

8.5 There is no definition of 'function'. It is suggested that a good working definition for 'function' in this context is 'power or duty'. But in the absence of a statutory definition, the exact limit of the term 'function' is uncertain. The use of the term echoes section 12 of the Landlord and Tenant (Covenants) Act 1995, which provides for the transmissibility of covenants with management companies which relate to 'any function with respect to all or any of the demised premises'.

8.6 In the case of *Francia Properties Limited v Aristou*,[1] the judge held that the reference in section 97(2) of the CLRA 2002 to 'empowered' means that 'management functions' is wider than merely 'obligations' or 'duties' and includes 'powers'.

---

1 *Francia Properties Limited v Aristou* [2017] L & TR 5.

'relating to'

8.7 Section 96(1) of the CLRA 2002 provides that sections 96 and 97 apply 'in relation to functions relating to the whole or any part of the premises'. In the case of *Settlers Court RTM Company Limited v First Port Property Services Limited*,[2] Lord Briggs commented on 'functions relating to' in that context. He said at [39]:

> 'functions relating to' does not on its own spell out how close or tenuous that relationship has to be. Nor does the similar phrase in section 71(1), but that section is in my view purely introductory. To find out how close that relationship needs to be one must have regard to the whole of the Chapter to construe that key phrase purposively and in its context. That exercise reveals numerous signposts, all pointing to the need for a very close connection, sufficient to confine the right to manage to functions which the (necessarily) single-building RTM company can properly perform on its own, for the benefit and under the supervision of those tenants who will be directly affected by that performance.

'management functions'

8.8 Section 96(5) of the CLRA 2002 provides as follows:

> 'Management functions' are functions with respect to services, repairs, maintenance, improvements, insurance and management.

'services'

8.9 This would include all the usual services provided by a landlord, such as cleaning, heating, grounds maintenance, gardening, caretakers and porters, lighting, door entry systems, aerials.

'repairs, maintenance'

8.10 This refers to repair and maintenance required under the lease. This might include major works to the building and grounds, cyclical maintenance and repair or replacement of plant, such as air conditioning, lifts and boilers.

---

2 *Settlers Court RTM Company Limited v First Port Property Services Limited* [2022] UKSC 1, [2022] 1 WLR 519.

'improvements'

8.11 If the lease allows the landlord to recover the cost of improvements then the carrying out of improvements would be within the scope of the functions carried out by the RTM company.

'insurance'

8.12 This is self-explanatory. It means arranging insurance for the premises in respect of which the right to manage has been acquired.

'management'

8.13 This is the vaguest category. It would include the collection of the service charges, keeping records, preparing accounts, provision of information required by statute, and day-to-day management of the building.

'a person who is landlord under a lease of the whole or any part of the premises ...'

8.14 This wording makes clear that the management functions of a landlord under a lease of only part of the premises will be transferred. A tenant of part of the premises may also be a landlord of that part if other tenants have rights of way or use over that part. This point is illustrated by the facts in the case of *Lexham House RTM v European Investments & Development*.[3] In that case, the top floor flats had an easement to use the roof of the premises. The freeholder granted a lease of the roof to a company. The Upper Tribunal (Lands Chamber) held that the company lessee was a landlord on the basis that it held the reversion to an easement to use the roof granted for a term to each of the top floor lessees – *Nevill Long & Company (Boards) Limited v Firmenich & Co*[4] applied.

'under the lease'

8.15 It is only a management function which a landlord has 'under the lease' which becomes a function of the RTM company (section 96(2) of

---

3 *Lexham House RTM v European Investments & Development* [2019] UKUT 390 (LC), [2019] 12 WLUK 290.

4 *Nevill Long & Company (Boards) Limited v Firmenich & Company* [1983] 2 EGLR 76.

the CLRA 2002). The former President of the Upper Tribunal (Lands Chamber) described the effect of these provisions as follows:

> The effect of these provisions is to transfer to the RTM company the management functions that the landlord had under the lease and to make the tenant liable to the RTM company rather than to the landlord in respect of the tenant's obligations under the lease. The provisions thus effect a transfer of rights and duties that are contained in the lease. They do not modify those rights and duties, nor do they create new ones. The liability of the tenant to the landlord in respect of service charges is to be ascertained purely by reference to the terms of the lease, and the fact that the management functions are exercisable by an RTM company does not affect the construction of the lease under these provisions.[5]

8.16 In that passage, the judge focussed on 'rights and duties' but as mentioned in para 8.5, 'function' includes powers as well as rights. In the case of powers, the words 'under the lease' have an important limiting effect. A landlord has power to do anything to retained property which is not restricted by the lease, but it is considered that to be a power 'under the lease' there must be an express provision referable to the power.

8.17 This point is illustrated by the express reference in section 96(5) of the CLRA 2002 to improvements. A lease will rarely put an obligation on a landlord to carry out improvements. If there is reference in a lease to improvements at all, it is usually a provision which allows the landlord to recover the cost of improvements to common parts from the tenants. Where a lease contains such a provision, it seems fairly clear that the RTM company would be permitted to carry out improvements and to recover the cost from the tenants. The more difficult case is where the lease is silent as to improvements. In that case, although the landlord has power to carry out improvements, it is thought that it is not a power 'under the lease' and thus the RTM company would not be able to carry out improvements.

8.18 Section 96(2) of the CLRA 2002 provides that it is the management functions which the landlord 'has' under the lease which are transferred. It is unclear whether the functions transferred are those which the landlord had as at the date of acquisition or whether it is the functions which the landlord has for the time being (or rather, would have, but for the statutory

---

5 *Wilson v Lesley Place (RTM) Company Limited* [2010] UKUT 342 (LC), [2011] L & TR 11 at [13].

transfer) which are transferred. The use of the word 'has' suggests that it is the latter, so that if one or more leases are later varied the management functions may be widened or narrowed as a result. Potentially, this is open to abuse in that it gives the landlord an opportunity to create burdensome functions after the right to manage has been exercised.

'are instead functions of the RTM company'

8.19 It is these words which effect the statutory transfer of functions from the landlord or third party to the RTM company. The scope of the management functions derives from the lease, but the basis of the RTM company's authority to execute those functions and its liability in the case of failure to comply with covenants is statutory. This is also clear from the wording of section 97(1) of the CLRA 2002, which refers to 'an obligation owed by the RTM company by virtue of section 96 to a tenant'.

Release of landlord from liability under the lease

8.20 The corollary of the transfer of the management functions is that the landlord is released from liability in relation to the same. This is achieved by section 96(4) of the CLRA 2002, which provides that 'any provisions of the lease making provision about the relationship of a person who is landlord under the lease ... in relation to such functions do not have effect'.

Transfer of functions operates to exclude the landlord from management functions

8.21 The landlord is not entitled to do anything which the RTM company is required or empowered to do under the lease, unless the company agrees, although the landlord may insure all or any part of the premises at his or her own expense (section 97(2) and (3) of the CLRA 2002).

8.22 As pointed out in paras 8.15–8.18, the functions transferred to the RTM are the management functions 'under the lease'. The RTM company may exercise management functions over retained property, but this will not necessarily prevent the landlord from developing retained premises. In the case of *Francia Properties v Aristos Aristou*,[6] the Recorder held (at [77]) that a landlord could develop retained areas where he takes all

---

6 *Francia Properties Limited v Aristou* [2017] L & TR 5.

reasonable steps to minimise the disturbance to the management functions of the RTM both during and after the works.

Pre-existing Landlord and Tenant Act 1987 manager

8.23 Where there is a pre-existing manager appointed by the tribunal under Part II of the Landlord and Tenant Act 1987 (LTA 1987) there is a transfer of management functions to the RTM company, but the appointment does not come to an end and the manager will retain any functions which are not conferred on the RTM company.[7]

EXCEPTIONS

Partial exception for business leases and short leases

8.24 There is no transfer of functions with respect to a matter concerning only a part of the premises consisting of a flat or other unit not held under a lease by a qualifying tenant (section 96(6)(a) of the CLRA 2002). Units let on a business tenancy and flats let directly by the freeholder on a short lease are not units held under a lease by a qualifying tenant. The position in relation to short leases is dealt with at paras 8.35–8.40. It is sometimes said that business leases are exempt, but they are only partially exempt. *Prima facie* there is a transfer of the landlord's functions, but functions which concern only the business premises are not transferred. So if the ground floor of a mixed-use building is let on a business tenancy, then there is no transfer of any repairing responsibility relating to the repair of the internal parts of the ground floor unit, but responsibility for repair of the roof of the building is transferred to the RTM company since that is not 'a matter concerning only a part of the premises consisting of a flat or other unit not held under a lease by a qualifying tenant' (section 96(6)(a)).

Re-entry

8.25 Functions relating to re-entry or forfeiture are expressly excluded from transfer to the RTM company (section 96(6)(b) of the CLRA 2002). But this does not exclude an RTM company from applying for a determination of breach under section 168(4).[8]

---

7 *Benthan v Lindsay Court (St Annes) RTM Company Limited* [2021] UKUT 4 (LC), [2021] L & TR 11.

8 *Eastpoint Block A RTM Company Limited v Otubaga* [2023] EWCA Civ 879, [2023] 1 WLR 3896.

'Whole or any part of the premises'

8.26 Section 96(1) of the CLRA 2002 provides that sections 96 and 97 apply in relation to management functions relating to 'the whole or any part of the premises'. In the context, it would seem that 'the premises' means the premises the subject of the claim to right to manage. That might seem like a statement of the obvious, but it is useful to clarify the point where the right to manage has been acquired in respect of only part of a building. Assuming that 'premises' does have this meaning, then the purpose of section 96(1) is to make clear that there is only a transfer of management functions in relation to that part.

Shared appurtenant property

8.27 Further, the decision in the case of *Settlers Court RTM Company Limited and Others v FirstPort Property Services Limited*[9] makes clear that the right to manage is confined to that which the RTM company could manage on its own, namely, the structure and facilities within the building (or part thereof) constituting the relevant premises, and facilities outside it which were exclusively used by the occupants of the relevant premises. So the RTM company would not acquire a right to manage over shared appurtenant property.

8.28 Nor in a multi-block estate can a group of RTM companies enter into and enforce agreements to manage the estate as a whole and recover estate-wide maintenance costs from the lessees of the blocks, see the case of *G & A Gorrara Limited v Kenilworth Court Block E RTM Company Limited*:[10]

> It is now well-established that an RTM company takes on management functions in relation to one building only (Ninety Broomfield Road) and in relation to property that is appurtenant to that one building only (Settlers Court). It would make no sense at all for the RTM company to have power in addition to enforce obligations in relation to a different block.

---

9 *Settlers Court RTM Company Limited v FirstPort Property Services Limited* [2022] UKSC 1, [2022] 1 WLR 519.

10 *G & A Gorrara Limited v Kenilworth Court Block E RTM Company Limited* [2022] UKUT 90 (LC), [2022] L & TR 29 at [60].

Newly developed parts

8.29 One moot point which arises in practice relates to the development of new parts of a building. Take, for example, where the landlord wishes to excavate beneath the building to create a basement or to develop a flat roof. The new basement or the new rooftop development did not exist when the right to manage was acquired. In that case, are the management functions in relation to those new areas vested in the RTM company or the landlord? The case of *Dartmouth Court Blackheath Limited v Berisworth Limited*[11] lends a clue to the probable answer. In that case, Warren J held, in the context of Part 1 of the LTA 1987, that the world 'building' includes the airspace necessary to enable maintenance to be carried out. On the same reasoning, the right to manage extends to any airspace development, and by extension of the same reasoning to any subsoil development. In the case of *Francia Properties v Aristou*,[12] the Recorder accepted (at [64]) that the RTM company had control over the roof of the premises by reason of the management functions exercised by it, but held that this did not prevent the landlord from developing the roof and airspace by erecting a new flat on the roof. Further, it was held in the case of *LM Homes Limited v Queen Court Freehold Company Limited*,[13] that for the purposes of the Leasehold Reform Housing and Urban Development Act 1993 (LRHUDA 1993), 'the airspace and the sub-soil form part of the 'premises' to the freehold of which the qualifying tenants are entitled'.

8.30 It is thought that the management functions of the RTM company would extend to the newly created parts once built, on the basis that section 96(2) of the CLRA 2002 refers to the transfer of management functions 'which a person who is landlord ... has under the lease'. Use of the word 'has' suggests it is the functions of the landlord for the time being (rather than the functions exercised at the date of acquisition of the right to manage) which are transferred.

---

11 *Dartmouth Court Blackheath Limited v Berisworth Limited* [2008] EWHC 350 (Ch), [2008] L & TR 12.

12 *Francia Properties Limited v Aristou* [2017] L & TR 5.

13 *LM Homes Limited v Queen Court Freehold Company Limited* [2020] EWCA Civ 371, [2020] 2 WLR 1135.

Implied right of entry but no transfer of possession of all retained parts

8.31 The landlord does not need to reserve a right to enter retained parts of an estate which do not form part of the building in relation to which the right to manage has been acquired, i.e. any part which is not demised under any individual lease; the landlord is entitled to possession of those parts. In order to properly exercise its management functions, the RTM company will need access to those parts and there must be an implied right of entry in relation to such retained parts. But that does not necessarily mean that possession or control over all retained areas is transferred to the RTM company. For example, if the retained parts of a block included a car park which the landlord had used wholly for his or her own purposes and without any rights granted to the residential tenants, the RTM company might have a right of entry to the car park ancillary to its management functions, such as keeping the block in repair, but it would not be empowered to exclude the landlord from the car park or control access thereto.

Aggregative transfer of functions

8.32 Section 96(2) of the CLRA 2002 provides that management functions 'which a person who is landlord under a lease of the whole or any part of the premises has under the lease are instead functions of the RTM company'. This means that the management functions of each person who is a landlord of the whole or part of the premises are aggregated and vested in the RTM company. Often, those functions will completely overlap, but they may not where there are multiple intermediate interests of different parts.

8.33 Take, for example, a mansion block where there is: a freeholder; a head lessee; a long lessee of each flat; and where several of the flat lessees have sub-let on assured shorthold tenancies. The management functions of *each* landlord in the title structure are transferred to the RTM company. The management functions of each landlord will not necessarily be coterminous. For instance, the freeholder may have a duty to repair the roof but the other landlords may not. The result in that case would be that the RTM company has the duty to repair the roof. So, in effect, the various powers and duties of the several landlords are aggregated and vested in the RTM company.

8.34 The hotchpotch of functions vested in the RTM company is further complicated by the provisions relating to short leases.

SHORT LEASES

8.35 The transfer of functions in relation to flats held on short leases is widened as explained in para 8.41. In respect of flats let on short leases, each of those lessees is a landlord and there is a partial transfer of functions, limited by section 96(6)(a) of the CLRA 2002. However, paragraph 3 of Schedule 7 alters the position in relation to the obligations imposed on a lessor by virtue of section 11 of the Landlord and Tenant Act 1985 (LTA 1985). Section 11 primarily applies to a lease of a dwelling-house granted for a term of less than 7 years (section 13(1) of the LTA 1985).

8.36 Section 11(1) of the LTA 1985 implies a covenant by the lessor:

(a) to keep in repair the structure and exterior of the dwelling-house (including drains, gutters and external pipes),
(b) to keep in repair and proper working order the installations in the dwelling-house for the supply of water, gas and electricity and for sanitation (including basins, sinks, baths and sanitary conveniences, but not other fixtures, fittings and appliances for making use of the supply of water, gas or electricity), and
(c) to keep in repair and proper working order the installations in the dwelling-house for space heating and heating water.

8.37 The CLRA 2002 provides that the obligations imposed on a lessor by virtue of section 11 of the LTA 1985 are, so far as they relate to any flat or other unit contained in the premises, instead, obligations of the RTM company (paragraph 3(1) of Schedule 7 to the CLRA 2002). It then goes on to state that the RTM company owes to any person who is in occupation of a flat or other unit contained in the premises otherwise than under a lease the same obligations as would be imposed on it by virtue of section 11 of the LTA 1985 if that person were a lessee under a lease of the flat or other unit (paragraph 3(2) of Schedule 7 to the CLRA 2002). So, in the example given above, if the freeholder or a flat lessee allows a relative to occupy a flat, that occupier would be owed a duty by the RTM company to comply with section 11 of the LTA 1985 notwithstanding the absence of such an obligation between the occupier and the person permitting occupation.

8.38 This is subject to the caveat that the obligations of the RTM company do not apply to 'an obligation to the extent that it relates to a matter concerning only the flat or other unit concerned' (paragraph 3(3) of Schedule 7 to the CLRA 2002). So it would not apply to an implied obligation to repair a sink, or a boiler which served only one flat, but it would apply to the obligation to keep the structure and exterior in repair. This mirrors the limitation on the transfers of functions in section 96(6)(a).

8.39 The obligation imposed on the RTM company to a flat lessee under section 11 of the LTA 1985 is also owed to the lessor (paragraph 3(4) of Schedule 7 to the CLRA 2002). So, in the mansion block example given above, both the assured shorthold tenant and the flat lessee could sue the RTM company for failure to keep in repair a communal boiler, for example.

8.40 It is possible that these provisions could put the RTM company in a situation where it could not fully recover the cost of complying with the duties imposed upon it. Under an assured shorthold tenancy, it is very unusual for there to be an obligation for the tenant to pay a service charge. The usual position is that the tenant pays rent and the landlord covers the cost of complying with obligations under section 11 of the LTA 1985 out of the rent. Where the section 11 obligations are imposed on the RTM company there is no provision made for the RTM company to recover the cost. So, in the (admittedly unlikely) situation where the section 11 obligations were more extensive than the obligations imposed on the freeholder and/or the head lessee, the service charge provisions in the head lease and/or the flat leases would not provide a means of recovery.

Transfer of third-party functions

8.41 Management functions of any third party under a lease are also transferred to the RTM company (section 96(3) of the CLRA 2002), for example, a management company which is a third party to the lease. And the management company is released from liability on the basis that the 'provisions of the lease making provision about the relationship of ... a person who is party to the lease otherwise than as landlord or tenant, in relation to such functions do not have effect' (section 96(4)).

Management functions under collateral agreements

8.42 The transfer of functions of a landlord or a third party relate to the functions that person has 'under the lease'. 'Lease' is defined at section 112(2) of the CLRA 2002. The definition does not include a collateral agreement. The CLRA 2002 does not make any provision for the transfer of obligations arising under collateral agreements. Obligations under collateral agreements will generally run with the land.[14] The omission to provide for the transfer of obligations under collateral agreements is surprising and provides a means of avoidance of the CLRA 2002. The omission is odd because Chapter II of Part I of the LRHUDA 1993 has specific provisions dealing with collateral agreements and makes provision in respect of the same on an individual lease renewal.

Nature of obligation owed to landlord

8.43 There is no contract between the landlord and the RTM company and so the obligation created by section 97(1) of the CLRA 2002 cannot operate to imply an obligation into a contract in the way that section 11(1) of the LTA 1985 operates. So, it is thought that it creates a free-standing statutory obligation and that the cause of action is an action on a specialty (i.e. a cause of action based on a statute).

8.44 Section 97(1) of the CLRA 2002 provides that 'any obligation owed by the RTM company by virtue of section 96 to a tenant under a lease of the whole or any part of the premises is also owed to each person who is landlord under the lease'. Therefore, the RTM company owes a duty to each landlord in respect of the performance of transferred functions. This means that the responsibility of each person who is a landlord is aggregated and vested in the RTM company. The RTM company owes a duty to each of those landlords. As set out at para 8.33, the management functions of each landlord may differ and, where that is the case, the RTM company will owe a different duty to each landlord.

---

14 In respect of 'old' tenancies, i.e. those granted prior to the Landlord and Tenant (Covenants) Act 1995, see *Weg Motors v Hale* [1962] Ch 49. In respect of new tenancies, Landlord and Tenant (Covenants) Act 1995, s 3 provides that the benefit and burden of all landlord and tenant covenants pass on an assignment of a tenancy. 'Covenant' is defined to include a covenant contained in a collateral agreement.

Damages

8.45 On the basis that the landlord no longer owes a duty to the tenants in respect of transferred functions, he or she will not be suing the RTM company in a third-party capacity where claims are brought by the tenants for non-compliance with the management obligations in the lease. Any such claim would be brought against the RTM company. This suggests that the landlord's claim is likely to be in respect of damage to the value of his or her reversion or damage to retained property.

8.46 An example may help to illustrate these points. An RTM company has acquired the right to manage in respect of a mansion block which comprises four commercial units on the ground floor and four stories of residential accommodation above comprising 30 flats. The title structure is as follows. There is a freeholder, an intermediate lessee of the residential parts comprising ground floor entrance and four stories above, and an intermediate lessee of the commercial parts comprising ground floor shops. Each of these landlords has covenanted to keep the roof in repair. There are individual long leases of 30 flats and business tenants of four commercial units. Two of the flats are let on assured shorthold tenancies. The roof leaks and the RTM company fails to repair it. The RTM company owes an obligation to:

(a) each long lessee of a flat as tenant;
(b) each tenant under an assured shorthold tenancy;
(c) each of the two long lessees, who have sub-let on assured shorthold tenancies, in their capacity as a landlord under section 97(1) of the CLRA 2002;
(d) the business tenant of each commercial unit;
(e) each intermediate lessee both as landlord under section 97(1) and as tenant under each intermediate lease;
(f) the freeholder under section 97(1).

ENFORCEMENT OF TENANT COVENANTS

Transferred covenants

What is a transferred covenant?

8.47 The functions of the RTM company are functions in respect of 'services, repairs, maintenance, improvements, insurance and management'.

The RTM company is given power to enforce corresponding duties on the tenant in relation to those functions by section 97(4) of the CLRA 2002.

8.48 Section 97(4) of the CLRA 2002 provides that:

> (4) So far as any function of a tenant …
>
> (a) relates to the exercise of any function under the lease which is a function of the RTM company … and
> (b) is exercisable in relation to a person who is landlord …
>
> it is instead exercisable in relation to the RTM company.

8.49 So, put simply, where previously the tenant owed any duty to the landlord in relation to a management function, after the acquisition date the duty is owed to the RTM company. This provision makes the payment of service charges and other sums referable to transferred functions formerly due from the tenant to the landlord, due from the tenant to the RTM company. Section 97(5) of the CLRA 2002 limits recovery to costs incurred after the right to manage was acquired.

8.50 The term ‘function’ is used presumably to make clear that there is a transfer of powers in addition to obligations, but it is difficult to think of an example of where it means anything other than an obligation. The CLRA 2002 later abandons this terminology (at section 100) and draws a distinction between transferred and untransferred tenant *covenants*. In the language of that part of the CLRA 2002, the obligations to pay service charges and insurance rent are ‘transferred covenants’.

8.51 Section 97(4) of the CLRA 2002 applies to functions of a tenant under a lease which relate to the exercise of any function which is a function of the RTM company, i.e. functions relating to services, repairs, maintenance, improvements, insurance and management. It provides that if previously that tenant’s function was exercisable in relation to the landlord, ‘it is instead exercisable in relation to the RTM company’. It is easy to see how the section is intended to work in the case of positive covenants. Take the obligation to pay service charges. It is section 97(4) which operates to make those service charges payable to the RTM company as opposed to the landlord. Where a tenant has covenanted not to do something it is less clear that section 97(4) applies because in ordinary language one would not describe a covenant not to do something as a function of a tenant exercisable in relation to the landlord.

8.52 As noted at para 8.19, there is no transfer to the RTM company of functions relating to re-entry or forfeiture. It is thought that the landlord will, therefore, retain the ability to forfeit in relation to non-payment of service charges (and other transferred covenants) notwithstanding that by virtue of section 97(4) of the CLRA 2002 the money is payable (or duty owed) to the RTM company rather than to the landlord. This is on the basis that the lease is likely to be drafted in terms which allow the landlord to forfeit for any breach of covenant. If that is the case, it would not matter whether the duty under that covenant is to pay money to the landlord or (by the statutory transfer of functions) to the RTM company; in either case, failure to pay results in a breach of the lease. This is consistent with George Bartlett QC's observation in the case of *Wilson v Lesley Place (RTM) Company Limited*[15] that the rights and duties transferred are those under the lease and that the RTM legislation does not create new duties. It is also consistent with the RTM company's duty to monitor and report breaches of covenant to the landlord.

8.53 The landlord's functions in relation to approvals are also transferred to the RTM company, but there is a specific code relating to approvals under section 98 and section 99 of the CLRA 2002, which are discussed at para 8.74.

Set-off

8.54 Generally speaking, a claim for service charges may be set off against an unliquidated claim for damages for breach of the landlord's repairing obligations and the covenant for quiet enjoyment, as in the case of *Filross Securities v Midgeley*.[16] But a claim for damages against a previous landlord may not be set off against a successor landlord's claim for rent arrears which have accrued due after the reversion has been assigned to him, as in the case of *Edlington Properties v JH Fenner & Co*.[17]

---

15 *Wilson v Lesley Place (RTM) Company Limited* [2010] UKUT 342 (LC), [2011] L & TR 11.

16 *Filross Securities v Midgeley* [1998] 3 EGLR 43.

17 *Edlington Properties v JH Fenner & Company* [2006] EWCA Civ 403, [2006] 1 WLR 1583.

8.55 It was held in the case of *Maunder Taylor v Blaquiere*[18] that a claim by a tenant for damages for disrepair against the landlord may not be set off against a claim for unpaid service charges brought by a manager appointed under Part II of the LTA 1987. The rationale is that the manager's right to the money claimed from the tenant arose from his appointment as manager by the court and not from the lease and that, accordingly, there was no mutuality between the manager's claim and that of the tenant, and no set-off was possible.

8.56 In the case of transferred covenants, the RTM company is not enforcing the covenants on behalf of the landlord. The effect of section 97(4) of the CLRA 2002 is that the tenants' covenants relating to management are no longer enforceable by the landlord. The duty to pay service charges after the acquisition date is owed to the RTM company. It is therefore thought that both, because the RTM company is in the position of a successor (per *Edlington Properties*) and because of the want of mutuality (because the RTM company is not acting on behalf of the landlord), there is no set-off.

8.57 It is difficult to see a reason in principle why the tenant should not be able to set-off a claim for unliquidated damages for breach of the repairing obligations of the RTM company in the period since the acquisition date.

Examples of transferred covenants

8.58 Transferred covenants are the corollary of transferred functions so they would include covenants to pay for services, repairs, maintenance, improvements, insurance and management.

UNTRANSFERRED COVENANTS

8.59 Untransferred tenant covenants are covenants which are not exercisable in relation to the RTM company by virtue of section 97(4) of the CLRA 2002. So they are, broadly speaking, the other tenant covenants in the lease which do not relate to the management functions transferred

[18] *Maunder Taylor v Blaquiere* [2002] EWCA Civ 1633, [2003] 1 WLR 379.

to the RTM company. It was said in the case of *G & A Gorrara Limited v Kenilworth Court Block E RTM Company Limited*:[19]

> 'Untransferred covenants' are covenants such as the obligation not to cause a nuisance, or not to use the premises for anything except a private residence. The usefulness of the RTM company being able to enforce such covenants is obvious.

8.60 The majority of tenant covenants commonly found in a lease are likely to be untransferred.

8.61 The obligation under such untransferred covenants is still owed to the landlord, but the covenants are enforceable both by the RTM company, as well as by any other person (for example landlord or third party) by whom they were enforceable prior to the company acquiring the right to manage (section 100(2) of the CLRA 2002). They are enforceable in the same manner as they were enforceable by that other person save that the RTM company may not exercise any function of re-entry or forfeiture (section 100(3)).

8.62 It is clear that in the absence of an equivalent provision to section 97(4) of the CLRA 2002, which makes a covenant to pay service charges payable to the landlord a covenant to pay service charges to the RTM company, that the untransferred covenants are still owed to the landlord (or third party) as provided for in the lease. An example illustrates the point: if the lease provides that on assignment of the lease the lessee must notify the landlord and pay an administration fee to the landlord, then the lessee must still notify the landlord and pay the fee to the landlord. The only change is that the covenant to do so is now enforceable both by the landlord, and the RTM company.

8.63 Any power of entry under a lease of a person who is a landlord or a third party to enter the demised premises to check whether a tenant is complying with any untransferred covenant is exercisable by the RTM company as well as by the landlord or third party (section 100(5) of the CLRA 2002).

---

[19] *G & A Gorrara Limited v Kenilworth Court Block E RTM Company Limited* [2022] UKUT 90 (LC), [2022] L & TR 29.

Set-off

8.64 In relation to untransferred covenants, the position in relation to set-off is less clear. It is less likely to be relevant in that the main covenants on the part of the tenant to pay sums of money are transferred covenants. The covenant to pay rent is not a transferred covenant and so the tenant could claim a right of set-off against a claim for rent. There is no reason why a tenant could not set-off an unliquidated claim for damages for breach of the landlord's repairing obligations, which related to the period prior to the acquisition date, against a claim for rent by the landlord. In relation to a claim for disrepair arising after the acquisition date it is thought that the tenant would struggle to set-off a claim for damages against the landlord as the landlord no longer has an obligation to keep the premises in repair.

RTM company's duty to monitor and report

8.65 The RTM company must keep under review whether 'tenant covenants' of leases of the whole or any part of the premises are being complied with and report to any person who is a landlord under such a lease any failure to comply with any tenant covenant of the lease (section 101(2) of the CLRA 2002).

8.66 'Tenant covenants' are defined so as to include both transferred and untransferred covenants (section 100(4) of the CLRA 2002).

8.67 The report must be made within 3 months of the breach of covenant coming to the attention of the RTM company (section 101(3) of the CLRA 2002).

8.68 However, the RTM company need not report to a landlord a failure to comply with a tenant covenant if the breach has been remedied, reasonable compensation has been paid or the landlord has notified the RTM company that it need not report to him or her certain breaches (section 101(4) of the CLRA 2002).

8.69 The CLRA 2002 does not state the consequence of non-compliance by the RTM company in relation to its obligation to monitor and report. However, it is to be noted that the *Service Charge Residential Management Code* (RICS, 3rd edn, 2016) applies to RTM companies and that, pursuant to section 24(2)(ac) of the LTA 1987, failure to comply with that Code is one of the grounds upon which a tribunal may be asked to appoint a manager under Part II of the LTA 1987.

Ground rent

8.70 It is commonly said that the RTM company does not have the right to collect ground rent. Technically, the position is that the obligation to pay rent is an untransferred covenant. The rent is still payable to the landlord, but in default of payment both the landlord and the RTM company may enforce the covenant. Furthermore, the RTM company would be under an obligation to monitor payment by the tenant, but as the rent is still payable to the landlord it is difficult to see how, practically, it can do that.

Problems

8.71 As untransferred covenants are enforceable both by the RTM company and the landlord, there is potential for conflict. It is not unknown in the law of landlord and tenant for two or more persons to have concurrent rights. The position commonly arises in tripartite leases where covenants are made by the tenant with both the landlord and the management company. Similarly, where there is a letting scheme a tenant often covenants both with the landlord and the other tenants. In those situations there is more than one party with the benefit of the covenant. Under the RTM provisions, the position is different as the landlord retains the benefit of untransferred covenants, but they become enforceable by both the landlord and the RTM company.

8.72 The potential for conflict arises out of the alternative routes which may be taken to enforce covenants. It will be recalled that the RTM company may not exercise 'any function of re-entry or forfeiture'. The usual and most efficacious method employed by landlords where a tenant is in breach of covenant is to bring proceedings under section 168(4) of the CLRA 2002 for a determination that breach of covenant has occurred, as a prelude to serving a notice under section 146(1) of the Law of Property Act 1925. An RTM company may avail itself of the procedure under section 168 of the CLRA 2002,[20] but as it has no right to serve a notice under section 146 of the Law of Property Act 1925 or forfeit the

---

[20] *Eastpoint Block A RTM Company Limited v Otubaga* [2023] EWCA Civ 879, [2023] 1 WLR 3896.

lease, it might choose to seek an injunction. Enforcing a covenant through seeking an injunction is a recognition of the continuance in force of the lease, and would be inconsistent with the landlord seeking to forfeit the lease. There is, therefore, scope for conflict.

8.73 As the benefit of untransferred covenants remains vested in the landlord, and it is only the right to sue which is shared with the RTM, it is thought that the landlord retains a unilateral right to waive a breach of an untransferred covenant or to vary the covenant. This raises the prospect of the RTM company taking enforcement proceedings only to be confronted by a settlement between the landlord and tenant, whereby the former waives the breach or varies the lease.

FUNCTIONS RELATING TO APPROVALS

8.74 Section 98 of the CLRA 2002 provides for the transfer of functions relating to approvals. It is as follows:

> (1) This section and section 99 apply in relation to the grant of approvals under long leases of the whole or any part of the premises; but nothing in this section or section 99 applies in relation to an approval concerning only a part of the premises consisting of a flat or other unit not held under a lease by a qualifying tenant.
>
> (2) Where a person who is—
>
> (a) landlord under a long lease of the whole or any part of the premises, or
>
> (b) party to such a lease otherwise than as landlord or tenant,
>
> has functions in relation to the grant of approvals to a tenant under the lease, the functions are instead functions of the RTM company.
>
> (3) Accordingly, any provisions of the lease making provision about the relationship of—
>
> (a) a person who is landlord under the lease, and
>
> (b) a person who is party to the lease otherwise than as landlord or tenant,
>
> in relation to such functions do not have effect.
>
> (4) The RTM company must not grant an approval by virtue of subsection (2) without having given—

(a) in the case of an approval relating to assignment, underletting, charging, parting with possession, the making of structural alterations or improvements or alterations of use, 30 days' notice, or
(b) in any other case, 14 days' notice,

to the person who is, or each of the persons who are, landlord under the lease.

(5) Regulations increasing the period of notice to be given under subsection (4)(b) in the case of any description of approval may be made by the appropriate national authority.

(6) So far as any function of a tenant under a long lease of the whole or any part of the premises—

(a) relates to the exercise of any function which is a function of the RTM company by virtue of this section, and
(b) is exercisable in relation to a person who is landlord under the lease or party to the lease otherwise than as landlord or tenant,

it is instead exercisable in relation to the RTM company.

(7) In this Chapter 'approval' includes consent or licence and 'approving' is to be construed accordingly; and an approval required to be obtained by virtue of a restriction entered on the register of title kept by the Chief Land Registrar is, so far as relating to a long lease of the whole or any part of any premises, to be treated for the purposes of this Chapter as an approval under the lease.

8.75 Section 99 of the CLRA 2002 supplements section 98. It is as follows:

(1) If a person to whom notice is given under section 98(4) objects to the grant of the approval before the time when the RTM company would first be entitled to grant it, the RTM company may grant it only—

(a) in accordance with the written agreement of the person who objected, or
(b) in accordance with a determination of (or on an appeal from) the appropriate tribunal.

(2) An objection to the grant of the approval may not be made by a person unless he could withhold the approval if the function of granting it were exercisable by him (and not by the RTM company).

(3) And a person may not make an objection operating only if a condition or requirement is not satisfied unless he could grant the approval

subject to the condition or requirement being satisfied if the function of granting it were so exercisable.

(4) An objection to the grant of the approval is made by giving notice of the objection (and of any condition or requirement which must be satisfied if it is not to operate) to—

(a) the RTM company, and
(b) the tenant,

and, if the approval is to a tenant approving an act of a sub-tenant, to the sub-tenant.

(5) An application to the appropriate tribunal for a determination under subsection (1)(b) may be made by—

(a) the RTM company,
(b) the tenant,
(c) if the approval is to a tenant approving an act of a sub-tenant, the sub-tenant, or
(d) any person who is landlord under the lease.

Premises to which section 98 applies

8.76 Section 98 of the CLRA 2002 applies in relation to the grant of approvals under long leases of the whole or any part of the premises.

8.77 It does not apply in relation to an approval concerning only a part of the premises consisting of a flat or other unit not held under a lease by a qualifying tenant (section 98(1) of the CLRA 2002).

Transfer of functions

8.78 Where a landlord or a third party to a lease has functions in relation to the grant of approvals to a tenant under the lease, section 98(2) of the CLRA 2002 provides that those functions are instead functions of the RTM company. Any provisions of a lease making provision to the contrary are of no effect (section 98(3)).

8.79 It is to be noted that the transfer is limited to the grant of approvals 'under the lease'. It is thought that this limits the application of section 98 of the CLRA 2002 to where the lease provides that the landlord has a power to grant or withhold consent. So, for example, if the lease includes an absolute covenant against alterations, there is no 'function' which is transferred. The RTM company does not have power to give consent to alterations. The landlord retains the power to enter into a deed of variation permitting the tenant to do works which would otherwise contravene the absolute covenant.

8.80 There is one exception to the requirement that the approval be 'under the lease'. An approval required to be obtained by virtue of a restriction entered on the Title Register kept by the Chief Land Registrar is, so far as relating to a long lease of the whole or any part of any premises, to be treated as an approval under the lease (section 98(7) of the CLRA 2002).

8.81 Section 98(7) of the CLRA 2002 provides as follows:

> (7) ... an approval required to be obtained by virtue of a restriction entered on the register of title kept by the Chief Land Registrar is, so far as relating to a long lease of the whole or any part of the premises, to be treated for the purposes of this Chapter as an approval under the lease.

8.82 Where the RTM has been acquired by a RTM company, the consent or certificate required by the restriction where this is required in respect of the landlord's management functions must be given by the RTM company.

8.83 The disposition for registration, provided it is caught by the restriction, should be accompanied by a conveyancer's certificate confirming that:

> X [*the person named in the restriction*] is landlord [*or state other*] under the lease dated [*insert details*] made between [*insert details*];
> Y [*the RTM company giving the consent or certificate required by the restriction*] is a right to manage company and has acquired the right to manage in respect of X's [*landlord*] management functions under the lease; and
> the notice required by section 98 of the Commonhold and Leasehold Reform Act 2002 was given by Y in respect of the [*consent or certificate, as appropriate*] required under the terms of the restriction and the requisite notice period has elapsed without an objection having been made.

8.84 For further information, consult HMLR, Practice guide 27: the leasehold reform legislation (updated 22 April 2025).

8.85 Any obligation on a tenant to obtain approval from the landlord under a long lease becomes an obligation to obtain approval from the RTM company (section 98(5) of the CLRA 2002).

Section 19 of the Landlord and Tenant Act 1927

8.86 Section 19(1) of the Landlord and Tenant Act 1927 provides that where a lease contains a covenant against alienation without consent, that covenant shall be deemed to be subject to a proviso that such licence should not be unreasonably withheld. The RTM provisions amend this section so that references to the 'landlord' or 'lessor' are to be read as references to the RTM company. Similar provision is made in respect of section 19(3) (which applies to covenants against alteration of user) (paragraphs (2) and (4) of Schedule 7 to the CLRA 2002).

8.87 As originally drafted, both section 19(2) of the Landlord and Tenant Act 1927 (covenants against improvement) and section 19(3) (covenants against change of user) allow the landlord to require as a condition of consent payment of a reasonable sum in respect of any damage to or diminution in the value of the premises or neighbouring premises belonging to the landlord. Where there is an RTM company in place, those provisions apply as if the reference to payment of such a sum were omitted. So where previously a landlord could have reasonably withheld consent unless the tenant paid a sum of money referable to the diminution in value of neighbouring premises, the RTM company is able to grant consent without including such a condition. Indeed, it would seem that it could not include such a provision.

Requirement to give notice before granting an approval

Notice

8.88 The RTM company must not grant an approval without having given: (a) in the case of an approval relating to assignment, underletting, charging, parting with possession, the making of structural alterations or improvements or alterations of use, 30 days' notice; or (b) in any other case, 14 days' notice, to the person who is, or each of the persons who are, landlord under the lease (section 98(4) of the CLRA 2002). Where there are intermediate interests then the RTM will be obliged to give notice to more than one landlord.

8.89 The CLRA 2002 contains no express provision for an RTM company to which an application for consent to an alienation is made to give notice of it to the landlord; however, a duty to do so arises under section 2 of the Landlord and Tenant Act 1988.[21] In that case, the lessee applied for consent to assignment to the RTM company, which neither informed the landlord nor addressed the application. The Court of Appeal held (at [51]) that the RTM company had not unreasonably refused to give consent. As the RTM company was prohibited by section 98(4) of the CLRA 2002 in the clearest terms from giving consent until it had given 30 days' notice to the landlord, a refusal or failure to give consent in the meantime could not in law be unreasonable. The tenant's remedy lay under section 107 of the CLRA 2002, which entitles 'any person interested' to apply to the appropriate tribunal for an order requiring 'a person who has failed to comply with a requirement imposed on him by, under or by virtue of any provision of this Chapter to make good the default within such time as is specified in the order'.

Objection

8.90 If a person to whom notice is given under section 98(4) of the CLRA 2002 objects to the grant of the approval before the time when the RTM company would first be entitled to grant it (i.e. 30 days or 14 days, depending on the nature of the approval), the RTM company may grant it only: (a) in accordance with the written agreement of the person who objected; or (b) in accordance with a determination of (or on an appeal from) the appropriate tribunal.

Grounds of objection

8.91 There are no new grounds upon which the landlord may object. A person may only object to the grant of approval if he or she could have withheld the approval but for the transfer of the approval function to the RTM company (section 99(2) of the CLRA 2002).

---

21 *Reiner v Triplark Limited* [2018] EWCA Civ 2151, [2019] 1 WLR 2003 at [46].

8.92 Similarly, the landlord cannot ask for conditions to be imposed unless he could previously have granted the approval subject to the condition or requirement being satisfied (section 99(3) of the CLRA 2002).

8.93 The landlord has to give notice of the objection (and of any condition or requirement which must be satisfied if it is not to operate) to the RTM company, and the tenant, and, if the approval is to a tenant approving an act of a sub-tenant, to the sub-tenant (section 99(4) of the CLRA 2002).

8.94 If there is no agreement after a landlord has objected then an application may be made by the RTM company, the tenant, a relevant sub-tenant or any person who is the landlord under the lease (section 99(5) of the CLRA 2002).

8.95 It may be problematic for the RTM company to recover the costs of any application to the tribunal. Although the RTM company is entitled to recover the service charge from tenants, many leases will not have apposite wording to recover the costs of such an application. In the case of *Geyfords Limited v O'Sullivan*,[22] the Upper Tribunal (Lands Chamber) rejected the landlord's attempt to recover the cost of tribunal proceedings under a generally worded clause. One of the matters considered relevant was that the lease was drawn up at a time in the 1970s when proceedings for non-payment or service charge disputes would have taken place in the county court, where the winning party can expect to recover costs. It was not contemplated that a 'no costs' tribunal would have been involved. A similar point can be made in respect of an application to the tribunal under section 99 of the CLRA 2002. In *56 Westbourne Terrace RTM Company Limited v Polturak*,[23] the Upper Tribunal, exercising the jurisdiction to vary long leases under section 35(2)(e) of the Landlord and Tenant Act 1987, varied a lease to allow an RTM company to recover legal costs of service charge proceedings against defaulting leaseholders. It is conceivable that similar applications could be made in other cases under section 35(2)(e), which permits a lease variation where the lease fails to make satisfactory provision for 'the recovery by one party to the lease

---

22 *Geyfords Limited v O'Sullivan* [2015] UKUT 683 (LC), [2015] 12 WLUK 611.

23 *56 Westbourne Terrace RTM Company Limited v Polturak* [2025] UKUT 88 (LC), [2025] L & TR 17.

from another party to it of expenditure incurred or to be incurred by him, or on his behalf, for the benefit of that other party or of a number of persons who include that other party'. This is a developing area.

Examples

8.96 The following examples may help to illustrate the points made above:

- A lease contains a covenant not to carry out structural alterations without consent. The tenant must seek consent from the RTM company. The RTM company must notify the landlord. If the landlord objects then consent may only be given if the landlord gives written consent or in accordance with a determination of the tribunal.
- A lease contains an absolute covenant against carrying out structural alterations. There is no approval function under the lease and therefore there is no transfer of a relevant function to the RTM company. The covenant is, therefore, an untransferred covenant. The RTM company must monitor and report any breach of covenant to the landlord and has power to enforce the covenant. The landlord can also enforce the covenant by seeking a determination under section 168 of the CLRA 2002 as a prelude to forfeiture. It is thought that the landlord may also waive the breach and/or vary the covenant. If the landlord varies the covenant or gives consent despite absolute prohibition and charges a premium, there is no obligation to share this with RTM company.

What if the RTM company refuses consent and the landlord wants to give consent?

8.97 There is no duty to notify the landlord where the RTM company refuses consent and similarly there is no opportunity for the landlord to challenge the refusal in the tribunal. It may, however, be possible for the landlord to vary the lease to allow the works in question or waive any breach. In relation to a variation it could be said that this is inconsistent with the statutory transfer of the approval function to the RTM company. In relation to waiver, it is thought that although the approval function is transferred to the RTM company the covenant not to alter/alienate, etc without consent is still an untransferred covenant and it would therefore be permissible for the landlord to waive any breach.

LANDLORD CONTRIBUTIONS TO SERVICE CHARGES IN RESPECT OF EXCLUDED UNITS

8.98 Section 103 of the CLRA 2002 places landlords under an obligation to meet any shortfall in the costs recovered by the RTM company caused by the proportions payable by tenants under their leases failing to add up to 100 per cent of the total. It is in the following terms:

> (1) This section applies where—
>
> (a) the premises contain at least one flat or other unit not subject to a lease held by a qualifying tenant (an 'excluded unit'),
> (b) the service charges payable under leases of flats contained in the premises which are so subject fall to be calculated as a proportion of the relevant costs, and
> (c) the proportions of the relevant costs so payable, when aggregated, amount to less than the whole of the relevant costs.
>
> (2) Where the premises contain only one excluded unit, the person who is the appropriate person in relation to the excluded unit must pay to the RTM company the difference between—
>
> (a) the relevant costs, and
> (b) the aggregate amount payable in respect of the relevant costs under leases of flats contained in the premises which are held by qualifying tenants.
>
> (3) Where the premises contain more than one excluded unit, each person who is the appropriate person in relation to an excluded unit must pay to the RTM company the appropriate proportion of that difference.
> (4) And the appropriate proportion in the case of each such person is the proportion of the internal floor area of all of the excluded units which is internal floor area of the excluded unit in relation to which he is the appropriate person.
> (5) The appropriate person in relation to an excluded unit—
>
> (a) if it is subject to a lease, is the landlord under the lease,
> (b) if it is subject to more than one lease, is the immediate landlord under whichever of the leases is inferior to all the others, and
> (c) if it is not subject to any lease, is the freeholder.

8.99 Where the premises which are subject to the right to manage contain at least one flat or other unit not subject to a lease held by a qualifying tenant then that unit is known as an 'excluded unit' (section 103(1) of the CLRA 2002).

8.100 Where the following conditions in section 103(1) of the CLRA 2002 are satisfied then the RTM company is entitled to a payment from the 'appropriate person':

(a) the premises contain at least one excluded unit;
(b) the service charges payable under the leases of flats contained in the premises fall to be calculated as a proportion of the relevant costs; and
(c) the proportions of the relevant costs so payable, when aggregated, amount to less than the whole of the relevant costs.

8.101 The 'appropriate person' is the immediate landlord or, if the unit is not subject to a lease, the freeholder (section 103(5) of the CLRA 2002).

8.102 Where there is only one excluded unit, the appropriate person pays the difference between the relevant costs incurred by the RTM company and the aggregate amount payable by the qualifying tenants (section 103(2) of the CLRA 2002).

8.103 Where there is more than one excluded unit, each person who is an appropriate person pays an appropriate proportion towards the shortfall calculated by reference to the floor area of the excluded units (section 103(3) and (4) of the CLRA 2002). This is so even if it leads to odd results. Say there are ten flats, one of which is an excluded unit and the service charge payable by the remaining nine is not calculated on floor area and adds up to 90 per cent. If the floor of the area of the excluded unit is 15 per cent of the total floor area then the landlord pays 15 per cent.

8.104 Paragraph 4(3) of Schedule 7 to the CLRA 2002 provides that references to a tenant of a dwelling in sections 18–30 of the LTA 1985 include a person who is landlord under a lease of the whole or any part of the premises so that sums paid by him in pursuance of section 103 of the CLRA 2002 are service charges. This provision imports wholesale all the tenant protective aspects of that legislation. The landlord may rely on the reasonableness provisions of section 19 of the LTA 1985 and is entitled to be consulted in respect of major works, and is also entitled to request a summary of relevant costs under section 21 of the LTA 1985, etc.

BUILDING SAFETY ACT 2022

8.105 As set out above, the effect of section 96 of the CLRA 2002 is that there is a statutory transfer of management obligations under the lease, but the Building Safety Act 2022 (BSA 2002) imposes additional obligations on RTM companies over and above obligations arising from the lease. This is not the place for an exhaustive review of those provisions, but some of the more significant obligations are set out in paras 8.106–8.112.

8.106 Part 4 of the BSA 2022 imposes obligations on the 'accountable person' in relation to 'higher risk buildings'. Section 72 states as follows:

> (1) In this Part an 'accountable person' for a higher-risk building is—
>
> (a) a person who holds a legal estate in possession in any part of the common parts (subject to subsection (2)), or
> (b) a person who does not hold a legal estate in any part of the building but who is under a relevant repairing obligation in relation to any part of the common parts.
>
> This subsection is subject to subsection (5) (special rule for commonhold land).
>
> (2) A person ('the estate owner') who holds a legal estate in possession in the common parts of a higher-risk building or any part of them ('the relevant common parts') is not an accountable person for the building by virtue of subsection (1)(a) if—
>
> (a) each long lease of which the estate owner is lessor provides that a particular person, who does not hold a legal estate in any part of the building, is under a relevant repairing obligation in relation to all of the relevant common parts, or
> (b) all repairing obligations relating to the relevant common parts which would otherwise be obligations of the estate owner are functions of an RTM company.

8.107 In most cases, an RTM company will be 'a person who does not hold a legal estate in any part of the building but who is under a relevant repairing obligation in relation to any part of the common parts' and thus an 'accountable person'. Broadly speaking, the accountable person is the entity responsible for meeting the statutory obligations under Part 4 of the BSA 2022 for occupied higher-risk buildings. Reference should be made to specialist works in relation to the detailed obligations of 'an accountable person' and of 'the principal accountable person'.

8.108 As from a dated to be appointed it is proposed that the LTA 1985 should be amended by the addition of section 30E, which is intended to allow the recovery of costs incurred in complying with the obligations imposed on an accountable person under the BSA 2022. The section is in the following terms:

> **30E Liability for remuneration of building safety director of resident management company etc**
>
> (1) This section applies to a lease of premises which consist of or include a dwelling in a higher-risk building if—
>
> (a) the landlord is an accountable person for the building,
>
> (b) the landlord is—
>
> (i) a resident management company within the meaning of section 111 of the Building Safety Act 2022, or
>
> (ii) an RTM company within the meaning of Chapter 1 of Part 2 of the Commonhold and Leasehold Reform Act 2002 (right to manage), and
>
> (c) the tenant is liable to pay a service charge.
>
> (2) The lease has effect—
>
> (a) as if it contained provision authorising the appointment of a person (whether or not a leaseholder or a resident of the building) as a director of the landlord for a building safety purpose,
>
> (b) as if the matters for which the service charge is payable under the lease included remunerating any director of the landlord appointed for a building safety purpose (insofar as this would not otherwise be the case), and

(c) where the lease contains different methods for apportioning different relevant costs (within the meaning of section 18), as if it provided that any costs for which the tenant is liable by virtue only of paragraph (b) to be apportioned in the same way as costs incurred in connection with insuring the building.

(3) In this section—

'building safety purpose' means the purpose of supporting the landlord in complying with its duties under Part 4 of the Building Safety Act 2022 or under regulations made under that Part;
'landlord' includes any person who has a right under the lease to enforce payment of a service charge;
'service charge' has the meaning given by section 18;
'tenant' includes any person who has an obligation under the lease to pay a service charge.

Remediation orders under the Building Safety Act 2022

8.109 Sections 116–125 of, and Schedule 8 to, the BSA 2022 make provision in relation to remediation of certain defects in buildings. In particular, those provisions include protections from liability for leaseholders in specific circumstances. Regulations 3–5 of the Building Safety (Leaseholder Protections) (Information etc) (England) Regulations 2022 (SI 2022/859) make provision for recovery of amounts as between landlords where, because of provisions in Schedule 8 to the BSA 2022, a service charge cannot be claimed from a leaseholder under a lease. In those regulations, the person seeking the remediation order is referred to as 'L'. The point to note is that 'L' also includes an RTM company.

8.110 The material effect of this is that where there is a shortfall in service charge recovery for remediation works, because certain sums cannot be recovered from leaseholders, the RTM company may seek recovery of such sums from the 'responsible landlord' and other persons identified in paragraphs 3, 4 and 5 of the Building Safety (Leaseholder Protections) (Information etc) (England) Regulations 2022.

Section 161 of the Building Safety Act 2022: liability of officers of body corporate – partial exemption for 'relevant company'

8.111 This section provides that, where a corporate body commits a criminal offence under Part 2 or Part 4 of the BSA 2022, any director, manager, secretary or other similar officer of that body is also deemed to have committed that offence in certain circumstances. Those circumstances are where the individual has consented to or connived in the commission of the offence or where the offence is attributable to any neglect on his or her part. Section 40 makes similar provision in respect of the criminal offences in the Building Act 1984.

8.112 Section 161(4) of the BSA 2022 provides an exception where a 'relevant company' appoints a paid director for a building safety purpose. In this case, all unpaid directors of the company will be relieved of their personal criminal liability for breaches of Part 4 duties. 'Relevant company' includes an RTM company (section 161(5)(b)).

LIABILITY OF THE LANDLORD AND THE RTM COMPANY UNDER OTHER STATUTES

8.113 Section 102(1) of the CLRA 2002 gives effect to Schedule 7, which amends the effect of various other statutory provisions where a company has acquired the right to manage. As mentioned at para 8.21 when the right to manage has been exercised, the landlord under a lease is not entitled to do anything which the RTM company is required or empowered to do under the lease (section 97(2)). In some cases, the amendments made by Schedule 7 are intended to impose liability on an RTM company where previously the landlord was liable. This reflects the landlord's inability to carry out acts which the RTM company is required or empowered to do. Where they have not already been explained above, the effect of these provisions is summarised below.

8.114 There are a number of statutory obligations of one kind or another on owners or managers of property which are not mentioned in Schedule 7 to the CLRA 2002, and in those cases, it may be unclear whether it is the landlord or the RTM company which is liable and, if the former, whether his or her inability to act provides a statutory defence. Some instances of this nature are explored in Chapter 10.

Defective premises

8.115 Section 4 of the Defective Premises Act 1972 casts a duty of care on the landlord where the lease puts an obligation on him or her to maintain or repair the premises. The duty is recast as a duty on the RTM company (paragraph 2 of Schedule 7 to the CLRA 2002).

Service charges

8.116 Sections 18–30 of the LTA 1985 have effect with the modification that the references to the landlord are to be taken as references to the RTM company (paragraph 4 of Schedule 7 to the CLRA 2002). Additionally, references to a tenant of a dwelling include a landlord who is obliged to contribute in relation to an excluded unit.

Right to request information on insurance

8.117 Similar provision is made in relation to section 30A of, and the Schedule to, the LTA 1985, which concern the rights of the tenants in relation to insurance (paragraph 5 of Schedule 7 to the CLRA 2002). References to the landlord are to be taken as references to the RTM company, and references to a tenant of a dwelling include a landlord who is obliged to contribute in relation to an excluded unit.

Managing agents

8.118 Section 30B of the LTA 1985 (recognised tenants' associations to be consulted about landlord's managing agents) has effect as if references to the landlord were to the RTM company (and as if subsection (6) were omitted) (paragraph 6 of Schedule 7 to the CLRA 2002).

Right of first refusal

8.119 Where section 5 of the LTA 1987 (right of first refusal: requirement that landlord serve offer notice on tenant) requires the landlord to serve an offer notice on the qualifying tenants of the flats contained in the premises, he or she must serve a copy of the offer notice on the RTM company (paragraph 7 of Schedule 7 to the CLRA 2002).

Appointment of a manager under Part II of the Landlord and Tenant Act 1987

8.120 Paragraph 8 of Schedule 7 to the CLRA 2002 preserves the right to apply for a manager when there is an RTM company, and provides that references to the landlord are to the RTM company. It makes other changes to the provisions of Part II; in particular, it creates a power when making an order appointing a manager to make an order that the right to manage the premises is to cease to be exercisable by the RTM company (paragraph 8(7) of Schedule 7, amending section 24 of the LTA 1987).

Right to acquire landlord's interest

8.121 One positive effect of the right to manage, from the point of view of the landlord, is that whilst there is an RTM company in place, Part III of the LTA 1987, which permits compulsory acquisition by the tenants of the landlord's interest, does not apply (paragraph 9 of Schedule 7 to the CLRA 2002). This makes sense as the tenants need to prove that the landlord is at fault. If there is an RTM company then the landlord is prohibited from exercising management functions so it would be unfair to allow acquisition due to the faults of the RTM company.

Variation of leases

8.122 Sections 35, 36, 38 and 39 of the LTA 1987 (variation of long leases relating to flats) have effect as if references to a party to a long lease (apart from those in section 38(8)) included the RTM company (paragraph 10 of Schedule 7 to the CLRA 2002).

Service charges to be held in trust

8.123 Sections 42–42B of the LTA 1987 (service charge contributions to be held in trust and in designated account) have effect with the modification that references to the payee are to the RTM company (paragraph 11 of Schedule 7 to the CLRA 2002). The definition of 'tenant' in section 42(1) of the LTA 1987 does not apply. References to a tenant of a dwelling include a person who is landlord under a lease of the whole or any part of the premises. The reference in section 42(2) to sums paid to the payee by the contributing tenants by way of relevant service charges includes payments made to the RTM company under section 94 (accrued uncommitted service charges) or section 103 (landlord contribution to service charge in respect of excluded units). Section 42A(5) applies as if paragraph (a) were omitted and the person referred to in paragraph (b) were a person who receives service charges on behalf of the RTM company.

Information to be furnished to tenants

8.124 Sections 46–48 of the LTA 1987 (information to be furnished to tenants) have effect with the modification that references to the landlord include the RTM company (paragraph 12 of Schedule 7 to the CLRA 2002). So both the RTM company and the landlord should serve notices under section 48 of the LTA 1997, one to allow recovery of service charges and the other for rent.

8.125 It is also provided that references to a tenant include a person who is landlord under a lease of the whole or any part of the premises; and, in relation to such a person, the reference in section 47(4) of the LTA 1987 to sums payable to the landlord under the terms of the tenancy are to sums paid by him or her under section 103 of the CLRA 2002.

Landlord and Tenant Act 1988

8.126 The Landlord and Tenant Act 1988 (statutory duties in connection with covenants against assigning, etc) has effect with the modification that the reference in section 1(2)(b) to the covenant is to the covenant as it has effect subject to section 98 (paragraph 13 of Schedule 7 to the CLRA 2002). References in section 3(2), (4) and (5) of the Landlord and Tenant Act 1988 (qualified duty to approve consent by another) to the landlord are to be taken as referring to the RTM company.

Tenants' right to management audit

8.127 Chapter 5 of Part 1 (tenants' right to management audit by landlord) of the LRHUDA 1993 has effect with the modification that references to the landlord (other than the references in section 76(1) and (2) to 'the same landlord') are to the RTM company (paragraph 14 of Schedule 7 to the CLRA 2002). References to a tenant include a person who is landlord under a lease of the whole or any part of the premises and has to make payments under section 103 of the CLRA 2002. Section 80(5) of the LRHUDA 1993 applies as if the reference to a person who receives rent were to a person who receives service charges.

Right to appoint surveyor

8.128 Section 84 of, and Schedule 4 to (apart from paragraph 7), the Housing Act 1996 (right of recognised tenants' association to appoint surveyor to advise on matters relating to service charges) have effect as if references to the landlord were to the RTM company (paragraph 15 of Schedule 7 to the CLRA 2002). Section 84(5) of, and paragraph 4(5) of Schedule 4 to, the Housing Act 1996 apply as if the reference to a person who receives rent were to a person who receives service charges.

Administration charges

8.129 Schedule 11 to the CLRA 2002 has effect as if references to the landlord (or a party to a lease) included the RTM company (paragraph 16 of Schedule 7). This makes sense as the definition of an administration charge is wide enough to include a sum which is payable to an RTM company, for instance, a clause requiring an amount to be paid in respect of a failure to pay service charges on the due date (which would fall within paragraph 1(c) of Schedule 11).

LEASE VARIATION TO PERMIT COST RECOVERY

8.130 In *56 Westbourne Terrace RTM Company Limited v Polturak*,[24] the Upper Tribunal (Lands Chamber), exercising the jurisdiction to vary long leases under section 35(2)(e) of the Landlord and Tenant Act 1987, varied a lease to allow an RTM company to recover legal costs of service charge proceedings against defaulting leaseholders. In *Eastern Pyramid Group Corp SA v Spire House RTM Company Limited*,[25] the Upper Tribunal held that the First-tier Tribunal (Property Chamber) had jurisdiction to vary long leases under section 35(2)(e) of the Landlord and Tenant Act 1987 to enable an RTM company to remove a limitation on advance service charge payments so that it could recover the cost of significant repair work in advance. Without advance payment, the RTM company could not undertake the emergency work as it had no assets other than the service charge contributions.

---

[24] *56 Westbourne Terrace RTM Company Limited v Polturak* [2025] UKUT 88 (LC), [2025] L & TR 17.

[25] *Eastern Pyramid Group Corp SA v Spire House RTM Company Limited* [2025] UKUT 292 (LC), [2025] 9 WLUK 80.

Chapter 9

Cessation of the Right to Manage

SUMMARY

9.1 This chapter examines the cessation of the right to manage. Section 105 of the Commonhold and Leasehold Reform Act 2002 (CLRA 2002) contemplates the right to manage coming to an end by agreement, on the winding up of the RTM company, appointment of a receiver or manager in relation to the RTM company, a voluntary arrangement in relation to the RTM company being approved under the Insolvency Act 1986, or the RTM company being struck off the Companies Register. Further, the right to manage ceases to be exercisable if a manager is appointed under Part 2 of the Landlord and Tenant Act 1987 (LTA 1987). Lastly, the right to manage ceases to be exercisable if the RTM company ceases to be an RTM company in relation to the premises.

CESSATION BY AGREEMENT

9.2 Management by the RTM company may be brought to an end by agreement. What is required is for the RTM company and each person who is landlord under a lease of the whole or any part of the premises to enter into an agreement for the right to manage the premises to cease to be exercisable by the RTM company (section 105(2) of the CLRA 2002). Obviously, it would be sensible for such an agreement to specify a date upon which the right to manage should cease and to provide for ancillary matters, such as the transfer of documents and payment of any accrued uncommitted service charges held by the RTM company.

CESSATION ON WINDING UP, ETC OF THE RTM COMPANY

9.3 Section 105(3) states that the right to manage ceases to be exercisable by the RTM company if:

> (a) a winding-up order … is made, or a resolution for voluntary winding-up is passed, with respect to the RTM company, or the RTM company enters administration,
> (b) a receiver or a manager of the RTM company's undertaking is duly appointed, or possession is taken, by or on behalf of the holders of any debentures secured by a floating charge, of any property of the RTM company comprised in or subject to the charge,
> (c) a voluntary arrangement proposed in the case of the RTM company for the purposes of Part 1 of the Insolvency Act 1986 (c. 45) is approved under that Part of that Act, or
> (d) the RTM company's name is struck off the register under section 1000, 1001 or 1003 of the Companies Act 2006.

9.4 Although an RTM company will have control over the service charge fund, it can only use that fund for the purposes envisaged by the lease. The RTM provisions create new opportunities for litigation which would not have been in the contemplation of the parties when the lease was entered into. For example, the RTM company cannot grant an approval where a landlord has objected without the landlord's written consent or a favourable determination under section 99(1) of the CLRA 2002 by the First-tier Tribunal (Property Chamber). Most leases will not be drawn in such a way as to allow the service charges to be spent on litigation by an RTM company against a landlord. Such litigation would have to be funded by a call on its members. There is therefore a significant risk that an RTM could end up in a situation where it had debts and members unwilling to fund the company.

Struck off company restored

9.5 In the case of *AB&R RTM Company Limited v Rovergrange Limited*,[1] an RTM company which had been struck off the Companies Register and dissolved pursuant to section 1000 of the Companies Act

---

1 *AB & R RTM Company Limited v Rovergrange Limited*, LON/00AM/LRM/2017/0005, FTT (PC), 12 April 2017, [2017] 4 WLUK 282.

2006 was subsequently reinstated and restored to the Register. It was held that it was entitled to take back the management of the property.

CESSATION ON THE APPOINTMENT OF A MANAGER UNDER THE LANDLORD AND TENANT ACT 1987

9.6 As noted in Chapter 8, the appointment of a manager provisions of Part 2 of the LTA 1987 apply to premises where an RTM company has been appointed. But an existing order appointing a manager under the LTA 1987 cannot be varied to bring RTM premises within the ambit of the order. In the case of *Benthan v Lindsay Court (St Annes) RTM Company Limited*,[2] it was held that an order under Part 2 appointing a person as manager of blocks of residential flats could not be varied so as to extend his management powers to include a block of flats in respect of which a third party had acquired a right to manage under the CLRA 2002. An order depriving the RTM company of management powers over the property, where that party was not bound by the initial appointment of the manager, was not a variation but a new order. The specific requirements of the LTA 1987 had to be satisfied before someone could be deprived of their right and responsibility to manage their own property.

9.7 The right to manage the premises ceases to be exercisable by the RTM company if a manager is appointed under Part 2 of the LTA 1987 to act in relation to the premises, or any premises containing or contained in the premises, and begins so to act, or if an order made under section 24 of the LTA 1987 (as amended by paragraph 8(7) of Schedule 7 to the CLRA 2002) that the right to manage the premises is to cease to be exercisable by the RTM company takes effect (section 105(4) of the CLRA 2002).

CESSATION ON THE RTM COMPANY CEASING TO BE AN RTM COMPANY

9.8 The right to manage the premises ceases to be exercisable by the RTM company if it ceases to be an RTM company in relation to the premises (section 105(5) of the CLRA 2002). Whereas section 105(3) deals with the right to manage ceasing where the company is to be

2 *Benthan v Lindsay Court (St Annes) RTM Company Limited* [2021] UKUT 4 (LC), [2021] L & TR 11.

wound up, this provision is intended to deal with the situation where the company will continue but has ceased to be an RTM company. Section 73(2) states that, *prima facie*, a company is an RTM company in relation to premises if:

(a) it is a private company limited by guarantee, and
(b) its articles of association state that its object, or one of its objects, is the acquisition and exercise of the right to manage the premises.

9.9 There are, however, exceptions. A company is not an RTM company if it is a commonhold association (within the meaning of Part 1 of the CLRA 2002). Similarly, if the freehold of any premises is transferred to a company which is an RTM company in relation to the premises, or any premises containing or contained in the premises, it ceases to be an RTM company when the transfer is executed (section 73(5)).

9.10 The CLRA 2002 does not state that an RTM company will cease to be an RTM company if the initial qualifying criteria in section 72 cease to apply, for instance, because the number of flats held by qualifying tenants falls below two-thirds of the total number of flats contained in the premises or because the percentage of parts used for commercial purposes increases as a result of a change of use or a redevelopment of part of the premises. Nor does the CLRA 2002 state that the right to manage will cease in such circumstances, and it is therefore thought that the right would continue.

9.11 Prior to the decision of the Court of Appeal in *Triplerose Limited v Ninety Broomfield Road RTM Company Limited*,[3] it was thought that the right to manage could be exercised by a single RTM company in respect of more than one self-contained building or part of a building. In that case, the Court of Appeal decided the contrary. Many RTM companies were set up and purportedly exercised and purportedly acquired the right to manage in respect of more than one block. Similarly, as a result of the decision in *FirstPort Property Services Limited v Settlers Court RTM Company Limited*,[4] an RTM company may only acquire the right to manage property which is immediately appurtenant to the block in

---

3 *Triplerose Limited v Ninety Broomfield Road RTM Company Limited* [2015] EWCA Civ 282, [2016] 1 WLR 275.

4 *FirstPort Property Services Limited v Settlers Court RTM Company Limited* [2022] UKSC 1, [2022] 1 WLR 519.

question. Prior to the decision, many RTM companies managed communal property shared by several blocks. In those cases where the landlord went along with the acquisition of the right to manage, it is likely that there is an estoppel by convention. Those cases will have to be approached on a case-by-case basis.

Consequences of cessation

Immediate consequences

9.12 All the operative provisions of the right set out in sections 96–103 of the CLRA 2002 (i.e. the transfer of management functions and approval functions, the enforcement of tenant covenants and the payment by the landlord of contributions to service charges) apply only so long as the right to manage has not ceased to be exercisable (section 95).

9.13 There is no equivalent in reverse providing for the service of 'contractor notices' and 'contract notices' as provided for under section 91 and section 92 of the CLRA 2002. As explained in Chapter 5, sections 91 and 92 contain an obligation on the manager of the premises prior to the acquisition of the right to manage to serve 'contractor notices' on the contractor party and 'contract notices' on the RTM company. The purpose behind the service of contractor notices and contract notices is to require the manager to make the RTM company aware of all of the existing management contracts relating to the premises in advance of the acquisition date.

9.14 If matters are proceeding in an orderly fashion and the fact that the RTM company will shortly cease to exercise the right to manage is foreseen, then the RTM company can by agreement with the landlord or third-party manager under the lease hand back management before the event causing cessation to take effect. Under section 97(2) of the CLRA 2002, a landlord or third-party manager under the lease is generally prohibited from doing anything which the RTM company is 'required or empowered to do', but there is an exception where it is done in accordance with an agreement with the RTM company.

9.15 The reverse of this is that the general prohibition on landlords and third-party managers ceases to have effect on cessation because the RTM company at that point will no longer be 'required or empowered to do' anything. So unless powers have already been handed back, there will be a return to the *status quo ante* under the lease at that point in time.

9.16 It may be that a third-party manager under the lease was a company which was wound up or allowed to be struck off when the RTM company acquired the right to manage. Well-drafted tripartite leases provide that, in the event of the third-party manager ceasing to exist, the landlord will be obliged to carry out its functions. In the event of a lacuna arising in relation to management then the tenants should consider whether the conditions are fulfilled for an application for the appointment of a manager under the LTA 1987. Failing that, the tenants might consider forming a new RTM company and applying to the tribunal to disapply the cooling-off period (see paras 9.19–9.22).

Frustration of contracts

9.17 If a party to a contract is placed, by events outside his or her control, in the position of being unable to fulfil his or her obligations or role under that contract, the normal effect of contract law will be that the contract falls as frustrated. One such case is where the operation of the law intervenes to prevent someone being able to fulfil part of a contract. Although the events leading up to an event causing cessation might be within the control of the RTM company, the loss of the right to manage on the happening of such an event occurs by operation of law and the likely result is that contracts entered into by the RTM company will be frustrated.

9.18 In practical terms, a person contracting with the RTM company will have little interest in pursuing the RTM company because of the limited liability of members and the fact that once it loses the right to manage it loses control of the service charge fund and thus the ability to pay bills. Where the solvency of the RTM company is in question, prudent directors will pay close regard to the rules relating to trading while insolvent and the resultant personal liability.

Cooling-off period

9.19 Where a right to manage ceases to be exercisable there is a statutory cooling-off period.

9.20 Paragraph 5 of Schedule 6 to the CLRA 2002 provides as follows:

> 5(1) This Chapter does not apply to premises falling within section 72(1) at any time if—
>
> (a) the right to manage the premises is at that time exercisable by a RTM company, or
> (b) that right has been so exercisable but has ceased to be so exercisable less than four years before that time.

9.21 The cooling-off period does not apply where the right to manage the premises ceases to be exercisable by reason of the fact that the RTM company acquires the freehold. So in such a case, a new RTM claim can be made immediately.

9.22 The appropriate tribunal also has a power to disapply paragraph 5 of Schedule 6 to the CLRA 2002. The appropriate tribunal may, on an application made by an RTM company, determine that paragraph 5(1)(b) is not to apply in any case if it considers that it would be unreasonable for it to apply in the circumstances of the case.

Appendix 1

The Right to Manage (Prescribed Particulars and Forms) (England) Regulations 2010 (SI 2010/825)

Made	*17th March 2010*
Laid before Parliament	*24th March 2010*
Coming into force	*19th April 2010*

The Secretary of State(1), in exercise of the powers conferred by sections 78(2)(d) and (3), 80(8) and (9), 84(2), 92(3) and (7) and 178(1)(a), (b) and (c) of the Commonhold and Leasehold Reform Act 2002(2), makes the following Regulations:

Citation, commencement and application

1.—(1) These Regulations may be cited as the Right to Manage (Prescribed Particulars and Forms) (England) Regulations 2010 and shall come into force on 19th April 2010.
(2) These Regulations apply in relation to premises in England only.

(1) By virtue of section 179(1) of the Commonhold and Leasehold Reform Act 2002 (c. 15), the Secretary of State is 'the appropriate national authority' as respects England. The powers conferred by sections 78(2)(d) and (3), 80(8) and (9), 84(2) and 92(3)(e) and (7)(b) of that Act are exercisable, as respects Wales, by the National Assembly for Wales.

(2) 2002 c. 15.

Interpretation

2. In these Regulations—

'the 2002 Act' means the Commonhold and Leasehold Reform Act 2002;

'landlord', in relation to RTM premises, means a person who is landlord under a lease of the whole or any part of the premises(1);

'RTM premises' means premises as regards which a RTM company intends to acquire the right to manage(2);

'third party', in relation to RTM premises, means a person who is party to a lease of the whole or any part of the premises otherwise than as landlord or tenant(3).

(1) As to 'landlord' *see also* section 112(2), (3) and (5) of the 2002 Act.
(2) As to 'RTM company', *see* sections 71(1) and 73 of the 2002 Act. As to 'right to manage' *see* section 71(2) of that Act.
(3) As to 'tenant' *see* section 112(2), (3) and (5) of the 2002 Act.

Additional content of notice of invitation to participate

3. (1) A notice of invitation to participate shall contain, in addition to the statements and information referred to in section 78(2)(a) to (c) of the 2002 Act (notice inviting participation), the particulars mentioned in paragraph (2).

(2) The particulars referred to in paragraph (1) are—

(a) the RTM company's registered number(1), the address of its registered office and the names of its directors and if applicable, secretary;

(b) the names of the landlord and any third party;

(c) a statement that, subject to the exclusions mentioned in sub-paragraph (e), if the right to manage is acquired by the RTM company, the company will be responsible for—

(i) the discharge of the landlord's duties under the lease; and

(ii) the exercise of his powers under the lease,

with respect to services, repairs, maintenance, improvements, insurance and management;

(d) a statement that, subject to the exclusion mentioned in sub-paragraph (e)(ii), if the right to manage is acquired by the RTM company, the company may enforce untransferred tenant covenants(2);

(e) a statement that, if the right to manage is acquired by the RTM company, the company will not be responsible for the discharge of the landlord's duties or the exercise of his powers under the lease—

(i) with respect to a matter concerning only a part of the premises consisting of a flat or other unit not subject to a lease held by a qualifying tenant(3); or
(ii) relating to re-entry or forfeiture;

(f) a statement that, if the right to manage is acquired by the RTM company, the company will have functions under the statutory provisions referred to in Schedule 7 to the 2002 Act;
(g) a statement that the RTM company intends or, as the case may be, does not intend, to appoint a managing agent; and—

(i) if it does so intend, a statement—

(aa) of the name and address of the proposed managing agent (if known); and
(bb) if it be the case, that the person is the landlord's managing agent; or

(ii) if it does not so intend, the qualifications or experience (if any) of the existing members of the RTM company in relation to the management of residential property;

(h) a statement that, where the RTM company gives a claim notice, a person who is or has been a member of the company may be liable for costs incurred by the landlord and others in consequence of the notice;
(i) a statement that, if the recipient of the notice (of invitation to participate) does not fully understand its purpose or implications, he is advised to seek professional help; and
(j) the information provided in the notes to the form set out in Schedule 1 to these Regulations.

(1) *See* section 15 of the Companies Act 2006 (c. 46).
(2) As to 'untransferred tenant covenants' *see* section 100(4) of the 2002 Act.

(3) As to premises to which Chapter 1 of Part 2 of the 2002 Act applies, *see* section 72 (and Schedule 6). As to 'flat' and 'unit' *see* section 112(1). As to 'lease' *see* section 112(2). As to 'qualifying tenant', *see* sections 75 and 112(4) and (5).

Additional content of claim notice

4. A claim notice shall contain, in addition to the particulars required by section 80(2) to (7) (contents of claim notice) of the 2002 Act—

(a) a statement that a person who—

(i) does not dispute the RTM company's entitlement to acquire the right to manage(1); and
(ii) is the manager party under a management contract(2) subsisting immediately before the date specified in the claim notice,

must, in accordance with section 92 of the 2002 Act (duties to give notice of contracts), give a notice to the RTM company and to the person who is the contractor party;

(b) a statement that, from the acquisition date(3), landlords under leases of the whole or any part of the premises to which the claim notice relates are entitled to be members of the RTM company;

(c) a statement that the notice is not invalidated by any inaccuracy in any of the particulars required by section 80(2) to (7) of the 2002 Act or this regulation, but that a person who is of the opinion that any of the particulars contained in the claim notice are inaccurate may—

(i) identify the particulars in question to the RTM company by which the notice was given; and
(ii) indicate the respects in which they are considered to be inaccurate;

(d) a statement that a person who receives the notice but does not fully understand its purpose, is advised to seek professional help; and

(e) the information provided in the notes to the form set out in Schedule 2 to these Regulations.

(1) As to the circumstances in which there is no dispute about entitlement; *see* section 90(3) of the 2002 Act.
(2) As to 'manager party' *see* section 91(2) and (4) of the 2002 Act. As to 'management contract' *see* section 91(2) of that Act.
(3) *See* section 90 of the 2002 Act.

Additional content of counter-notice

5. A counter-notice shall contain (in addition to the statement referred to in paragraph (a) or (b) of section 84(2) (counter-notices) of the 2002 Act)—

(a) a statement that, where the RTM company has been given one or more counter-notices containing such a statement as is mentioned in paragraph (b) of section 84(2) of the 2002 Act, the company may apply to a […]* tribunal for a determination that, on the date on which notice of the claim was given, the company was entitled to acquire the right to manage the premises specified in the claim notice;
(b) a statement that, where the RTM company has been given one or more counter-notices containing such a statement as is mentioned in paragraph (b) of section 84(2) of the 2002 Act, the company does not acquire the right to manage the premises specified in the claim notice unless—

(i) on an application to a […]* tribunal, it is finally determined(1) that the company was entitled to acquire the right to manage the premises; or
(ii) the person by whom the counter-notice was given agrees, or the persons by whom the counter-notices were given agree, in writing that the company was so entitled; and

(c) the information provided in the notes to the form set out in Schedule 3 to these Regulations.

(1) *See* section 84(7) and (8) of the 2002 Act.

AMENDMENTS

* Words revoked by Transfer of Tribunal Functions Order 2013 (SI 2013/1036), Sch 2(1), para 42 (1 July 2013: revocation has effect subject to transitional provisions and savings specified in SI 2013/1036, art 6(3) and Sch 3).

Additional content of contractor notice

6. A contractor notice(1) shall contain (in addition to the particulars referred to in paragraphs (a) to (d) of section 92(3) (duties to give notice of contracts) of the 2002 Act) the statement that, should the person to whom the notice is given wish to provide to the RTM company services which, as the contractor party, it has provided to the manager party(2) under the contract, it is advised to contact the RTM company at the address given in the notice.

(1) *See* section 92(1)(a) of the 2002 Act.
(2) *See* section 91(2)(a) of the 2002 Act.

Additional content of contract notice

7. A contract notice shall contain (in addition to the particulars referred to in section 92(7)(a) of the 2002 Act)—

- (a) the address of the person who is the contractor party, or sub-contractor party(1), under the contract of which particulars are given in the notice; and
- (b) a statement that, should the RTM company wish to avail itself of the services which the contractor party, or sub-contractor party, has provided to the manager party under that contract, it is advised to contact the contractor party, or sub-contractor party, at the address given in the notice.

(1) As to 'sub-contractor party' *see* section 92(4) of the 2002 Act.

Form of notices

8.—(1) Notices of invitation to participate shall be in the form set out in Schedule 1 to these Regulations.
(2) Claim notices shall be in the form set out in Schedule 2 to these Regulations.
(3) Counter-notices shall be in the form set out in Schedule 3 to these Regulations.

Revocation and transitional provision

9.—(1) The Right to Manage (Prescribed Particulars and Forms) (England) Regulations 2003 ('the 2003 Regulations') are revoked(1).
(2) Any notice served under the 2003 Regulations will be treated on or after the coming into force of these Regulations as if it had been served under them.

(1) SI 2003/1988.

Ian Austin
Parliamentary Under Secretary of State
Department for Communities and Local Government

17th March 2010

SCHEDULE 1
FORM OF NOTICE OF INVITATION TO PARTICIPATE

Regulations 3 and 8(1)

COMMONHOLD AND LEASEHOLD REFORM ACT 2002

NOTICE OF INVITATION TO PARTICIPATE IN RIGHT TO MANAGE

To [*name and address*] (See Note 1 below)

1. *[*name*] 'RTM company' ('the company'), a private company limited by guarantee, of [*address of registered office*], and of which the registered number is [*number under Companies Act 2006*], is authorised by its articles of association to acquire and exercise the right to manage [*name of premises to which notice relates*] ('the premises'). The company intends to acquire the right to manage the premises.

2. The company's articles of association accompany this notice.

*The company's articles of association may be inspected at [*address for inspection*] between [*specify times*]. (See Note 2 below) At any time within the period of seven days beginning with the day after this notice is given, a copy of the articles of association may be ordered from [*specify address*] on payment of [*specify fee*]. (See Note 3 below)

**Delete one of these statements, as the circumstances require.*

3. The names of—

(a) the members of the company;
(b) the company's directors; and
(c) if the company has a secretary, the name of that person

are set out in the Schedule below.

4. The names of the landlord and of the person (if any) who is party to a lease of the whole or any part of the premises otherwise than as landlord or tenant are [*specify*].

5. Subject to the exclusions mentioned in paragraph 7, if the right to manage is acquired by the company, the company will be responsible for—

(a) the discharge of the landlord's duties under the lease; and
(b) the exercise of his powers under the lease,

with respect to services, repairs, maintenance, improvements, insurance and management.

6. Subject to the exclusion mentioned in paragraph 7(b), if the right to manage is acquired by the company, the company may enforce untransferred tenant covenants. (See Note 4 below)

7. If the right to manage is acquired by the company, the company will not be responsible for the discharge of the landlord's duties or the exercise of his powers under the lease—

(a) with respect to a matter concerning only a part of the premises consisting of a flat or other unit not subject to a lease held by a qualifying tenant; or
(b) relating to re-entry or forfeiture.

8. If the right to manage is acquired by the company, the company will have functions under the statutory provisions referred to in Schedule 7 to the Commonhold and Leasehold Reform Act 2002. (See Note 5 below)

9. *The company intends to appoint a managing agent within the meaning of section 30B(8) of the Landlord and Tenant Act 1985. [*If known, give the name and address of the proposed managing agent here. If that person is the current managing agent, that fact must also be stated here.*]

*The company does not intend to appoint a managing agent within the meaning of section 30B(8) of the Landlord and Tenant Act 1985. [*If any existing member of the company has qualifications or experience in* *relation to the management of residential property, give details in the Schedule below.*]

**Delete one of these statements, as the circumstances require.*

10. If the company gives notice of its claim to acquire the right to manage the premises (a 'claim notice'), a person who is or has been a member of the company may be liable for costs incurred by the landlord and others in consequence of the claim notice. (See Note 6 below)

11. You are invited to become a member of the company. (See Note 7 below)

12. If you do not fully understand the purpose or implications of this notice you are advised to seek professional help.

SCHEDULE

The names of the members of the company are: [*state names of company members*] The names of the company's directors are: [*state directors' names*]

[*If applicable*] The name of the company's secretary is: [*state company secretary's name*]

[*If applicable; see the second alternative in paragraph 9 above*] The following member[s] of the company [has][have] qualifications or experience in relation to the management of residential property: [*give details*]

Signed by authority of the company,
[*Signature of authorised member or officer*]

[*Insert date*]

NOTES

1. The notice inviting participation must be sent to each person who is at the time the notice is given a qualifying tenant of a flat in the premises but who is not already, and has not agreed to become, a member of the company. A qualifying

tenant is defined in section 75 of the Commonhold and Leasehold Reform Act 2002 ('the 2002 Act').

2. The specified times must be periods of at least 2 hours on each of at least 3 days (including a Saturday or Sunday or both) within the 7 days beginning with the day following that on which the notice is given.

3. The ordering facility must be available throughout the 7 day period referred to in Note 2. The fee must not exceed the reasonable cost of providing the ordered copy.

4. An untransferred tenant covenant is a covenant in a tenant's lease that he must comply with, but which can be enforced by the company only by virtue of section 100 of the 2002 Act.

5. The functions relate to matters such as repairing obligations, administration and service charges, and information to be furnished to tenants. Details may be obtained from the RTM company.

6. If the claim notice is at any time withdrawn, deemed to be withdrawn or otherwise ceases to have effect, each person who is or has been a member of the company is liable (except in the circumstances mentioned at the end of this note) for reasonable costs incurred by—

- (a) the landlord,
- (b) any person who is party to a lease of the whole or any part of the premises otherwise than as landlord or tenant, or
- (c) a manager appointed under Part 2 of the Landlord and Tenant Act 1987 to act in relation to the premises to which this notice relates, or any premises containing or contained in the premises to which this notice relates,

in consequence of the claim notice.

A current or former member of the company is liable both jointly with the company and every other person who is or has been a member of the company, and individually. However, a former member is not liable if he has assigned the lease by virtue of which he was a qualifying tenant to another person and that other person has become a member of the company.

7. All qualifying tenants of flats contained in the premises are entitled to be members. Landlords under leases of the whole or any part of the premises are also entitled to be members, but only once the right to manage has been acquired by the company. An application for membership may be made in accordance with the company's articles of association which, if they do not accompany this notice, may be inspected as mentioned in paragraph 2 of the notice.

8. If the right to manage is acquired by the company, the company must report to any person who is landlord under a lease of the whole or any part of premises any failure to comply with any tenant covenant of the lease unless, within the period

of three months beginning with the day on which the failure to comply comes to the attention of the company—

(a) the failure has been remedied,
(b) reasonable compensation has been paid in respect of the failure, or
(c) the landlord has notified the company that it need not report to him failures of the description of the failure concerned.

9. If the right to manage is acquired by the company, management functions of a person who is party to a lease of the whole or any part of the premises otherwise than as landlord or tenant will become functions of the company. The company will be responsible for the discharge of that person's duties under the lease and the exercise of his powers under the lease, with respect to services, repairs, maintenance, improvements, insurance and management. However, the company will not be responsible for matters concerning only a part of the premises consisting of a flat or other unit not subject to a lease held by a qualifying tenant, or relating to re-entry or forfeiture.
10. If the right to manage is acquired by the company, the company will be responsible for the exercise of the powers relating to the grant of approvals to a tenant under the lease, but will not be responsible for the exercise of those powers in relation to an approval concerning only a part of the premises consisting of a flat or other unit not subject to a lease held by a qualifying tenant.

SCHEDULE 2
FORM OF CLAIM NOTICE

Regulations 4 and 8(2)

COMMONHOLD AND LEASEHOLD REFORM ACT 2002

CLAIM NOTICE

To [*name and address*] (See Note 1 below)

1. [*Name of RTM company*] ('the company'), of [*address of registered office*], and of which the registered number is [*number under Companies Act 2006*], in accordance with Chapter 1 of Part 2 of the Commonhold and Leasehold Reform Act 2002 ('the 2002 Act') claims to acquire the right to manage [*name of premises to which notice relates*] ('the premises').

2. The company claims that the premises are ones to which Chapter 1 of the 2002 Act applies on the grounds that [*state grounds*]. (See Note 2 below)

3. The full names of each person who is both—

(a) the qualifying tenant of a flat contained in the premises, and
(b) a member of the company,

and the address of that person's flat are set out in Part 1 of the Schedule below.

4. There are set out, in Part 2 of the Schedule, in relation to each person named in Part 1 of the Schedule—

(a) the date on which that person's lease was entered into,
(b) the term for which it was granted,
(c) the date of commencement of the term
(d) *such other particulars of the lease as are necessary to identify it.

**may be ignored if no other particulars need to be given.*

5. If you are—

(a) landlord under a lease of the whole or any part of the premises,
(b) party to such a lease otherwise than as landlord or tenant, or
(c) a manager appointed under Part 2 of the Landlord and Tenant Act 1987 to act in relation to the premises, or any premises containing or contained in the premises,

you may respond to this claim notice by giving a counter-notice under section 84 of the 2002 Act. A counter-notice must be in the form set out in Schedule 3 to the Right to Manage (Prescribed Particulars and Forms) (England) Regulations 2010. It must be given to the company, at the address in paragraph 1, not later than [*specify date not earlier than one month after the date on which the claim notice is given*]. If you do not fully understand the purpose or implications of this notice you are advised to seek professional help.

6. The company intends to acquire the right to manage the premises on [*specify date, being at least three months after that specified in paragraph 5*].

7. If you are a person to whom paragraph 5 applies and—

(a) you do not dispute the company's entitlement to acquire the right to manage; and
(b) you are the manager party under a management contract subsisting immediately before the date specified in this notice,

you must, in accordance with section 92 (duties to give notice of contracts) of the 2002 Act, give a notice in relation to the contract to the person who is the contractor party in relation to the contract and to the company. (See Note 3 below).

8. From the date on which the company acquires the right to manage the premises, landlords under leases of the whole or any part of the premises are entitled to be members of the company (See Note 4 below).

9. This notice is not invalidated by any inaccuracy in any of the particulars required by section 80(2) to (7) of the 2002 Act or regulation 5 of the Right to Manage (Prescribed Particulars and Forms) (England) Regulations

2010. If you are of the opinion that any of the particulars contained in the claim notice are inaccurate you may notify the company of the particulars in question, indicating the respects in which you think that they are inaccurate.

SCHEDULE

PART 1

Full names and addresses of persons who are both qualifying tenants and members of the company

[*set out here the particulars required by paragraph 3 above*]

PART 2

Particulars of leases of persons named in Part 1

[*set out here the particulars required by paragraph 4 above*]

Signed by authority of the company,
[*Signature of authorised member or officer*]

[*Insert date*]

NOTES

1. A claim notice (a notice in the form set out in Schedule 2 to the Right to Manage (Prescribed Particulars and Forms) (England) Regulations 2010 of a claim to exercise the right to manage specified premises) must be given to each person who, on the date on which the notice is given, is—

- (a) landlord under a lease of the whole or any part of the premises to which the notice relates,
- (b) party to such a lease otherwise than as landlord or tenant, or
- (c) a manager appointed under Part 2 of the Landlord and Tenant Act 1987 to act in relation to the premises, or any premises containing or contained in the premises.

But notice need not be given to such a person if he cannot be found, or if his identity cannot be ascertained. If that means that there is no one to whom the notice must be given, the company may apply to a […]* tribunal for an order that the company is to acquire the right to manage the premises. In that case, the procedures specified in section 85 of the 2002 Act (landlords etc not traceable) will apply.

2. The relevant provisions are contained in section 72 of the 2002 Act (premises to which Chapter 1 applies). The company is advised to consider, in particular, Schedule 6 to the 2002 Act (premises excepted from Chapter 1).

3. The terms ‘management contract’, ‘manager party’ and ‘contractor party’ are defined in section 91(2) of the 2002 Act (notices relating to management contracts).

4. Landlords under leases of the whole or any part of the premises are entitled to be members of the company, but only once the right to manage has been acquired by the company. An application for membership may be made in accordance with the company’s articles of association, which may be inspected at the company’s registered office, free of charge, at any reasonable time.

AMENDMENTS

* Words revoked by Transfer of Tribunal Functions Order 2013 (SI 2013/1036), Sch 2(1), para 43 (1 July 2013: revocation has effect subject to transitional provisions and savings specified in SI 2013/1036, art 6(3) and Sch 3).

SCHEDULE 3
FORM OF COUNTER-NOTICE

Regulations 5 and 8(3)

COMMONHOLD AND LEASEHOLD REFORM ACT 2002

COUNTER-NOTICE

To [*name and address*] (See Note 1 below)

1. *I admit that, on [*insert date on which claim notice was given*], [*insert name of company by which claim notice was given*] ('the company') was entitled to acquire the right to manage the premises specified in the claim notice.

*I allege that, by reason of [*specify provision of Chapter 1 of Part 2 of the Commonhold and Leasehold Reform Act 2002 relied on*], on [*insert date on which claim notice was given*], [*insert name of company by which claim notice was given*] ('the company') was not entitled to acquire the right to manage the premises specified in the claim notice.

**Delete one of these statements, as the circumstances require.*

2. If the company has been given one or more counter-notices containing such a statement as is mentioned in paragraph (b) of subsection (2) of section 84 of the Commonhold and Leasehold Reform Act 2002, the company may apply to a […]* tribunal for a determination that, on the date on which notice of the claim was given, the company was entitled to acquire the right to manage the premises specified in the claim notice (See Note 2 below).

3. If the company has been given one or more counter-notices containing such a statement as is mentioned in paragraph (b) of subsection (2) of section 84 of the Commonhold and Leasehold Reform Act 2002, the company does not acquire the right to manage those premises unless—

(a) on an application to a […]* tribunal, it is finally determined that the company was entitled to acquire the right to manage the premises; or
(b) the person by whom the counter-notice was given agrees, or the persons by whom the counter-notices were given agree, in writing that the company was so entitled. (See Note 3 below)

Signed:
[*Signature of person on whom claim notice served, or of agent of such person. Where an agent signs, insert also 'Duly authorised agent of [insert name of person on whom claim notice served]'*]

Address:
[*Give the address to which future communications relating to the subject-matter of the notice should be sent*]

Date:
[*Insert date*]

OR

Signed by authority of the company on whose behalf this notice is given
[*Signature of authorised member or officer and statement of position in company*]

Address:
[*Give the address to which future communications relating to the subject-matter of the notice should be sent*]

Date:
[*Insert date*]

NOTES

1. The counter-notice is to be given to the company that gave the claim notice. The company's name and address are given in that notice.
2. An application to a […]* tribunal must be made within the period of two months beginning with the day on which the counter-notice (or, where more than one, the last of the counter-notices) was given.
3. For the time at which an application is finally determined, see section 84(7) and (8) of the Commonhold and Leasehold Reform Act 2002.

AMENDMENTS

* Words revoked by Transfer of Tribunal Functions Order 2013 (SI 2013/1036), Sch 2(1), para 44 (1 July 2013: revocation has effect subject to transitional provisions and savings specified in SI 2013/1036, art 6(3) and Sch 3).

EXPLANATORY NOTE

(This note is not part of the Regulations)

These Regulations supplement Chapter 1 of Part 2 of the Commonhold and Leasehold Reform Act 2002 ('the 2002 Act'). That Chapter makes provision for the acquisition and exercise of rights in relation to the management of premises to which the Chapter applies by a company which may acquire and exercise those rights ('RTM company').

It was decided not to amend the 2003 Regulations but to revoke and replace them because the Department recognised that they are likely to be used by people who do not have access to professional advice. The Department considered it would be confusing for applicants to try and access two sets of regulations in order to set up their Right to Manage Company.

Before a RTM company can acquire the right to manage premises, it must give notice ('notice of invitation to participate') to those tenants of flats contained in the premises who are 'qualifying tenants' (see section 75 of the 2002 Act) of its intention to acquire the right. The notice must invite the recipients of it to become members of the RTM company. Regulation 3, to which Schedule 1 is also relevant, prescribes requirements, in addition to those specified in section 78 of the Act, as regards the contents of the notice.

Once the RTM company has given notice of invitation to participate, it may make a claim to acquire the right to manage. The claim is required to be made by notice ('claim notice'), that is to be given to each person who is—

(a) landlord under a lease of the whole or any part of the premises to which the notice relates,
(b) party to such a lease otherwise than as landlord or tenant, or
(c) a manager appointed under Part 2 of the Landlord and Tenant Act 1987 to act in relation to the premises, or any premises containing or contained in the premises.

Regulation 4, to which Schedule 2 is also relevant, prescribes requirements as regards the contents of the notice in addition to those specified in section 80 of the 2002 Act.

A person who receives a claim notice may respond by giving the RTM company a counter-notice, in which the RTM company's claim is either admitted or opposed. Regulation 5, to which Schedule 3 is also relevant, prescribes requirements as regards the contents of the notice. These are in addition to those specified in section 84 of the Act.

If a person who is entitled to receive a claim notice is also party to a contract under which the other party to the contract agrees to provide services, or do other things, in connection with any matter relating to a function that will be the function of the RTM company once it acquires the right to manage the premises, that person must give notice to the other party to the contract ('contractor notice') and to the RTM company ('contract notice'). Regulations 6 and 7 prescribe requirements, in addition to those specified in section 92 of the Act, as regards contractor notices and contract notices, respectively. Regulation 8 prescribes the form of invitations to participate, claim notices and counter-notices. Forms of contractor notices and contract notices are not prescribed.

An impact assessment has not been prepared for this document.

Appendix 2

The Right to Manage (Prescribed Particulars and Forms) (Wales) Regulations 2011 (SI 2011/2684)

Made	*5 November 2011*
Laid before the National Assembly for Wales	*8 November 2011*
Coming into force	*30 November 2011*

The Welsh Ministers make the following Regulations in exercise of the powers conferred upon the National Assembly for Wales by sections 78(2)(d) and (3), 80(8) and (9), 84(2), 92(3) and (7) and 178(1)(a), (b), (c) and 179(1) of the Commonhold and Leasehold Reform Act 2002(1) and section 26(3) of the Welsh Language Act 1993(2) and now vested in them(3).

(1) 2002 c. 15.
(2) 1993 c. 38.
(3) By virtue of paragraph 30 of Schedule 11 to the Government of Wales Act 2006 (c. 32) the functions formerly exercised by the National Assembly for Wales as the 'appropriate national authority' under section 179(1) of the Commonhold and Leasehold Reform Act 2002 are now vested in the Welsh Ministers. The National Assembly for Wales (Transfer of Functions) Order 1999 (S.I. 1999/672), article 2(b), Schedule 1, directed that the power in section 26(3) of the Welsh Language Act 1993 be exercisable, in relation to Wales, by the National Assembly for Wales concurrently with any Minister of the Crown by whom the power was exercisable. The power was transferred to the Welsh Ministers by virtue of section 162(3) of, and paragraph 30(1) of Schedule 11 to, the Government of Wales Act 2006.

Title, commencement and application

1.—(1) The title of these Regulations is the Right to Manage (Prescribed Particulars and Forms) (Wales) Regulations 2011 and they come into force on 30 November 2011.

(2) These Regulations apply in relation to premises in Wales.

Interpretation

2. In these Regulations—

'the 2002 Act' ('*Deddf 2002*') means the Commonhold and Leasehold Reform Act 2002;

'landlord', ('*landlord*') in relation to RTM premises, means a person who is landlord under a lease of the whole or any part of the premises(1);

'RTM premises' ('*mangre RTM*') means premises as regards which a Right to Manage company ('RTM company') intends to acquire the right to manage(2);

'third party' ('*trydydd parti*'), in relation to RTM premises, means a person who is party to a lease of the whole or any part of the premises otherwise than as landlord or tenant(3).

(1) For the definition of 'landlord' *see also* section 112(2), (3) and (5) of the 2002 Act.
(2) *See* sections 71(1) and 73 of the 2002 Act. As to 'right to manage' *see* section 71(2) of the 2002 Act.
(3) *See* section 112(2), (3) and (5) of the 2002 Act.

Additional content of notice of invitation to participate

3.—(1) A notice of invitation to participate must contain, in addition to the statements and information referred to in section 78(2)(a) to (c) of the 2002 Act (notice inviting participation), the particulars mentioned in paragraph (2).
(2) The particulars referred to in paragraph (1) are—

(a) the RTM company's registered number(1), the address of its registered office and the names of its directors and, if applicable, secretary;
(b) the names of the landlord and any third party;
(c) a statement that, subject to the exclusions mentioned in sub-paragraph (e), if the right to manage is acquired by the RTM company, the company will be responsible for—

    (i) the discharge of the landlord's duties under the lease; and
    (ii) the exercise of his or her powers under the lease,

with respect to services, repairs, maintenance, improvements, insurance and management;

(d) a statement that, subject to the exclusion mentioned in sub-paragraph (e)(ii), if the right to manage is acquired by the RTM company, the company may enforce untransferred tenant covenants(2);

(e) a statement that, if the right to manage is acquired by the RTM company, the company will not be responsible for the discharge of the landlord's duties or the exercise of his or her powers under the lease—

   (i) with respect to a matter concerning only a part of the premises consisting of a flat or other unit not subject to a lease held by a qualifying tenant(3); or

   (ii) relating to re-entry or forfeiture;

(f) a statement that, if the right to manage is acquired by the RTM company, the company will have functions under the statutory provisions referred to in Schedule 7 to the 2002 Act;

(g) a statement that the RTM company intends or, as the case may be, does not intend, to appoint a managing agent; and—

   (i) if it does so intend, a statement—

      (aa) of the name and address of the proposed managing agent (if known); and

      (bb) if it is the case, that the person is the landlord's managing agent; or

   (ii) if it does not so intend, the qualifications or experience (if any) of the existing members of the RTM company in relation to the management of residential property;

(h) a statement that, where the RTM company gives a claim notice(4), a person who is or has been a member of the company may be liable for costs incurred by the landlord and others in consequence of the notice;

(i) a statement that, if the recipient of the notice (of invitation to participate) does not fully understand its purpose or implications, he or she is advised to seek professional help; and

(j) the information provided in the notes to the form set out in Schedule 1 to these Regulations.

(1) *See* section 1066 of the Companies Act 2006 (c. 46).
(2) *See* section 100(4) of the 2002 Act.
(3) As to premises to which Chapter 1 of Part 2 of the 2002 Act applies, *see* section 72 (and Schedule 6). As to 'flat' and 'unit' *see* section 112(1). As to 'lease' *see* section 112(2). As to 'qualifying tenant' *see* sections 75 and 112(4) and (5).
(4) *See* section 79(1) of the 2002 Act.

Additional content of claim notice

4. A claim notice must contain, in addition to the particulars required by section 80(2) to (7) (contents of claim notice) of the 2002 Act—

(a) a statement that a person who—

(i) does not dispute the RTM company's entitlement to acquire the right to manage(1); and
(ii) is the manager party under a management contract(2) subsisting immediately before the date specified in the claim notice,

must, in accordance with section 92 of the 2002 Act (duties to give notice of contracts), give a notice to the RTM company and to the person who is the contractor party(3);
(b) a statement that, from the acquisition date(4), landlords under leases of the whole or any part of the premises to which the claim notice relates are entitled to be members of the RTM company;
(c) a statement that the notice is not invalidated by any inaccuracy in any of the particulars required by section 80(2) to (7) of the 2002 Act or this regulation, but that a person who is of the opinion that any of the particulars contained in the claim notice are inaccurate may—

(i) identify the particulars in question to the RTM company by which the notice was given; and
(ii) indicate the respects in which they are considered to be inaccurate;

(d) a statement that a person who receives the notice but does not fully understand its purpose, is advised to seek professional help; and

(e) the information provided in the notes to the form set out in Schedule 2 to these Regulations.

(1) As to the circumstances in which there is no dispute about entitlement, *see* section 90(3) of the 2002 Act.
(2) *See* section 91(2) and (4) of the 2002 Act.
(3) *See* section 91(2)(b) of the 2002 Act.
(4) *See* section 90 of the 2002 Act.

Additional content of counter-notice

5. A counter-notice must contain (in addition to the statement referred to in section 84(2(a) and (b) (counter-notices) of the 2002 Act)—

(a) a statement that, where the RTM company has been given one or more counter-notices containing such a statement as is mentioned in section 84(2)(b) of the 2002 Act, the company may apply to a leasehold valuation tribunal for a determination that, on the date on which notice of the claim was given, the company was entitled to acquire the right to manage the premises specified in the claim notice;

(b) a statement that, where the RTM company has been given one or more counter-notices containing such a statement as is mentioned in section 84(2)(b) of the 2002 Act, the company does not acquire the right to manage the premises specified in the claim notice unless—

(i) on an application to a leasehold valuation tribunal, it is finally determined(1) that the company was entitled to acquire the right to manage the premises; or

(ii) the person by whom the counter-notice was given agrees, or the persons by whom the counter-notices were given agree, in writing, that the company was so entitled; and

(c) the information provided in the notes to the form set out in Schedule 3 to these Regulations.

(1) *See* section 84(7) and (8) of the 2002 Act.

Additional content of contractor notice

6.—(1) A contractor notice(1) must contain (in addition to the particulars referred to in paragraphs (a) to (d) of section 92(3) (duties to give notice of contracts) of the 2002 Act) the statement that, should the person to whom the notice is given wish to provide to the RTM company services which, as the contractor party, it has provided to the manager party under the contract, it is advised to contact the RTM company at the address given in the notice; and
(2) the information provided in the notes to the form set out in Schedule 4 to these Regulations.

(1) *See* section 92(1)(a) of the 2002 Act.

Additional content of contract notice

7. A contract notice(1) must contain (in addition to the particulars referred to in section 92(7)(a) of the 2002 Act)—

(a) the address of the person who is the contractor party, or sub-contractor party(2), under the contract of which particulars are given in the notice;
(b) a statement that, should the RTM company wish to avail itself of the services which the contractor party, or sub-contractor party, has provided to the manager party under that contract, it is advised to contact the contractor party, or sub-contractor party, at the address given in the notice; and
(c) The information provided in the notes to the form set out in Schedule 5 to these Regulations.

(1) *See* section 92(1)(b) of the 2002 Act.
(2) *See* section 92(4) of the 2002 Act.

Form of notices

8.—(1) Notices of invitation to participate must be in the form set out in Schedule 1 to these Regulations or a form to the like effect provided that it contains all of the prescribed particulars as set out in regulation 3.
(2) Claim notices must be in the form set out in Schedule 2 to these Regulations or a form to the like effect provided that it contains all of the prescribed particulars as set out in regulation 4.

(3) Counter-notices must be in the form set out in Schedule 3 to these Regulations or a form to the like effect provided that it contains all of the prescribed particulars as set out in regulation 5.
(4) Contractor notices must be in the form set out in Schedule 4 to these Regulations or a form to the like effect provided that it contains all of the prescribed particulars as set out in regulation 6.
(5) Contract notices must be in the form set out in Schedule 5 to these Regulations or a form to the like effect provided that it contains all of the prescribed particulars as set out in regulation 7.

Revocations and transitional provisions

9.—(1) The Right to Manage (Prescribed Particulars and Forms) (Wales) Regulations 2004(1) ('the 2004 Regulations') are revoked.
(2) Any notice served under the 2004 Regulations will be treated on or after the coming into force of these Regulations as if it had been served under them.

(1) S.I. 2004/678 (W.66).

Huw Lewis
Minister for Housing, Regeneration and Heritage, one of the Welsh Ministers

5 November 2011

SCHEDULE 1
FORM OF NOTICE OF INVITATION TO PARTICIPATE

Regulations 3 and 8(1)

COMMONHOLD AND LEASEHOLD REFORM ACT 2002

NOTICE OF INVITATION TO PARTICIPATE IN RIGHT TO MANAGE

To [*name and address*] (see Note 1 below)

1.
[*Name of RTM company*]
('the company'), a private company limited by guarantee, of
[*address of registered office*]

and of which the registered number is
[*number under Companies Act 2006*]

is authorised by its articles of association to acquire and exercise the right to manage
[*name of premises to which notice relates*]
('the premises').

2. The company intends to acquire the right to manage the premises.

Either

3.1 The company's articles of association, accompany this notice.

☐ Yes. [*Tick if this is the case and proceed to paragraph 4.*] (See Note 2 below)

Or

3.2 The company's articles of association, may be inspected in accordance with the arrangements in the following paragraph.

☐ Yes. [*Tick if the statement above applies and complete the remainder of this paragraph 3.*] (See Note 2)

3.2.1 At
[*address for inspection*]

3.2.2 between
[*specify times*]. (See Note 3 below)

3.2.3 At any time within the period of seven days beginning with the day after this notice is given, a copy of the articles of association may be ordered from
[*specify address*]

3.2.4 on payment of
[*specify fee*]. (See Note 4 below)

4. The names of—

(a) the members of the company;
(b) the company's directors; and
(c) if the company has a secretary, the name of that person are set out in the Schedule below.

5. The names of the landlord and of the person (if any) who is party to a lease of the whole or any part of the premises otherwise than as landlord or tenant are:
[*specify*]

6. Subject to the exclusions mentioned in paragraph 8, if the right to manage is acquired by the company, the company will be responsible for—

(a) the discharge of the landlord's duties under the lease; and
(b) the exercise of his or her powers under the lease,

with respect to services, repairs, maintenance improvements, insurance and management.

7. Subject to the exclusion mentioned in paragraph 8(b), if the right to manage is acquired by the company, the company may enforce untransferred tenant covenants. (See Note 5 below)

8. If the right to manage is acquired by the company, the company will not be responsible for the discharge of the landlord's duties or the exercise of his or her powers under the lease—

(a) with respect to a matter concerning only part of the premises consisting of a flat or other unit not subject to a lease held by a qualifying tenant; or
(b) relating to re-entry or forfeiture.

9. If the right to manage is acquired by the company, the company will have functions under the statutory provisions referred to in Schedule 7 to the Commonhold and Leasehold Reform Act 2002. (See Note 6 below)

Either—

9.1 The company intends to appoint a managing agent within the meaning of section 30B(8) of the Landlord and Tenant Act 1985.

☐ Yes. [*Tick if the statement above applies. If you tick this box, proceed to paragraph 9.2. If you do not tick this box, proceed to paragraph 9.4.*]

9.2 If known, give the name and address of the proposed managing agent below. Proceed to paragraph 9.3.
[*Name and address of the proposed managing agent*]

9.3 The person named in paragraph 9.2 above is the current managing agent.

☐ Yes. [*Tick if the statement above applies.*
Proceed to paragraph 10 whether or not the statement above applies.]

Or

9.4 The company does not intend to appoint a managing agent within the meaning of section 30B(8) of the Landlord and Tenant Act 1985

☐ Yes. [*Tick if the statement above applies [If any existing member of the company has qualifications or experience in relation to the management of residential property, give details in paragraph 4 of the Schedule below.]*]

10. If the company gives notice of its claim to acquire the right to manage the premises (a 'claim notice'), a person who is or has been a member of the company may be liable for costs incurred by the landlord and others in consequence of the claim notice. (See Note 7 below)

11. You are invited to become a member of the company. (See Note 8 below)

12. If you do not fully understand the purpose or implications of this notice you are advised to seek professional help.

SCHEDULE

1. The names of the members of the company are [*state names of company members*]:

2. The names of the company's directors are: [*state director's names (if applicable)*]

3. The name of the company's secretary is: [*company secretary's name*]

[*If applicable complete the following information.*] (See paragraph 9.4 above)

4. The following member[s] of the company [has][have] qualifications or experience in relation to the management of residential property:

(1)
[*Name of member*]

[*qualification in relation to the management of residential property*]

[*Number of years experience in relation to the management of residential property*]

[*address[es] of [property][properties] and dates when experience acquired*]

(2) [*repeat as above as necessary*]

Signed by authority of the company,
[*Signature of authorised member or officer*]

[*Insert date*]

NOTES

1. The notice inviting participation must be sent to each person who is at the time the notice is given a qualifying tenant of a flat in the premises but who is not already, and has not agreed to become, a member of the company. A qualifying tenant is defined in section 75 of the Commonhold and Leasehold Reform Act 2002 ('the 2002 Act').
2. The notice must either (a) be accompanied by a copy of the articles of association of the RTM company or (b) include a statement about inspection and copying the Articles of Association of the RTM company giving the information specified in paragraph 3 of the notice.
3. The specified times must be periods of at least 2 hours on each of at least 3 days (including a Saturday or Sunday or both) within the 7 days beginning with the day following that on which the notice is given.
4. The ordering facility must be available throughout the 7 day period referred to in Note 3. The fee must not exceed the reasonable cost of providing the ordered copy.
5. An untransferred tenant covenant is a covenant in a tenant's lease that he must comply with, but which can be enforced by the company only by virtue of section 100 of the 2002 Act.
6. The functions relate to matters such as repairing obligations, administration and service charges, and information to be furnished to tenants. Details may be obtained from the RTM company.
7. If the claim notice is at any time withdrawn, deemed to be withdrawn or otherwise ceases to have effect, each person who is or has been a member of the company is liable (except in the circumstances mentioned at the end of this note) for reasonable costs incurred by—

(a) the landlord,
(b) any person who is party to a lease of the whole or any part of the premises otherwise than as landlord or tenant, or
(c) a manager appointed under Part 2 of the Landlord and Tenant Act 1987 to act in relation to the premises to which this notice relates, or any premises containing or contained in the premises to which this notice relates,

in consequence of the claim notice.
A current or former member of the company is liable both jointly with the company and every other person who is or has been a member of the company, and individually. However, a former member is not liable if he has assigned the lease by virtue of which he was a qualifying tenant to another person and that other person has become a member of the company.
8. All qualifying tenants of flats contained in the premises are entitled to be members. Landlords under leases of the whole or any part of the premises are also

entitled to be members, but only once the right to manage has been acquired by the company. An application for membership may be made in accordance with the company's articles of association which, if they do not accompany this notice, may be inspected as mentioned in paragraph 3.2 of the notice.

9. If the right to manage is acquired by the company, the company must report to any person who is landlord under a lease of the whole or any part of premises any failure to comply with any tenant covenant of the lease unless, within the period of three months beginning with the day on which the failure to comply comes to the attention of the company—

(a) the failure has been remedied,
(b) reasonable compensation has been paid in respect of the failure, or
(c) the landlord has notified the company that it need not report to him failures of the description of the failure concerned.

10. If the right to manage is acquired by the company, management functions of a person who is party to a lease of the whole or any part of the premises otherwise than as landlord or tenant will become functions of the company. The company will be responsible for the discharge of that person's duties under the lease and the exercise of his or her powers under the lease, with respect to services, repairs, maintenance, improvements, insurance and management. However, the company will not be responsible for matters concerning only a part of the premises consisting of a flat or other unit not subject to a lease held by a qualifying tenant, or relating to re-entry or forfeiture.

11. If the right to manage is acquired by the company, the company will be responsible for the exercise of the powers relating to the grant of approvals to a tenant under the lease, but will not be responsible for the exercise of those powers in relation to an approval concerning only a part of the premises consisting of a flat or other unit not subject to a lease held by a qualifying tenant.

SCHEDULE 2
FORM OF CLAIM NOTICE

Regulations 4 and 8(2)

COMMONHOLD AND LEASEHOLD REFORM ACT 2002

CLAIM NOTICE

To [*Name and address*] (See Note 1 below)

1.
[*name of RTM company*]
('the company'), of

[*address of registered office*]

and of which the registered number is
[*number under Companies Act 2006*]

in accordance with Chapter 1 of Part 2 of the Commonhold and Leasehold Reform Act 2002 ('the 2002 Act') claims to acquire the right to manage
[*name of premises to which notice relates*]
('the premises').

2. The company claims that the premises are ones to which Chapter 1 of the 2002 Act applies on the grounds that [state grounds] (See Note 2 below)

3. The full names of each person who is both—

(a) the qualifying tenant of a flat contained in the premises; and
(b) a member of the company,

and the address of that person's flat are set out in Part 1 of the Schedule below.

4. There are set out, in Part 2 of the Schedule, in relation to each person named in Part 1 of the Schedule—

(a) the date on which that person's lease was entered into;
(b) the term for which it was granted;
(c) the date of commencement of the term
*(d) such other particulars of that person's lease as are necessary to identify it.

**(d) may be ignored if no other particulars need to be given.*

5. If you are—

(a) landlord under a lease of the whole or any part of the premises;
(b) party to such a lease otherwise than as landlord or tenant; or
(c) a manager appointed under Part 2 of the Landlord and Tenant Act 1987 to act in relation to the premises; or any premises containing or contained in the premises,

you may respond to this claim notice by giving a counter-notice under section 84 of the 2002 Act. A counter-notice must be in the form set out in Schedule 3 to the Right to Manage (Prescribed Particulars and Forms) (Wales) Regulations 2011. It must be given to the company, at the address in paragraph 1, not later than
[*specify date not earlier than one month after the date on which the claim notice is given.*]

If you do not fully understand the purpose or implications of this notice you are advised to seek professional help.

6. The company intends to acquire the right to manage the premises on [*specify date, being at least three months after that specified in paragraph 5.*]

7. If you are a person to whom paragraph 5 applies and—

(a) you do not dispute the company's entitlement to acquire the right to manage; and
(b) you are the manager party under a management contract subsisting immediately before the date specified in this notice,

you must, in accordance with section 92 (duties to give notice of contracts) of the 2002 Act, give a notice in relation to the contract to the person who is the contractor party in relation to the contract and to the company. (See Note 3 below).

8. From the date on which the company acquires the right to manage the premises, landlords under leases of the whole or any part of the premises are entitled to be members of the company (See Note 4 below).

9. This notice is not invalidated by any inaccuracy in any of the particulars required by section 80(2) to (7) of the 2002 Act or regulation 4 of the Right to Manage (Prescribed Particulars and Forms) (Wales) Regulations 2011. If you are of the opinion that any of the particulars contained in the claim notice are inaccurate you may notify the company of the particulars in question, indicating the respects in which you think that they are inaccurate.

SCHEDULE

PART 1

Full names and addresses of persons who are both qualifying tenants and members of the company
[*set out here the particulars required by paragraph 3 above*]

PART 2

Particulars of leases of persons named in Part 1

[*Set out in this table the particulars required by paragraph 4 above and repeat as necessary for each person named in the Schedule*] [*Name of person referred to in Part 1 of this Schedule*] [*date on which lease was entered into*] [*term of years for which lease was granted*]

[*date of commencement of term*] [*such other particulars as are necessary to identify the lease. This section should not be completed if it is possible to identify the lease from the remainder of the information in this table*]

Signed by authority of the company,
Signature of authorised member or officer]

[*Insert date*]

NOTES

1. A claim notice (a notice in the form set out in Schedule 2 to the Right to Manage (Prescribed Particulars and Forms) (Wales) Regulations 2011 of a claim to exercise the right to manage specified premises) must be given to each person who, on the date on which the notice is given, is—

(a) landlord under a lease of the whole or any part of the premises to which the notice relates,
(b) party to such a lease otherwise than as landlord or tenant, or
(c) a manager appointed under Part 2 of the Landlord and Tenant Act 1987 to act in relation to the premises, or any premises containing or contained in the premises.

But notice need not be given to such a person if that person cannot be found, or if that person's identity cannot be ascertained. If that means that there is no one to whom the notice must be given, the company may apply to a leasehold valuation tribunal for an order that the company is to acquire the right to manage the premises. In that case, the procedures specified in section 85 of the 2002 Act (landlords etc. not traceable) will apply.
2. The relevant provisions are contained in section 72 of the 2002 Act (premises to which Chapter 1 applies). The company is advised to consider, in particular, Schedule 6 to the 2002 Act (premises excepted from Chapter 1).
3. The terms 'management contract', 'manager party' and 'contractor party' are defined in section 91(2) of the 2002 Act (notices relating to management contracts).
4. Landlords under leases of the whole or any part of the premises are entitled to be members of the company, but only once the right to manage has been acquired by the company. An application for membership may be made in accordance with the company's articles of association, which may be inspected at the company's registered office, free of charge, at any reasonable time.

SCHEDULE 3
FORM OF COUNTER NOTICE

Regulations 5 and 8(3)

COMMONHOLD AND LEASEHOLD REFORM ACT 2002

COUNTER-NOTICE

To

[*name and address*] (See Note 1 below)

Either

1.1 I admit that, on
[*insert date on which claim notice was given*],

[*insert name of company by which claim notice was given*]
('the company') was entitled to acquire the right to manage the premises specified in the claim notice.

☐ Yes. [*Tick if the statement above applies and proceed to paragraph 2.*]

Or

1.2 I allege that, by reason of
[*specify provision of Chapter 1 of Part 2 of the Commonhold and Leasehold Reform Act 2002 relied on*]

on
[*insert date on which claim notice was given*]

[*insert name of company by which claim notice was given*]
('the company') was not entitled to acquire the right to manage the premises specified in the claim notice.

☐ Yes. [*Tick if the statement in paragraph 1.2 applies.*]

2. If the company has been given one or more counter-notices containing such a statement as is mentioned in section 84 (2) (b) of the Commonhold and Leasehold Reform Act 2002, the company may apply to a leasehold valuation tribunal for a determination that, on the date on which notice of the claim was given, the company was entitled to acquire the right to manage the premises specified in the claim notice (See Note 2 below).

3. If the company has been given one or more counter-notices containing such a statement as is mentioned in section 84(2)(b) of the Commonhold and Leasehold Reform Act 2002, the company does not acquire the right to manage those premises unless—

(a) on an application to a leasehold valuation tribunal, it is finally determined that the company was entitled to acquire the right to manage the premises; or
(b) the person by whom the counter-notice was given agrees, or the persons by whom the counter-notices were given agree, in writing that the company was so entitled. (See Note 3 below)

Either

Signed:
[*Signature of person on whom claim notice served, or of agent of such person Where an agent signs, insert also.*]

Duly authorised agent of
[*insert name of person on whom claim notice served*]

Address:
[*Give the address to which future communications relating to the subject-matter of the notice should be sent*]

[*Date*]

Or

Signed by authority of the company on whose behalf this notice is given
[*Signature of authorised member or officer and statement of position in company*]

Address
[*Give the address to which future communications relating to the subject-matter of the notice should be sent*]

Date [*Insert date*]

NOTES

1. The counter-notice is to be given to the company that gave the claim notice. The company's name and address are given in that notice.
2. An application to a leasehold valuation tribunal must be made within the period of two months beginning with the day on which the counter-notice (or, where more than one, the last of the counter-notices) was given.
3. For the time at which an application is finally determined, see section 84(7) and (8) of the Commonhold and Leasehold Reform Act 2002.

SCHEDULE 4
FORM OF CONTRACTOR NOTICE

Regulations 6 and 8(4)

COMMONHOLD AND LEASEHOLD REFORM ACT 2002

CONTRACTOR NOTICE

To
[*name and address*] (See Note 1 below)

1. This notice is given in relation to the management contract, details of which are given in the Schedule to this notice ('the contract') (See Note 2 below)

2. The right to manage
[*give the address of the premises which the RTM company is to acquire the right to manage*] (See Note 3 below)

('the premises') is to be acquired by
[*state name of RTM company*]
('the company').

3. The registered office of the company is
[*registered office address of RTM company*]

4. The date of acquisition of the right to manage the premises by the company is
[*date of acquisition*]

5. If you wish to provide to the company services which as the contractor party you have provided to the manager party under the contract you are advised to contact the company at the address given in paragraph 2 above. (See Note 1 below)

Either

Signed:
[*signature on behalf of company*]

Duly authorised officer of:
[*name of company giving the notice*]

Date:

Or

Signed:
[*signature*]

By or on behalf of
[*name of person/entity giving this notice*]

Date:

SCHEDULE

Insert details below as required by paragraph 1 above

Name of contract as set out in the contract documentation:

Premises to which the contract relates:

Parties to contract:

Date of contract:

Term of contract:

years and
months

Any other particulars necessary to identify the contract in relation to which this notice is given: [*This section should only be completed if the details above are not sufficient to identify the contract in question*]

NOTES

1. The contractor notice (a notice in the form set out in Schedule 4 to the Right to Manage (Prescribed Particulars and Forms) (Wales) Regulations 2011) ('the 2011 Regulations') is relevant when the right to manage certain premises is to be acquired by a Right to Manage company under the Commonhold and Leasehold Reform Act 2002 ('the 2002 Act'). The contractor notice must be sent by the manager party to the contractor party in relation to an existing management contract relating to the premises. The definition of 'existing management contract' is in section 91(3) of the 2002 Act. The definitions of 'manager party' and 'contractor party' are set out in section 91(2) of the 2002 Act. Section 92(2) of the 2002 Act sets out the time when such notices must be given.
2. If you are party to an existing management sub-contract with another person you must (a) send a copy of the contractor notice to the other party to the sub-contract and (b) give to the company a contract notice (a notice in the form set out in Schedule 5 to the 2011 Regulations) in relation to the existing management sub-contract in accordance with section 92(4) of the 2002 Act. Section 92(5) of that Act defines an existing management sub-contract.
Section 92(6) of the 2002 Act sets out the time when such notices must be given.
3. The RTM company is the company which is to acquire the right to manage premises in accordance with Part 2 of Chapter 1 of the 2002 Act.

SCHEDULE 5
FORM OF CONTRACT NOTICE

Regulation 7 and 8(5)

COMMONHOLD AND LEASEHOLD REFORM ACT 2002

CONTRACT NOTICE

To
[*name and address of RTM company*] (See Note 1 below)
('the company')

1. This notice is given in relation to the contract details of which are given in the Schedule to this notice ('the contract'). (See Note 2 below)

2. Should the company wish to avail itself of the services which the contractor party, or sub-contractor party, has provided to the manager party under the contract it is advised to contact the contractor party, or sub-contractor party

at
[*address at which person/entity giving this notice should be contacted*]

Either

Signed:
[*signature on behalf of company*]

Duly authorised officer of:
[*name of company giving the notice*]

Date:

Or

Signed:
[*signature*]

By or on behalf of:
[*name of person/entity giving this notice*]

Date:

SCHEDULE

Insert details required by paragraph 1 above

Name of contract:

Parties to contract (See Note 3 below):

(1)
[*contractor (or sub-contractor) party*]

(2)
[*manager party*]

Address of the contractor (or sub-contractor) party under the contract:

Date of contract:

Term of contract:

years and

months

NOTES

1. The contract notice (a notice in the form set out in Schedule 5 to the Right to Manage (Prescribed Particulars and Forms)(Wales) Regulations 2011) is relevant when the right to manage certain premises is to be acquired by a Right to Manage company ('RTM company') under Part 2 of Chapter 1 of the Commonhold and Leasehold Reform Act 2002 ('the 2002 Act'). The person who is the manager party in relation to an existing management contract must give to the RTM company a contract notice in accordance with section 92(1) of the 2002 Act. A person who receives a contractor notice who is also party to an existing management sub-contract must also give to the RTM company a contract notice in accordance with section 92(4) of the 2002 Act.

'Existing management contract', is defined in section 91(3) of the 2002 Act. An existing management sub-contract is defined in section 92(5) of the 2002 Act.
2. The time for giving a contract notice is set out in section 92(2) and 92(6) of the 2002 Act.
3. 'Contractor party' and 'manager party' are defined in section 91(2) of the 2002 Act and 'sub-contractor party' is defined in section 92(4) of that Act.

EXPLANATORY NOTE

(This note is not part of the Regulations)

These Regulations supplement Chapter 1 of Part 2 of the Commonhold and Leasehold Reform Act 2002 ('the 2002 Act'). That Chapter makes provision for the acquisition and exercise of rights in relation to the management of premises to which the Chapter applies by a company which may acquire and exercise those rights (known as a Right to Manage company or 'RTM company').

It was decided to revoke and replace rather than amend the existing Regulations, the Right to Manage (Prescribed Particulars and Forms) (Wales) Regulations 2004 (S.I. 2004/678). This was due to the fact that the Welsh Ministers recognised that these Regulations are likely to be used by people who do not have access to professional advice. The Welsh Ministers consider that it would be confusing for applicants to access two sets of regulations in order to set up their RTM company.

Before a RTM company can acquire the right to manage premises, it must give notice ('notice of invitation to participate') to those tenants of flats contained in the premises who are 'qualifying tenants' (see section 75 of the 2002 Act) of its intention to acquire the right. The notice must invite its recipients to become members of the RTM company. Regulation 3, to which Schedule 1 is also relevant, prescribes requirements, in addition to those specified in section 78 of the 2002 Act, as regards the contents of the notice.

Once the RTM company has given notice of invitation to participate, it may make a claim to acquire the right to manage. The claim is required to be made by notice ('claim notice'), which is to be given to each person who is—

- (a) a landlord under a lease of the whole or any part of the premises to which the notice relates;
- (b) party to such a lease otherwise than as landlord or tenant; or
- (c) a manager appointed under Part 2 of the Landlord and Tenant Act 1987 to act in relation to the premises, or any premises containing or contained in the premises.

Regulation 4, to which Schedule 2 to these Regulations is also relevant, prescribes requirements as regards the contents of the claim notice in addition to those specified in section 80 of the 2002 Act.

A person who receives a claim notice may respond by giving the RTM company a counter-notice, in which the RTM company's claim is either admitted or opposed. Regulation 5, to which Schedule 3 to these Regulations is also relevant, prescribes requirements as regards the contents of the counter notice. These are in addition to those specified in section 84 of the 2002 Act.

If a person who is entitled to receive a claim notice is also party to a contract under which the other party to the contract agrees to provide services, or do other things, in connection with any matter relating to a function that will be the function of the RTM company once it acquires the right to manage the premises, that person must give notice to the other party to the contract ('contractor notice') and to the RTM company ('contract notice'). Regulations 6 and 7, to which Schedules 4 and 5 apply respectively, prescribe requirements, in addition to those specified in section 92 of the Act, as regards contractor notices and contract notices.

Regulation 8 introduces the Schedules which provide template forms for the invitation to participate, claim notice, counter-notice, contractor notice and contract notices. Regulation 8 allows forms to the like effect to be used, provided they contain the relevant prescribed particulars.

Appendix 3

Commonhold and Leasehold Reform Act 2002 (Extracts)

PART 2
LEASEHOLD REFORM

CHAPTER 1
RIGHT TO MANAGE

INTRODUCTORY

71 The right to manage

(1) This Chapter makes provision for the acquisition and exercise of rights in relation to the management of premises to which this Chapter applies by a company which, in accordance with this Chapter, may acquire and exercise those rights (referred to in this Chapter as a RTM company).

(2) The rights are to be acquired and exercised subject to and in accordance with this Chapter and are referred to in this Chapter as the right to manage.

QUALIFYING RULES

72 Premises to which Chapter applies

(1) This Chapter applies to premises if—

(a) they consist of a self-contained building or part of a building, with or without appurtenant property,
(b) they contain two or more flats held by qualifying tenants, and
(c) the total number of flats held by such tenants is not less than two-thirds of the total number of flats contained in the premises.

(2) A building is a self-contained building if it is structurally detached.
(3) A part of a building is a self-contained part of the building if—

(a) it constitutes a vertical division of the building,
(b) the structure of the building is such that it could be redeveloped independently of the rest of the building, and
(c) subsection (4) applies in relation to it.

(4) This subsection applies in relation to a part of a building if the relevant services provided for occupiers of it—

(a) are provided independently of the relevant services provided for occupiers of the rest of the building, or
(b) could be so provided without involving the carrying out of works likely to result in a significant interruption in the provision of any relevant services for occupiers of the rest of the building.

(5) Relevant services are services provided by means of pipes, cables or other fixed installations.
(6) Schedule 6 (premises excepted from this Chapter) has effect.

73 RTM companies

(1) This section specifies what is a RTM company.
(2) A company is a RTM company in relation to premises if—

(a) it is a private company limited by guarantee, and
(b) its [(a)articles of association state] that its object, or one of its objects, is the acquisition and exercise of the right to manage the premises.

(3) But a company is not a RTM company if it is a commonhold association (within the meaning of Part 1).

(4) And a company is not a RTM company in relation to premises if another company is already a RTM company in relation to the premises or to any premises containing or contained in the premises.

(5) If the freehold of any premises is conveyed or transferred to a company which is a RTM company in relation to the premises, or any premises containing or contained in the premises, it ceases to be a RTM company when the conveyance or transfer is executed.

TEXTUAL AMENDMENTS

(a) Words in s 73(2)(b) substituted (1.10.2009) by The Companies Act 2006 (Consequential Amendments, Transitional Provisions and Savings) Order 2009 (SI 2009/1941), Sch 1 para 194(15) (with art 10)

74 RTM companies: membership and regulations

(1) The persons who are entitled to be members of a company which is a RTM company in relation to premises are—

(a) qualifying tenants of flats contained in the premises, and

(b) from the date on which it acquires the right to manage (referred to in this Chapter as the 'acquisition date'), landlords under leases of the whole or any part of the premises.

(2) The appropriate national authority shall make regulations about the content and form of the [(a)articles of association] of RTM companies.

(3) A RTM company may adopt provisions of the regulations for its [(b)articles].

(4) The regulations may include provision which is to have effect for a RTM company whether or not it is adopted by the company.

(5) A provision of the [(b)articles] of a RTM company has no effect to the extent that it is inconsistent with the regulations.

(6) The regulations have effect in relation to [(c)articles]—

(a) irrespective of the date of the [(d)articles], but

(b) subject to any transitional provisions of the regulations.

[(e)(7) Section 20 of the Companies Act 2006 (default application of model articles) does not apply to a RTM company.]

TEXTUAL AMENDMENTS

(a) Words in s 74(2) substituted (1.10.2009) by The Companies Act 2006 (Consequential Amendments, Transitional Provisions and Savings) Order 2009 (SI 2009/1941), Sch 1 para 194(16)(a) (with art 10)

(b) Words in s 74(3), (5) substituted (1.10.2009) by The Companies Act 2006 (Consequential Amendments, Transitional Provisions and Savings) Order 2009 (SI 2009/1941), Sch 1 para 194(16)(b) (with art 10)
(c) Words in s 74(6) substituted (1.10.2009) by The Companies Act 2006 (Consequential Amendments, Transitional Provisions and Savings) Order 2009 (SI 2009/1941), Sch 1 para 194(16)(c)(i) (with art 10)
(d) Words in s 74(6)(a) substituted (1.10.2009) by The Companies Act 2006 (Consequential Amendments, Transitional Provisions and Savings) Order 2009 (SI 2009/1941), Sch 1 para 194(16)(c)(ii) (with art 10)
(e) S 74(7) substituted (1.10.2009) by The Companies Act 2006 (Consequential Amendments, Transitional Provisions and Savings) Order 2009 (SI 2009/ 1941), Sch 1 para 194(16)(d) (with art 10)

75 Qualifying tenants

(1) This section specifies whether there is a qualifying tenant of a flat for the purposes of this Chapter and, if so, who it is.
(2) Subject as follows, a person is the qualifying tenant of a flat if he is tenant of the flat under a long lease.
(3) Subsection (2) does not apply where the lease is a tenancy to which Part 2 of the Landlord and Tenant Act 1954 (c. 56) (business tenancies) applies.
(4) Subsection (2) does not apply where—

    (a) the lease was granted by sub-demise out of a superior lease other than a long lease,
    (b) the grant was made in breach of the terms of the superior lease, and
    (c) there has been no waiver of the breach by the superior landlord.

(5) No flat has more than one qualifying tenant at any one time; and subsections (6) and (7) apply accordingly.
(6) Where a flat is being let under two or more long leases, a tenant under any of those leases which is superior to that held by another is not the qualifying tenant of the flat.
(7) Where a flat is being let to joint tenants under a long lease, the joint tenants shall (subject to subsection (6)) be regarded as jointly being the qualifying tenant of the flat.

76 Long leases

(1) This section and section 77 specify what is a long lease for the purposes of this Chapter.

(2) Subject to section 77, a lease is a long lease if—

(a) it is granted for a term of years certain exceeding 21 years, whether or not it is (or may become) terminable before the end of that term by notice given by or to the tenant, by re-entry or forfeiture or otherwise,

(b) it is for a term fixed by law under a grant with a covenant or obligation for perpetual renewal (but is not a lease by sub-demise from one which is not a long lease),

(c) it takes effect under section 149(6) of the Law of Property Act 1925 (c. 20) (leases terminable after a death or marriage [(a)or the formation of a civil partnership]),

(d) it was granted in pursuance of the right to buy conferred by Part 5 of the Housing Act 1985 (c. 68) or in pursuance of the right to acquire on rent to mortgage terms conferred by that Part of that Act,

(e) it is a shared ownership lease, whether granted in pursuance of that Part of that Act or otherwise, where the tenant's total share is 100 per cent., or

(f) it was granted in pursuance of that Part of that Act as it has effect by virtue of section 17 of the Housing Act 1996 (c. 52) (the right to acquire).

(3) 'Shared ownership lease' means a lease—

(a) granted on payment of a premium calculated by reference to a percentage of the value of the demised premises or the cost of providing them, or

(b) under which the tenant (or his personal representatives) will or may be entitled to a sum calculated by reference, directly or indirectly, to the value of those premises.

(4) 'Total share', in relation to the interest of a tenant under a shared ownership lease, means his initial share plus any additional share or shares in the demised premises which he has acquired.

TEXTUAL AMENDMENTS

(a) Words in s 76(2)(c) inserted (5.12.2005) by Civil Partnership Act 2004 (c. 33), ss 81, 263(2), Sch 8 para 64; SI 2005/3175, art 2(1), Sch 1

77 Long leases: further provisions

(1) A lease terminable by notice after [(a)a death, a marriage or the formation of a civil partnership] is not a long lease if—

(a) the notice is capable of being given at any time after the death or marriage of [(b), or the formation of a civil partnership by,] the tenant,
(b) the length of the notice is not more than three months, and
(c) the terms of the lease preclude both its assignment otherwise than by virtue of section 92 of the Housing Act 1985 (assignments by way of exchange) and the sub-letting of the whole of the demised premises.

(2) Where the tenant of any property under a long lease, on the coming to an end of the lease, becomes or has become tenant of the property or part of it under any subsequent tenancy (whether by express grant or by implication of law), that tenancy is a long lease irrespective of its terms.
(3) A lease—

(a) granted for a term of years certain not exceeding 21 years, but with a covenant or obligation for renewal without payment of a premium (but not for perpetual renewal), and
(b) renewed on one or more occasions so as to bring to more than 21 years the total of the terms granted (including any interval between the end of a lease and the grant of a renewal),

is to be treated as if the term originally granted had been one exceeding 21 years.
(4) Where a long lease—

(a) is or was continued for any period under Part 1 of the Landlord and Tenant Act 1954 (c. 56) or under Schedule 10 to the Local Government and Housing Act 1989 (c. 42), or
(b) was continued for any period under the Leasehold Property (Temporary Provisions) Act 1951 (c. 38),

it remains a long lease during that period.
(5) Where in the case of a flat there are at any time two or more separate leases, with the same landlord and the same tenant, and—

(a) the property comprised in one of those leases consists of either the flat or a part of it (in either case with or without appurtenant property), and
(b) the property comprised in every other lease consists of either a part of the flat (with or without appurtenant property) or appurtenant property only,

there shall be taken to be a single long lease of the property comprised in such of those leases as are long leases.

TEXTUAL AMENDMENTS

(a) Words in s 77(1) substituted (5.12.2005) by Civil Partnership Act 2004 (c. 33), ss 81, 263(2), Sch 8 para 65(a); SI 2005/3175, art 2(1), Sch 1
(b) Words in s 77(1)(a) inserted (5.12.2005) by Civil Partnership Act 2004 (c. 33), ss 81, 263(2), Sch 8 para 65(b); SI 2005/3175, art 2(1), Sch 1

CLAIM TO ACQUIRE RIGHT

78 Notice inviting participation

(1) Before making a claim to acquire the right to manage any premises, a RTM company must give notice to each person who at the time when the notice is given—

(a) is the qualifying tenant of a flat contained in the premises, but
(b) neither is nor has agreed to become a member of the RTM company.

(2) A notice given under this section (referred to in this Chapter as a 'notice of invitation to participate') must—

(a) state that the RTM company intends to acquire the right to manage the premises,
(b) state the names of the members of the RTM company,
(c) invite the recipients of the notice to become members of the company, and
(d) contain such other particulars (if any) as may be required to be contained in notices of invitation to participate by regulations made by the appropriate national authority.

(3) A notice of invitation to participate must also comply with such requirements (if any) about the form of notices of invitation to participate as may be prescribed by regulations so made.

(4) A notice of invitation to participate must either—

(a) be accompanied by a copy of the [(a)articles of association] of the RTM company, or

(b) include a statement about inspection and copying of the [(a)articles of association] of the RTM company.

(5) A statement under subsection (4)(b) must—

(a) specify a place (in England or Wales) at which the [(a)articles of association] may be inspected,

(b) specify as the times at which they may be inspected periods of at least two hours on each of at least three days (including a Saturday or Sunday or both) within the seven days beginning with the day following that on which the notice is given,

(c) specify a place (in England or Wales) at which, at any time within those seven days, a copy of the [(a)articles of association] may be ordered, and

(d) specify a fee for the provision of an ordered copy, not exceeding the reasonable cost of providing it.

(6) Where a notice given to a person includes a statement under subsection (4)(b), the notice is to be treated as not having been given to him if he is not allowed to undertake an inspection, or is not provided with a copy, in accordance with the statement.

(7) A notice of invitation to participate is not invalidated by any inaccuracy in any of the particulars required by or by virtue of this section.

TEXTUAL AMENDMENTS

(a) Words in s 78(4)(a),(b); (5)(a),(c) substituted (1.10.2009) by The Companies Act 2006 (Consequential Amendments, Transitional Provisions and Savings) Order 2009 (SI 2009/1941), Sch 1 para 194(17) (with art 10)

79 Notice of claim to acquire right

(1) A claim to acquire the right to manage any premises is made by giving notice of the claim (referred to in this Chapter as a 'claim

notice'); and in this Chapter the 'relevant date', in relation to any claim to acquire the right to manage, means the date on which notice of the claim is given.

(2) The claim notice may not be given unless each person required to be given a notice of invitation to participate has been given such a notice at least 14 days before.

(3) The claim notice must be given by a RTM company which complies with subsection (4) or (5).

(4) If on the relevant date there are only two qualifying tenants of flats contained in the premises, both must be members of the RTM company.

(5) In any other case, the membership of the RTM company must on the relevant date include a number of qualifying tenants of flats contained in the premises which is not less than one-half of the total number of flats so contained.

(6) The claim notice must be given to each person who on the relevant date is—

 (a) landlord under a lease of the whole or any part of the premises,
 (b) party to such a lease otherwise than as landlord or tenant, or
 (c) a manager appointed under Part 2 of the Landlord and Tenant Act 1987 (c. 31) (referred to in this Part as 'the 1987 Act') to act in relation to the premises, or any premises containing or contained in the premises.

(7) Subsection (6) does not require the claim notice to be given to a person who cannot be found or whose identity cannot be ascertained; but if this subsection means that the claim notice is not required to be given to anyone at all, section 85 applies.

(8) A copy of the claim notice must be given to each person who on the relevant date is the qualifying tenant of a flat contained in the premises.

(9) Where a manager has been appointed under Part 2 of the 1987 Act to act in relation to the premises, or any premises containing or contained in the premises, a copy of the claim notice must also be given to the (a)... tribunal or court by which he was appointed.

TEXTUAL AMENDMENTS

(a) Words in s 79(9) omitted (1.7.2013) by virtue of The Transfer of Tribunal Functions Order 2013 (SI 2013/1036), art 1, Sch 1 para 132 (with Sch 3)

80 Contents of claim notice

(1) The claim notice must comply with the following requirements.

(2) It must specify the premises and contain a statement of the grounds on which it is claimed that they are premises to which this Chapter applies.

(3) It must state the full name of each person who is both—

- (a) the qualifying tenant of a flat contained in the premises, and
- (b) a member of the RTM company,

and the address of his flat.

(4) And it must contain, in relation to each such person, such particulars of his lease as are sufficient to identify it, including—

- (a) the date on which it was entered into,
- (b) the term for which it was granted, and
- (c) the date of the commencement of the term.

(5) It must state the name and registered office of the RTM company.

(6) It must specify a date, not earlier than one month after the relevant date, by which each person who was given the notice under section 79(6) may respond to it by giving a counter-notice under section 84.

(7) It must specify a date, at least three months after that specified under subsection (6), on which the RTM company intends to acquire the right to manage the premises.

(8) It must also contain such other particulars (if any) as may be required to be contained in claim notices by regulations made by the appropriate national authority.

(9) And it must comply with such requirements (if any) about the form of claim notices as may be prescribed by regulations so made.

81 Claim notice: supplementary

(1) A claim notice is not invalidated by any inaccuracy in any of the particulars required by or by virtue of section 80.

(2) Where any of the members of the RTM company whose names are stated in the claim notice was not the qualifying tenant of a flat contained in the premises on the relevant date, the claim notice is not invalidated on that account, so long as a sufficient number of

qualifying tenants of flats contained in the premises were members of the company on that date; and for this purpose a 'sufficient number' is a number (greater than one) which is not less than one-half of the total number of flats contained in the premises on that date.

(3) Where any premises have been specified in a claim notice, no subsequent claim notice which specifies—

(a) the premises, or
(b) any premises containing or contained in the premises,

may be given so long as the earlier claim notice continues in force.

(4) Where a claim notice is given by a RTM company it continues in force from the relevant date until the right to manage is acquired by the company unless it has previously—

(a) been withdrawn or deemed to be withdrawn by virtue of any provision of this Chapter, or
(b) ceased to have effect by reason of any other provision of this Chapter.

82 Right to obtain information

(1) A company which is a RTM company in relation to any premises may give to any person a notice requiring him to provide the company with any information—

(a) which is in his possession or control, and
(b) which the company reasonably requires for ascertaining the particulars required by or by virtue of section 80 to be included in a claim notice for claiming to acquire the right to manage the premises.

(2) Where the information is recorded in a document in the person's possession or control, the RTM company may give him a notice requiring him—

(a) to permit any person authorised to act on behalf of the company at any reasonable time to inspect the document (or, if the information is recorded in the document in a form in which it is not readily intelligible, to give any such person access to it in a readily intelligible form), and

(b) to supply the company with a copy of the document containing the information in a readily intelligible form (a)....

(3) A person to whom a notice is given must comply with it within the period of 28 days beginning with the day on which it is given.

[(b)(4) The RTM company is liable for the reasonable costs incurred by a person in complying (in accordance with this section) with a notice under this section.

(5) Any question arising in relation to the amount of the costs payable by the RTM company is, in default of agreement, to be determined by the appropriate tribunal.]

TEXTUAL AMENDMENTS

(a) Words in s 82(2)(b) omitted (3.3.2025) by virtue of Leasehold and Freehold Reform Act 2024 (c. 22), ss 50(2)(a), 124(3); SI 2025/131, s 2(b)

(b) S 82(4),(5) inserted (3.3.2025) by Leasehold and Freehold Reform Act 2024 (c. 22), ss 50(2)(b), 124(3); SI 2025/131, reg 2(b)

83 Right of access

(1) Where a RTM company has given a claim notice in relation to any premises, each of the persons specified in subsection (2) has a right of access to any part of the premises if that is reasonable in connection with any matter arising out of the claim to acquire the right to manage.

(2) The persons referred to in subsection (1) are—

(a) any person authorised to act on behalf of the RTM company,

(b) any person who is landlord under a lease of the whole or any part of the premises and any person authorised to act on behalf of any such person,

(c) any person who is party to such a lease otherwise than as landlord or tenant and any person authorised to act on behalf of any such person, and

(d) any manager appointed under Part 2 of the 1987 Act to act in relation to the premises, or any premises containing or contained in the premises, and any person authorised to act on behalf of any such manager.

(3) The right conferred by this section is exercisable, at any reasonable time, on giving not less than ten days' notice—

(a) to the occupier of any premises to which access is sought, or
(b) if those premises are unoccupied, to the person entitled to occupy them.

84 Counter-notices

(1) A person who is given a claim notice by a RTM company under section 79(6) may give a notice (referred to in this Chapter as a 'counter-notice') to the company no later than the date specified in the claim notice under section 80(6).
(2) A counter-notice is a notice containing a statement either—

(a) admitting that the RTM company was on the relevant date entitled to acquire the right to manage the premises specified in the claim notice, or
(b) alleging that, by reason of a specified provision of this Chapter, the RTM company was on that date not so entitled,

and containing such other particulars (if any) as may be required to be contained in counter-notices, and complying with such requirements (if any) about the form of counter-notices, as may be prescribed by regulations made by the appropriate national authority.
(3) Where the RTM company has been given one or more counter-notices containing a statement such as is mentioned in sub-section (2)(b), the company may apply to [(a)the appropriate tribunal] for a determination that it was on the relevant date entitled to acquire the right to manage the premises.
(4) An application under subsection (3) must be made not later than the end of the period of two months beginning with the day on which the counter-notice (or, where more than one, the last of the counter-notices) was given.
(5) Where the RTM company has been given one or more counter-notices containing a statement such as is mentioned in sub-section (2)(b), the RTM company does not acquire the right to manage the premises unless—

(a) on an application under subsection (3) it is finally determined that the company was on the relevant date entitled to acquire the right to manage the premises, or
(b) the person by whom the counter-notice was given agrees, or the persons by whom the counter-notices were given agree, in writing that the company was so entitled.

(6) If on an application under subsection (3) it is finally determined that the company was not on the relevant date entitled to acquire the right to manage the premises, the claim notice ceases to have effect.
(7) A determination on an application under subsection (3) becomes final—

(a) if not appealed against, at the end of the period for bringing an appeal, or
(b) if appealed against, at the time when the appeal (or any further appeal) is disposed of.

(8) An appeal is disposed of—

(a) if it is determined and the period for bringing any further appeal has ended, or
(b) if it is abandoned or otherwise ceases to have effect.

TEXTUAL AMENDMENTS

(a) Words in s 84(3) substituted (1.7.2013) by The Transfer of Tribunal Functions Order 2013 (SI 2013/1036), art 1, Sch 1 para 133 (with Sch 3)

85 Landlords etc. not traceable

(1) This section applies where a RTM company wishing to acquire the right to manage premises—

(a) complies with subsection (4) or (5) of section 79, and
(b) would not have been precluded from giving a valid notice under that section with respect to the premises,

but cannot find, or ascertain the identity of, any of the persons to whom the claim notice would be required to be given by subsection (6) of that section.

(2) The RTM company may apply to [(a)the appropriate tribunal] for an order that the company is to acquire the right to manage the premises.

(3) Such an order may be made only if the company has given notice of the application to each person who is the qualifying tenant of a flat contained in the premises.

(4) Before an order is made the company may be required to take such further steps by way of advertisement or otherwise as is determined proper for the purpose of tracing the persons who are—

(a) landlords under leases of the whole or any part of the premises, or

(b) parties to such leases otherwise than as landlord or tenant.

(5) If any of those persons is traced—

(a) after an application for an order is made, but

(b) before the making of an order,

no further proceedings shall be taken with a view to the making of an order.

(6) Where that happens—

(a) the rights and obligations of all persons concerned shall be determined as if the company had, at the date of the application, duly given notice under section 79 of its claim to acquire the right to manage the premises, and

(b) the (b)... tribunal may give such directions as it thinks fit as to the steps to be taken for giving effect to their rights and obligations, including directions modifying or dispensing with any of the requirements imposed by or by virtue of this Chapter.

(7) An application for an order may be withdrawn at any time before an order is made and, after it is withdrawn, subsection (6)(a) does not apply.

(8) But where any step is taken for the purpose of giving effect to subsection (6)(a) in the case of any application, the application shall not afterwards be withdrawn except—

(a) with the consent of the person or persons traced, or

(b) by permission of the (c)... tribunal.

(9) And permission shall be given only where it appears just that it should be given by reason of matters coming to the knowledge of the RTM company in consequence of the tracing of the person or persons traced.

TEXTUAL AMENDMENTS

(a) Words in s 85(2) substituted (1.7.2013) by The Transfer of Tribunal Functions Order 2013 (SI 2013/1036), art 1, Sch 1 para 134(a) (with Sch 3)

(b) Words in s 85(6)(b) omitted (1.7.2013) by virtue of The Transfer of Tribunal Functions Order 2013 (SI 2013/1036), art 1, Sch 1 para 134(b) (with Sch 3)

(c) Words in s 85(8)(b) omitted (1.7.2013) by virtue of The Transfer of Tribunal Functions Order 2013 (SI 2013/1036), art 1, Sch 1 para 134(b) (with Sch 3)

86 Withdrawal of claim notice

(1) A RTM company which has given a claim notice in relation to any premises may, at any time before it acquires the right to manage the premises, withdraw the claim notice by giving a notice to that effect (referred to in this Chapter as a 'notice of withdrawal').

(2) A notice of withdrawal must be given to each person who is—

(a) landlord under a lease of the whole or any part of the premises,

(b) party to such a lease otherwise than as landlord or tenant,

(c) a manager appointed under Part 2 of the 1987 Act to act in relation to the premises, or any premises containing or contained in the premises, or

(d) the qualifying tenant of a flat contained in the premises.

87 Deemed withdrawal

(1) If a RTM company has been given one or more counter-notices containing a statement such as is mentioned in subsection (2)(b) of section 84 but either—

(a) no application for a determination under subsection (3) of that section is made within the period specified in subsection (4) of that section, or

(b) such an application is so made but is subsequently withdrawn,

the claim notice is deemed to be withdrawn.

(2) The withdrawal shall be taken to occur—

(a) if paragraph (a) of subsection (1) applies, at the end of the period specified in that paragraph, and
(b) if paragraph (b) of that subsection applies, on the date of the withdrawal of the application.

(3) Subsection (1) does not apply if the person by whom the counter-notice was given has, or the persons by whom the counter-notices were given have, (before the time when the withdrawal would be taken to occur) agreed in writing that the RTM company was on the relevant date entitled to acquire the right to manage the premises.
(4) The claim notice is deemed to be withdrawn if—

(a) a winding-up order (a)... is made, or a resolution for voluntary winding-up is passed, with respect to the RTM company, [(b)or the RTM company enters administration,]
(b) a receiver or a manager of the RTM company's undertaking is duly appointed, or possession is taken, by or on behalf of the holders of any debentures secured by a floating charge, of any property of the RTM company comprised in or subject to the charge,
(c) a voluntary arrangement proposed in the case of the RTM company for the purposes of Part 1 of the Insolvency Act 1986 (c. 45) is approved under that Part of that Act, or
(d) the RTM company's name is struck off the register under [(c)section 1000, 1001 or 1003 of the Companies Act 2006].

TEXTUAL AMENDMENTS
(a) Words in s 87(4)(a) omitted (15.9.2003) by virtue of The Enterprise Act 2002 (Insolvency) Order 2003 (SI 2003/2096), art 4, Sch para 39(a) (with art 6)
(b) Words in s 87(4)(a) added (15.9.2003) by The Enterprise Act 2002 (Insolvency) Order 2003 (SI 2003/2096), art 4, Sch para 39(b) (with art 6)
(c) Words in s 87(4)(d) substituted (1.10.2009) by The Companies Act 2006 (Consequential Amendments, Transitional Provisions and Savings) Order 2009 (SI 2009/1941), Sch 1 para 194(18) (with art 10)

[(a)87A Costs: general

(1) An RTM company and a member of an RTM company are not liable for any costs incurred by any other person in consequence of a claim notice given by the company in relation to any premises, except as set out in this section.

(2) A lease, transfer, contract or other arrangement is accordingly of no effect to the extent it would provide to the contrary.
(3) An RTM company is liable to a member of the company in respect of costs incurred by the member to the extent agreed between the company and the member.
(4) A member of an RTM company—

(a) is liable to the company in respect of costs incurred by the company to the extent agreed between the member and the company;
(b) is liable to another member of the company in respect of costs incurred by that other member to the extent agreed between the two members.

(5) An RTM company or a member of an RTM company are liable for costs incurred by another person in connection with proceedings before a court or tribunal if—

(a) the court or tribunal has power under another enactment to order that they pay those costs, and
(b) the court or tribunal makes such an order.

(6) An RTM company and a member of an RTM company are liable for costs incurred by another person in the circumstances referred to in section 87B.
(7) For the purposes of this section, 'member', in relation to an RTM company, means each person who is or has been a member of the RTM company.
(8) See also sections 20CA and 20J of the Landlord and Tenant Act 1985, which prevent costs in connection with a claim under this Chapter being recovered by way of a variable service charge (within the meaning of section 18 of that Act).

87B Power of tribunal to order costs where claim ceases

(1) The appropriate tribunal may, on the application of a person ('the applicant') that incurs costs in consequence of a claim notice given by an RTM company, order that the RTM company is liable to the applicant for the costs if all of the conditions in subsection (2) are met.

(2) The conditions are—

(a) the claim notice—

(i) is at any time withdrawn or deemed to be withdrawn by virtue of any provision of this Chapter, or
(ii) at any time ceases to have effect by reason of any other provision of this Chapter;

(b) the RTM company acts unreasonably in—

(i) giving the claim notice, or
(ii) not withdrawing it, causing it to be deemed withdrawn, or causing it to cease to have effect sooner;

(c) the applicant is—

(i) a landlord under a lease of the whole or any part of the premises,
(ii) party to such a lease otherwise than as landlord or tenant, or
(iii) a manager appointed under Part 2 of the 1987 Act to act in relation to the premises, or any premises containing or contained in the premises;

(d) the costs are incurred before the claim notice is withdrawn, is deemed withdrawn, or ceases to have effect;
(e) the costs are incurred other than in connection with proceedings before a court or tribunal;
(f) the costs are reasonably incurred.

(3) Where the appropriate tribunal orders that an RTM company is liable under subsection (1), each person who is or has been a member of the RTM company is also liable (jointly and severally with the RTM company and each other such person).
(4) But a person is not liable if—

(a) the lease by virtue of which they were a qualifying tenant has been assigned to another person, and
(b) that other person has become a member of the RTM company.

(5) The reference in subsection (4) to an assignment includes—

(a) an assent by personal representatives, and
(b) assignment by operation of law where the assignment is to a trustee in bankruptcy or to a mortgagee under section 89(2) of the Law of Property Act 1925 (foreclosure of leasehold mortgage).]

TEXTUAL AMENDMENTS

(a) Ss 87A, 87B inserted (3.3.2025) by Leasehold and Freehold Reform Act 2024 (c. 22), ss 50(3), 124(3); SI 2025/131, reg 2(b)

(a)88 Costs: general

...

TEXTUAL AMENDMENTS

(a) S 88 omitted (3.3.2025) by virtue of Leasehold and Freehold Reform Act 2024 (c. 22), ss 50(4), 124(3); SI 2025/131, reg 2(b)

(a)89 Costs where claim ceases

...

TEXTUAL AMENDMENTS

(a) S 89 omitted (3.3.2025) by virtue of Leasehold and Freehold Reform Act 2024 (c. 22), ss 50(4), 124(3); SI 2025/131, reg 2(b)

ACQUISITION OF RIGHT

90 The acquisition date

(1) This section makes provision about the date which is the acquisition date where a RTM company acquires the right to manage any premises.
(2) Where there is no dispute about entitlement, the acquisition date is the date specified in the claim notice under section 80(7).
(3) For the purposes of this Chapter there is no dispute about entitlement if—

(a) no counter-notice is given under section 84, or

(b) the counter-notice given under that section, or (where more than one is so given) each of them, contains a statement such as is mentioned in subsection (2)(a) of that section.

(4) Where the right to manage the premises is acquired by the company by virtue of a determination under section 84(5)(a), the acquisition date is the date three months after the determination becomes final.

(5) Where the right to manage the premises is acquired by the company by virtue of subsection (5)(b) of section 84, the acquisition date is the date three months after the day on which the person (or the last person) by whom a counter-notice containing a statement such as is mentioned in subsection (2)(b) of that section was given agrees in writing that the company was on the relevant date entitled to acquire the right to manage the premises.

(6) Where an order is made under section 85, the acquisition date is (subject to any appeal) the date specified in the order.

91 Notices relating to management contracts

(1) Section 92 applies where—

(a) the right to manage premises is to be acquired by a RTM company (otherwise than by virtue of an order under section 85), and

(b) there are one or more existing management contracts relating to the premises.

(2) A management contract is a contract between—

(a) an existing manager of the premises (referred to in this Chapter as the 'manager party'), and

(b) another person (so referred to as the 'contractor party'),

under which the contractor party agrees to provide services, or do any other thing, in connection with any matter relating to a function which will be a function of the RTM company once it acquires the right to manage.

(3) And in this Chapter 'existing management contract' means a management contract which—

(a) is subsisting immediately before the determination date, or
(b) is entered into during the period beginning with the determination date and ending with the acquisition date.

(4) An existing manager of the premises is any person who is—

(a) landlord under a lease relating to the whole or any part of the premises,
(b) party to such a lease otherwise than as landlord or tenant, or
(c) a manager appointed under Part 2 of the 1987 Act to act in relation to the premises, or any premises containing or contained in the premises.

(5) In this Chapter 'determination date' means—

(a) where there is no dispute about entitlement, the date specified in the claim notice under section 80(6),
(b) where the right to manage the premises is acquired by the company by virtue of a determination under section 84(5)(a), the date when the determination becomes final, and
(c) where the right to manage the premises is acquired by the company by virtue of subsection (5)(b) of section 84, the day on which the person (or the last person) by whom a counter-notice containing a statement such as is mentioned in subsection (2)(b) of that section was given agrees in writing that the company was on the relevant date entitled to acquire the right to manage the premises.

92 Duties to give notice of contracts

(1) The person who is the manager party in relation to an existing management contract must give a notice in relation to the contract—

(a) to the person who is the contractor party in relation to the contract (a 'contractor notice'), and
(b) to the RTM company (a 'contract notice').

(2) A contractor notice and a contract notice must be given—

(a) in the case of a contract subsisting immediately before the determination date, on that date or as soon after that date as is reasonably practicable, and
(b) in the case of a contract entered into during the period beginning with the determination date and ending with the acquisition date, on the date on which it is entered into or as soon after that date as is reasonably practicable.

(3) A contractor notice must—

(a) give details sufficient to identify the contract in relation to which it is given,
(b) state that the right to manage the premises is to be acquired by a RTM company,
(c) state the name and registered office of the RTM company,
(d) specify the acquisition date, and
(e) contain such other particulars (if any) as may be required to be contained in contractor notices by regulations made by the appropriate national authority,

and must also comply with such requirements (if any) about the form of contractor notices as may be prescribed by regulations so made.

(4) Where a person who receives a contractor notice (including one who receives a copy by virtue of this subsection) is party to an existing management sub-contract with another person (the 'sub-contractor party'), the person who received the notice must—

(a) send a copy of the contractor notice to the sub-contractor party, and
(b) give to the RTM company a contract notice in relation to the existing management sub-contract.

(5) An existing management sub-contract is a contract under which the sub-contractor party agrees to provide services, or do any other thing, in connection with any matter relating to a function which will be a function of the RTM company once it acquires the right to manage and which—

(a) is subsisting immediately before the determination date, or

(b) is entered into during the period beginning with the determination date and ending with the acquisition date.

(6) Subsection (4) must be complied with—

(a) in the case of a contract entered into before the contractor notice is received, on the date on which it is received or as soon after that date as is reasonably practicable, and
(b) in the case of a contract entered into after the contractor notice is received, on the date on which it is entered into or as soon after that date as is reasonably practicable.

(7) A contract notice must—

(a) give particulars of the contract in relation to which it is given and of the person who is the contractor party, or sub-contractor party, in relation to that contract, and
(b) contain such other particulars (if any) as may be required to be contained in contract notices by regulations made by the appropriate national authority,

and must also comply with such requirements (if any) about the form of contract notices as may be prescribed by such regulations so made.

93 Duty to provide information

(1) Where the right to manage premises is to be acquired by a RTM company, the company may give notice to a person who is—

(a) landlord under a lease of the whole or any part of the premises,
(b) party to such a lease otherwise than as landlord or tenant, or
(c) a manager appointed under Part 2 of the 1987 Act to act in relation to the premises, or any premises containing or contained in the premises,

requiring him to provide the company with any information which is in his possession or control and which the company reasonably requires in connection with the exercise of the right to manage.
(2) Where the information is recorded in a document in his possession or control the notice may require him—

(a) to permit any person authorised to act on behalf of the company at any reasonable time to inspect the document (or, if the information is recorded in the document in a form in which it is not readily intelligible, to give any such person access to it in a readily intelligible form), and
(b) to supply the company with a copy of the document containing the information in a readily intelligible form.

(3) A notice may not require a person to do anything under this section before the acquisition date.
(4) But, subject to that, a person who is required by a notice to do anything under this section must do it within the period of 28 days beginning with the day on which the notice is given.

94 Duty to pay accrued uncommitted service charges

(1) Where the right to manage premises is to be acquired by a RTM company, a person who is—

(a) landlord under a lease of the whole or any part of the premises,
(b) party to such a lease otherwise than as landlord or tenant, or
(c) a manager appointed under Part 2 of the 1987 Act to act in relation to the premises, or any premises containing or contained in the premises,

must make to the company a payment equal to the amount of any accrued uncommitted service charges held by him on the acquisition date.
(2) The amount of any accrued uncommitted service charges is the aggregate of—

(a) any sums which have been paid to the person by way of service charges in respect of the premises, and
(b) any investments which represent such sums (and any income which has accrued on them),

less so much (if any) of that amount as is required to meet the costs incurred before the acquisition date in connection with the matters for which the service charges were payable.

(3) He or the RTM company may make an application to [(a)the appropriate tribunal] to determine the amount of any payment which falls to be made under this section.
(4) The duty imposed by this section must be complied with on the acquisition date or as soon after that date as is reasonably practicable.

TEXTUAL AMENDMENTS

(a) Words in s 94(3) substituted (1.7.2013) by The Transfer of Tribunal Functions Order 2013 (SI 2013/1036), art 1, Sch 1 para 136 (with Sch 3)

EXERCISING RIGHT

95 Introductory

Sections 96 to 103 apply where the right to manage premises has been acquired by a RTM company (and has not ceased to be exercisable by it).

96 Management functions under leases

(1) This section and section 97 apply in relation to management functions relating to the whole or any part of the premises.
(2) Management functions which a person who is landlord under a lease of the whole or any part of the premises has under the lease are instead functions of the RTM company.
(3) And where a person is party to a lease of the whole or any part of the premises otherwise than as landlord or tenant, management functions of his under the lease are also instead functions of the RTM company.
(4) Accordingly, any provisions of the lease making provision about the relationship of—

 (a) a person who is landlord under the lease, and
 (b) a person who is party to the lease otherwise than as landlord or tenant,

 in relation to such functions do not have effect.
(5) 'Management functions' are functions with respect to services, repairs, maintenance, improvements, insurance and management.
(6) But this section does not apply in relation to—

(a) functions with respect to a matter concerning only a part of the premises consisting of a flat or other unit not held under a lease by a qualifying tenant, or
(b) functions relating to re-entry or forfeiture.

(7) An order amending subsection (5) or (6) may be made by the appropriate national authority.

97 Management functions: supplementary

(1) Any obligation owed by the RTM company by virtue of section 96 to a tenant under a lease of the whole or any part of the premises is also owed to each person who is landlord under the lease.
(2) A person who is—

(a) landlord under a lease of the whole or any part of the premises,
(b) party to such a lease otherwise than as landlord or tenant, or
(c) a manager appointed under Part 2 of the 1987 Act to act in relation to the premises, or any premises containing or contained in the premises,

is not entitled to do anything which the RTM company is required or empowered to do under the lease by virtue of section 96, except in accordance with an agreement made by him and the RTM company.
(3) But subsection (2) does not prevent any person from insuring the whole or any part of the premises at his own expense.
(4) So far as any function of a tenant under a lease of the whole or any part of the premises—

(a) relates to the exercise of any function under the lease which is a function of the RTM company by virtue of section 96, and
(b) is exercisable in relation to a person who is landlord under the lease or party to the lease otherwise than as landlord or tenant,

it is instead exercisable in relation to the RTM company.
(5) But subsection (4) does not require or permit the payment to the RTM company of so much of any service charges payable by a tenant under a lease of the whole or any part of the premises as is required to meet costs incurred before the right to manage was acquired by the RTM

company in connection with matters for which the service charges are payable.

98 Functions relating to approvals

(1) This section and section 99 apply in relation to the grant of approvals under long leases of the whole or any part of the premises; but nothing in this section or section 99 applies in relation to an approval concerning only a part of the premises consisting of a flat or other unit not held under a lease by a qualifying tenant.

(2) Where a person who is—

(a) landlord under a long lease of the whole or any part of the premises, or
(b) party to such a lease otherwise than as landlord or tenant,

has functions in relation to the grant of approvals to a tenant under the lease, the functions are instead functions of the RTM company.

(3) Accordingly, any provisions of the lease making provision about the relationship of—

(a) a person who is landlord under the lease, and
(b) a person who is party to the lease otherwise than as landlord or tenant,

in relation to such functions do not have effect.

(4) The RTM company must not grant an approval by virtue of subsection (2) without having given—

(a) in the case of an approval relating to assignment, underletting, charging, parting with possession, the making of structural alterations or improvements or alterations of use, 30 days' notice, or
(b) in any other case, 14 days' notice,

to the person who is, or each of the persons who are, landlord under the lease.

(5) Regulations increasing the period of notice to be given under subsection (4)(b) in the case of any description of approval may be made by the appropriate national authority.

(6) So far as any function of a tenant under a long lease of the whole or any part of the premises—

(a) relates to the exercise of any function which is a function of the RTM company by virtue of this section, and
(b) is exercisable in relation to a person who is landlord under the lease or party to the lease otherwise than as landlord or tenant,

it is instead exercisable in relation to the RTM company.

(7) In this Chapter 'approval' includes consent or licence and 'approving' is to be construed accordingly; and an approval required to be obtained by virtue of a restriction entered on the register of title kept by the Chief Land Registrar is, so far as relating to a long lease of the whole or any part of any premises, to be treated for the purposes of this Chapter as an approval under the lease.

99 Approvals: supplementary

(1) If a person to whom notice is given under section 98(4) objects to the grant of the approval before the time when the RTM company would first be entitled to grant it, the RTM company may grant it only—

(a) in accordance with the written agreement of the person who objected, or
(b) in accordance with a determination of (or on an appeal from) [(a)the appropriate tribunal].

(2) An objection to the grant of the approval may not be made by a person unless he could withhold the approval if the function of granting it were exercisable by him (and not by the RTM company).

(3) And a person may not make an objection operating only if a condition or requirement is not satisfied unless he could grant the approval subject to the condition or requirement being satisfied if the function of granting it were so exercisable.

(4) An objection to the grant of the approval is made by giving notice of the objection (and of any condition or requirement which must be satisfied if it is not to operate) to—

(a) the RTM company, and
(b) the tenant,

and, if the approval is to a tenant approving an act of a sub-tenant, to the sub-tenant.

(5) An application to [(b)the appropriate tribunal] for a determination under subsection (1)(b) may be made by—

(a) the RTM company,
(b) the tenant,
(c) if the approval is to a tenant approving an act of a sub-tenant, the sub-tenant, or
(d) any person who is landlord under the lease.

TEXTUAL AMENDMENTS

(a) Words in s 99(1)(b) substituted (1.7.2013) by The Transfer of Tribunal Functions Order 2013 (SI 2013/1036), art 1, Sch 1 para 137 (with Sch 3)

(b) Words in s 99(5) substituted (1.7.2013) by The Transfer of Tribunal Functions Order 2013 (SI 2013/1036), art 1, Sch 1 para 137 (with Sch 3)

100 Enforcement of tenant covenants

(1) This section applies in relation to the enforcement of untransferred tenant covenants of a lease of the whole or any part of the premises.

(2) Untransferred tenant covenants are enforceable by the RTM company, as well as by any other person by whom they are enforceable apart from this section, in the same manner as they are enforceable by any other such person.

(3) But the RTM company may not exercise any function of re-entry or forfeiture.

(4) In this Chapter 'tenant covenant', in relation to a lease, means a covenant falling to be complied with by a tenant under the lease; and a tenant covenant is untransferred if, apart from this section, it would not be enforceable by the RTM company.

(5) Any power under a lease of a person who is—

(a) landlord under the lease, or
(b) party to the lease otherwise than as landlord or tenant,

to enter any part of the premises to determine whether a tenant is complying with any untransferred tenant covenant is exercisable by the RTM company (as well as by the landlord or party).

101 Tenant covenants: monitoring and reporting

(1) This section applies in relation to failures to comply with tenant covenants of leases of the whole or any part of the premises.

(2) The RTM company must—

(a) keep under review whether tenant covenants of leases of the whole or any part of the premises are being complied with, and

(b) report to any person who is landlord under such a lease any failure to comply with any tenant covenant of the lease.

(3) The report must be made before the end of the period of three months beginning with the day on which the failure to comply comes to the attention of the RTM company.

(4) But the RTM company need not report to a landlord a failure to comply with a tenant covenant if—

(a) the failure has been remedied,

(b) reasonable compensation has been paid in respect of the failure, or

(c) the landlord has notified the RTM company that it need not report to him failures of the description of the failure concerned.

102 Statutory functions

(1) Schedule 7 (provision for the operation of certain enactments with modifications) has effect.

(2) Other enactments relating to leases (including enactments contained in this Act or any Act passed after this Act) have effect with any such modifications as are prescribed by regulations made by the appropriate national authority.

103 Landlord contributions to service charges

(1) This section applies where—

(a) the premises contain at least one flat or other unit not subject to a lease held by a qualifying tenant (an 'excluded unit'),

(b) the service charges payable under leases of flats contained in the premises which are so subject fall to be calculated as a proportion of the relevant costs, and

(c) the proportions of the relevant costs so payable, when aggregated, amount to less than the whole of the relevant costs.

(2) Where the premises contain only one excluded unit, the person who is the appropriate person in relation to the excluded unit must pay to the RTM company the difference between—

(a) the relevant costs, and
(b) the aggregate amount payable in respect of the relevant costs under leases of flats contained in the premises which are held by qualifying tenants.

(3) Where the premises contain more than one excluded unit, each person who is the appropriate person in relation to an excluded unit must pay to the RTM company the appropriate proportion of that difference.
(4) And the appropriate proportion in the case of each such person is the proportion of the internal floor area of all of the excluded units which is internal floor area of the excluded unit in relation to which he is the appropriate person.
(5) The appropriate person in relation to an excluded unit—

(a) if it is subject to a lease, is the landlord under the lease,
(b) if it is subject to more than one lease, is the immediate landlord under whichever of the leases is inferior to all the others, and
(c) if it is not subject to any lease, is the freeholder.

SUPPLEMENTARY

104 Registration

(a) ...

TEXTUAL AMENDMENTS

(a) S 104 repealed (17.11.2004) by Commonhold and Leasehold Reform Act 2002 (c. 15), ss 180, 181, Sch 14; SI 2004/3056, art 2

105 Cessation of management

(1) This section makes provision about the circumstances in which, after a RTM company has acquired the right to manage any premises, that right ceases to be exercisable by it.

(2) Provision may be made by an agreement made between—

(a) the RTM company, and
(b) each person who is landlord under a lease of the whole or any part of the premises,

for the right to manage the premises to cease to be exercisable by the RTM company.

(3) The right to manage the premises ceases to be exercisable by the RTM company if—

(a) a winding-up order (a)... is made, or a resolution for voluntary winding-up is passed, with respect to the RTM company, [(b)or the RTM company enters administration,]
(b) a receiver or a manager of the RTM company's undertaking is duly appointed, or possession is taken, by or on behalf of the holders of any debentures secured by a floating charge, of any property of the RTM company comprised in or subject to the charge,
(c) a voluntary arrangement proposed in the case of the RTM company for the purposes of Part 1 of the Insolvency Act 1986 (c. 45) is approved under that Part of that Act, or
(d) the RTM company's name is struck off the register under [(c)section 1000, 1001 or 1003 of the Companies Act 2006].

(4) The right to manage the premises ceases to be exercisable by the RTM company if a manager appointed under Part 2 of the 1987 Act to act in relation to the premises, or any premises containing or contained in the premises, begins so to act or an order under that Part of that Act that the right to manage the premises is to cease to be exercisable by the RTM company takes effect.

(5) The right to manage the premises ceases to be exercisable by the RTM company if it ceases to be a RTM company in relation to the premises.

TEXTUAL AMENDMENTS

(a) Words in s 105(3)(a) omitted (15.9.2003) by virtue of The Enterprise Act 2002 (Insolvency) Order 2003 (SI 2003/2096), art 4, Sch para 40(a) (with art 6)

(b) Words in s 105(3)(a) added (15.9.2003) by The Enterprise Act 2002 (Insolvency) Order 2003 (SI 2003/2096), art 4, Sch para 40(b) (with art 6)

(c) Words in s 105(3)(d) substituted (1.10.2009) by The Companies Act 2006 (Consequential Amendments, Transitional Provisions and Savings) Order 2009 (SI 2009/1941), Sch 1 para 194(19) (with art 10)

106 Agreements excluding or modifying right

Any agreement relating to a lease (whether contained in the instrument creating the lease or not and whether made before the creation of the lease or not) is void in so far as it—

(a) purports to exclude or modify the right of any person to be, or do any thing as, a member of a RTM company,

(b) provides for the termination or surrender of the lease if the tenant becomes, or does any thing as, a member of a RTM company or if a RTM company does any thing, or

(c) provides for the imposition of any penalty or disability if the tenant becomes, or does any thing as, a member of a RTM company or if a RTM company does any thing.

107 [(a)Power of tribunal to order compliance]

(1) [(b)The [(c)appropriate tribunal]] may, on the application of any person interested, make an order requiring a person who has failed to comply with a requirement imposed on him by, under or by virtue of any provision of this Chapter to make good the default within such time as is specified in the order.

(2) An application shall not be made under subsection (1) unless—

(a) a notice has been previously given to the person in question requiring him to make good the default, and

(b) more than 14 days have elapsed since the date of the giving of that notice without his having done so.

[(d)(3) Where an order other than an order to pay a sum of money has been made under subsection (1) by the appropriate tribunal—

(a) a person may apply to the county court for enforcement of the order;
(b) the appropriate tribunal may by order transfer proceedings to the county court for enforcement of the order;

and the order is to be enforceable by the court in the same way as an order of the court.

(4) See section 176C for general provision about the enforcement of tribunal decisions and section 27 of the Tribunals, Courts and Enforcement Act 2007 for provision about the enforcement of an order to pay a sum of money.]

TEXTUAL AMENDMENTS

(a) S 107 heading substituted (3.3.2025) by Leasehold and Freehold Reform Act 2024 (c. 22), ss 51(4), 124(3); SI 2025/131, reg 2(c)
(b) Words in s 107(1) substituted (22.4.2014) by Crime and Courts Act 2013 (c. 22), s 61(3), Sch 9 para 52; SI 2014/954, art 2(c) (with art 3) (with transitional provisions and savings in SI 2014/956, arts 3-11)
(c) Words in s 107(1) substituted (3.3.2025) by Leasehold and Freehold Reform Act 2024 (c. 22), ss 51(2), 124(3); SI 2025/131, reg 2(c)
(d) S 107(3), (4) inserted (3.3.2025) by Leasehold and Freehold Reform Act 2024 (c. 22), ss 51(3), 124(3); SI 2025/131, reg 2(c)

108 Application to Crown

(1) This Chapter applies in relation to premises in which there is a Crown interest.
(2) There is a Crown interest in premises if there is in the premises an interest or estate—

(a) which is comprised in the Crown Estate,
(b) which belongs to Her Majesty in right of the Duchy of Lancaster,
(c) which belongs to the Duchy of Cornwall, or
(d) which belongs to a government department or is held on behalf of Her Majesty for the purposes of a government department.

(3) Any sum payable under this Chapter to a RTM company by the Chancellor of the Duchy of Lancaster may be raised and paid under section 25 of the Duchy of Lancaster Act 1817 (c. 97) as an expense incurred in improvement of land belonging to Her Majesty in right of the Duchy.

(4) Any sum payable under this Chapter to a RTM company by the Duke of Cornwall (or any other possessor for the time being of the Duchy of Cornwall) may be raised and paid under section 8 of the Duchy of Cornwall Management Act 1863 (c. 49) as an expense incurred in permanently improving the possessions of the Duchy.

109 Powers of trustees in relation to right

(1) Where trustees are the qualifying tenant of a flat contained in any premises, their powers under the instrument regulating the trusts include power to be a member of a RTM company for the purpose of the acquisition and exercise of the right to manage the premises.
(2) But subsection (1) does not apply where the instrument regulating the trusts contains an explicit direction to the contrary.
(3) The power conferred by subsection (1) is exercisable with the same consent or on the same direction (if any) as may be required for the exercise of the trustees' powers (or ordinary powers) of investment.
(4) The purposes—

(a) authorised for the application of capital money by section 73 of the Settled Land Act 1925 (c. 18), and
(b) authorised by section 71 of that Act as purposes for which moneys may be raised by mortgage,

include the payment of any expenses incurred by a tenant for life or statutory owner as a member of a RTM company.

110 Power to prescribe procedure

(1) Where a claim to acquire the right to manage any premises is made by the giving of a claim notice, except as otherwise provided by this Chapter—

(a) the procedure for giving effect to the claim notice, and
(b) the rights and obligations of all parties in any matter arising in giving effect to the claim notice,

shall be such as may be prescribed by regulations made by the appropriate national authority.

(2) Regulations under this section may, in particular, make provision for a person to be discharged from performing any obligations arising out of a claim notice by reason of the default or delay of some other person.

111 Notices

(1) Any notice under this Chapter—

(a) must be in writing, and
(b) may be sent by post.

(2) A company which is a RTM company in relation to premises may give a notice under this Chapter to a person who is landlord under a lease of the whole or any part of the premises at the address specified in subsection (3) (but subject to subsection (4)).
(3) That address is—

(a) the address last furnished to a member of the RTM company as the landlord's address for service in accordance with section 48 of the 1987 Act (notification of address for service of notices on landlord), or
(b) if no such address has been so furnished, the address last furnished to such a member as the landlord's address in accordance with section 47 of the 1987 Act (landlord's name and address to be contained in demands for rent).

(4) But the RTM company may not give a notice under this Chapter to a person at the address specified in subsection (3) if it has been notified by him of a different address in England and Wales at which he wishes to be given any such notice.
(5) A company which is a RTM company in relation to premises may give a notice under this Chapter to a person who is the qualifying tenant of a flat contained in the premises at the flat unless it has been notified by the qualifying tenant of a different address in England and Wales at which he wishes to be given any such notice.

INTERPRETATION

112 Definitions

(1) In this Chapter—

'appurtenant property', in relation to a building or part of a building or a flat, means any garage, outhouse, garden, yard or appurtenances belonging to, or usually enjoyed with, the building or part or flat,

[(a)'appropriate tribunal' means—

(a) in relation to premises in England, the First-tier Tribunal or, where determined by Tribunal Procedure Rules, the Upper Tribunal; and
(b) in relation to premises in Wales, a leasehold valuation tribunal;]

'copy', in relation to a document in which information is recorded, means anything onto which the information has been copied by whatever means and whether directly or indirectly,

'document' means anything in which information is recorded,

'dwelling' means a building or part of a building occupied or intended to be occupied as a separate dwelling,

'flat' means a separate set of premises (whether or not on the same floor)—

(a) which forms part of a building,
(b) which is constructed or adapted for use for the purposes of a dwelling, and
(c) either the whole or a material part of which lies above or below some other part of the building,

'relevant costs' has the meaning given by section 18 of the 1985 Act,

'service charge' has the meaning given by that section, and

'unit' means—

(a) a flat,
(b) any other separate set of premises which is constructed or adapted for use for the purposes of a dwelling, or

(c) a separate set of premises let, or intended for letting, on a tenancy to which Part 2 of the Landlord and Tenant Act 1954 (c. 56) (business tenancies) applies.

(2) In this Chapter 'lease' and 'tenancy' have the same meaning and both expressions include (where the context permits)—

(a) a sub-lease or sub-tenancy, and
(b) an agreement for a lease or tenancy (or for a sub-lease or sub-tenancy),

but do not include a tenancy at will or at sufferance.

(3) The expressions 'landlord' and 'tenant', and references to letting, to the grant of a lease or to covenants or the terms of a lease, shall be construed accordingly.

(4) In this Chapter any reference (however expressed) to the lease held by the qualifying tenant of a flat is a reference to a lease held by him under which the demised premises consist of or include the flat (whether with or without one or more other flats).

(5) Where two or more persons jointly constitute either the landlord or the tenant or qualifying tenant in relation to a lease of a flat, any reference in this Chapter to the landlord or to the tenant or qualifying tenant is (unless the context otherwise requires) a reference to both or all of the persons who jointly constitute the landlord or the tenant or qualifying tenant, as the case may require.

(6) In the case of a lease which derives (in accordance with section 77(5)) from two or more separate leases, any reference in this Chapter to the date of the commencement of the term for which the lease was granted shall, if the terms of the separate leases commenced at different dates, have effect as references to the date of the commencement of the term of the lease with the earliest date of commencement.

TEXTUAL AMENDMENTS

(a) Words in s 112(1) inserted (1.7.2013) by The Transfer of Tribunal Functions Order 2013 (SI 2013/1036), art 1, Sch 1 para 138 (with Sch 3)

113 Index of defined expressions

In this Chapter the expressions listed below are defined by the provisions specified.

Expression	**Interpretation provision**
Approval (and approving)	Section 98(7)
Appurtenant property	Section 112(1)
Acquisition date	Sections 74(1)(b) and 90
Claim notice	Section 79(1)
Contractor party	Section 91(2)(b)
Copy	Section 112(1)
Counter-notice	Section 84(1)
Date of the commencement of the term of a lease	Section 112(6)
Determination date	Section 91(5)
Document	Section 112(1)
Dwelling	Section 112(1)
Existing management contract	Section 91(3)
Flat	Section 112(1)
Landlord	Section 112(3) and (5)
Lease	Section 112(2) to (4)
Letting	Section 112(3)
Long lease	Sections 76 and 77
Manager party	Section 91(2)(a)
No dispute about entitlement	Section 90(3)
Notice of invitation to participate	Section 78
Notice of withdrawal	Section 86(1)
Premises to which this Chapter applies	Section 72 (and Schedule 6)
Qualifying tenant	Sections 75 and 112(4) and (5)
Relevant costs	Section 112(1)
Relevant date	Section 79(1)
Right to manage	Section 71(2)
RTM company	Sections 71(1) and 73
Service charge	Section 112(1)
Tenancy	Section 112(2)
Tenant	Section 112(3) and (5)
Tenant covenant	Section 100(4)
Unit	Section 112(1)

SCHEDULE 6
PREMISES EXCLUDED FROM RIGHT TO MANAGE

Section 72

Buildings with substantial non-residential parts

1(1) This Chapter does not apply to premises falling within section 72(1) if the internal floor area—

(a) of any non-residential part, or
(b) (where there is more than one such part) of those parts (taken together),

exceeds [(a)50%] of the internal floor area of the premises (taken as a whole).

(2) A part of premises is a non-residential part if it is neither—

(a) occupied, or intended to be occupied, for residential purposes, nor
(b) comprised in any common parts of the premises.

(3) Where in the case of any such premises any part of the premises (such as, for example, a garage, parking space or storage area) is used, or intended for use, in conjunction with a particular dwelling contained in the premises (and accordingly is not comprised in any common parts of the premises), it shall be taken to be occupied, or intended to be occupied, for residential purposes.

(4) For the purpose of determining the internal floor area of a building or of any part of a building, the floor or floors of the building or part shall be taken to extend (without interruption) throughout the whole of the interior of the building or part, except that the area of any common parts of the building or part shall be disregarded.

TEXTUAL AMENDMENTS

(a) Word in Sch 6 para 1(1) substituted (3.3.2025) by Leasehold and Freehold Reform Act 2024 (c. 22), ss 49, 124(3); SI 2025/131, reg 2(a)

Buildings with self-contained parts in different ownership

2 Where different persons own the freehold of different parts of premises falling within section 72(1), this Chapter does not apply to the premises if any of those parts is a self-contained part of a building.

Premises with resident landlord and no more than four units

3(1) This Chapter does not apply to premises falling within section 72(1) if the premises—

(a) have a resident landlord, and
(b) do not contain more than four units.

(2) Premises have a resident landlord if—

(a) the premises are not, and do not form part of, a purpose-built block of flats (that is, a building which, as constructed, contained two or more flats),
(b) a relevant freeholder, or an adult member of a relevant freeholder's family, occupies a qualifying flat as his only or principal home, and
(c) sub-paragraph (4) or (5) is satisfied.

(3) A person is a relevant freeholder, in relation to any premises, if he owns the freehold of the whole or any part of the premises.

(4) This sub-paragraph is satisfied if—

(a) the relevant freeholder, or
(b) the adult member of his family,

has throughout the last twelve months occupied the flat as his only or principal home.

(5) This sub-paragraph is satisfied if—

(a) immediately before the date when the relevant freeholder acquired his interest in the premises, the premises were premises with a resident landlord, and
(b) he, or an adult member of his family, entered into occupation of the flat during the period of 28 days beginning with that date

and has occupied the flat as his only or principal home ever since.

(6) 'Qualifying flat', in relation to any premises and a relevant freeholder or an adult member of his family, means a flat or other unit used as a dwelling—

(a) which is contained in the premises, and
(b) the freehold of the whole of which is owned by the relevant freeholder.

(7) Where the interest of a relevant freeholder in any premises is held on trust, the references in sub-paragraphs (2), (4) and (5)(b) to a relevant freeholder are to a person having an interest under the trust (whether or not also a trustee).
(8) A person is an adult member of another's family if he is—

(a) the other's spouse [(a)or civil partner],
(b) a son, daughter, son-in-law or daughter-in-law of the other, or of the other's spouse [(a)or civil partner], who has attained the age of 18, or
(c) the father or mother of the other or of the other's spouse [(a)or civil partner];

and 'son' and 'daughter' include stepson and stepdaughter ('son-in-law' and 'daughter-in-law' being construed accordingly).

TEXTUAL AMENDMENTS
(a) Words in Sch 6 para 3(8) inserted (5.12.2005) by Civil Partnership Act 2004 (c. 33), ss 81, 263(2), Sch 8 para 66; SI 2005/3175, art 2(1), Sch 1

Premises owned by local housing authority

4(1) This Chapter does not apply to premises falling within section 72(1) if a local housing authority is the immediate landlord of any of the qualifying tenants of flats contained in the premises.
(2) 'Local housing authority' has the meaning given by section 1 of the Housing Act 1985 (c. 68).

Premises in relation to which rights previously exercised

5(1) This Chapter does not apply to premises falling within section 72(1) at any time if—

(a) the right to manage the premises is at that time exercisable by a RTM company, or

(b) that right has been so exercisable but has ceased to be so exercisable less than four years before that time.

(2) Sub-paragraph (1)(b) does not apply where the right to manage the premises ceased to be exercisable by virtue of section 73(5).

(3) [(a)The appropriate tribunal] may, on an application made by a RTM company, determine that sub-paragraph (1)(b) is not to apply in any case if it considers that it would be unreasonable for it to apply in the circumstances of the case.

TEXTUAL AMENDMENTS

(a) Words in Sch 6 para 5(3) substituted (1.7.2013) by The Transfer of Tribunal Functions Order 2013 (SI 2013/1036), art 1, Sch 1 para 145 (with Sch 3)

SCHEDULE 7
RIGHT TO MANAGE: STATUTORY PROVISIONS

Section 102

Covenants not to assign etc.

1(1) Section 19 of the Landlord and Tenant Act 1927 (c. 36) (covenants not to assign without approval etc.) has effect with the modifications provided by this paragraph.

(2) Subsection (1) applies as if—

(a) the reference to the landlord, and
(b) the final reference to the lessor,

were to the RTM company.

(3) Subsection (2) applies as if the reference to the payment of a reasonable sum in respect of any damage to or diminution in the value of the premises or neighbouring premises belonging to the landlord were omitted.

(4) Subsection (3) applies as if—

(a) the first and final references to the landlord were to the RTM company, and
(b) the reference to the right of the landlord to require payment of a reasonable sum in respect of any damage to or diminution in the value of the premises or neighbouring premises belonging to him were omitted.

Defective premises

2(1) Section 4 of the Defective Premises Act 1972 (c. 35) (landlord's duty of care by virtue of obligation or right to repair demised premises) has effect with the modifications provided by this paragraph.

(2) References to the landlord (apart from the first reference in subsections (1) and (4)) are to the RTM company.

(3) The reference to the material time is to the acquisition date.

Repairing obligations [(a): England]

3(1) The obligations imposed on a lessor by virtue of section 11 (repairing obligations in short leases) of the Landlord and Tenant Act 1985 (c. 70) (referred to in this Part as 'the 1985 Act') are, so far as relating to any lease of any flat or other unit contained in the premises, instead obligations of the RTM company.

(2) The RTM company owes to any person who is in occupation of a flat or other unit contained in the premises otherwise than under a lease the same obligations as would be imposed on it by virtue of section 11 if that person were a lessee under a lease of the flat or other unit.

(3) But sub-paragraphs (1) and (2) do not apply to an obligation to the extent that it relates to a matter concerning only the flat or other unit concerned.

(4) The obligations imposed on the RTM company by virtue of sub-paragraph (1) in relation to any lease are owed to the lessor (as well as to the lessee).

(5) Subsections (3A) to (5) of section 11 have effect with the modifications that are appropriate in consequence of sub-paragraphs (1) to (3).

(6) The references in subsection (6) of section 11 to the lessor include the RTM company; and a person who is in occupation of a flat or other unit contained in the premises otherwise than under a lease has, in relation to the flat or other unit, the same obligation as that imposed on a lessee by virtue of that subsection.

(7) The reference to the lessor in section 12(1)(a) of the 1985 Act (restriction on contracting out of section 11) includes the RTM company.

TEXTUAL AMENDMENTS

(a) Word in Sch 7 para 3 heading inserted (1.12.2022) by The Renting Homes (Wales) Act 2016 (Consequential Amendments) Regulations 2022 (SI 2022/ 1166), regs 1(1), 27(2)(a)

Repairing obligations: Wales

[(a)3A(1)The obligations imposed on a landlord by virtue of section 91 (landlord's obligation: fitness for human habitation), section 92 (landlord's obligation to keep dwelling in repair) and section 93 (obligations under sections 91 and 92: supplementary) of the Renting Homes Wales Act 2016 (referred to in this paragraph as 'the 2016 Act') are, so far as relating to any occupation contract of any flat or other unit contained in the premises, instead obligations of the RTM company.

(2) The RTM company owes to any person who is in occupation of a flat or other unit contained in the premises otherwise than under an occupation contract the same obligations as would be imposed on it by virtue of sections 91, 92 and 93 of the 2016 Act if that person were a contract-holder under an occupation contract of the flat or other unit.

(3) But sub-paragraphs (1) and (2) do not apply to an obligation to the extent that it relates to a matter concerning only the flat or other unit concerned.

(4) The obligations imposed on the RTM company by virtue of sub-paragraph (1) in relation to any occupation contract are owed to the landlord (as well as to the contract-holder).

(5) Where appropriate, sections 95 to 97 of the 2016 Act have effect with such modifications as are necessary in consequence of sub-paragraphs (1) to (3).

(6) The references in section 98 of the 2016 Act to the landlord include the RTM company; and a person who is in occupation of a flat or other unit contained in the premises otherwise than under an occupation contract has, in relation to the flat or other unit, the same obligation as that imposed on a contract-holder by virtue of that section.

(7) In this paragraph, the following terms have the same meaning as in section 7 of the 2016 Act—

(a) 'contract-holder' (see section 7 (see also section 48) of that Act);

(b) 'occupation contract' (see section 7 of that Act).]

TEXTUAL AMENDMENTS

(a) Sch 7 para 3A inserted (1.12.2022) by The Renting Homes (Wales) Act 2016 (Consequential Amendments) Regulations 2022 (SI 2022/1166), regs 1(1), 27(2)(b)

Service charges

4(1) Sections 18 to 30 of the 1985 Act (service charges) have effect with the modifications provided by this paragraph.

(2) References to the landlord are to the RTM company.

(3) References to a tenant of a dwelling include a person who is landlord under a lease of the whole or any part of the premises (so that sums paid by him in pursuance of section 103 of this Act are service charges).

(4) Section 22(5) applies as if paragraph (a) were omitted and the person referred to in paragraph (b) were a person who receives service charges on behalf of the RTM company.

(5) Section 26 does not apply.

Right to request information on insurance

5(1) Section 30A of, and the Schedule to, the 1985 Act (rights of tenants with respect to insurance) have effect with the modifications provided by this paragraph.

(2) References to the landlord are to the RTM company.

(3) References to a tenant include a person who is landlord under a lease of the whole or any part of the premises and has to make payments under section 103 of this Act.

(4) Paragraphs 2(3) and 3(3) of the Schedule apply as if paragraph (a) were omitted and the person referred to in paragraph (b) were a person who receives service charges on behalf of the RTM company.

Managing agents

6 Section 30B of the 1985 Act (recognised tenants' associations to be consulted about landlord's managing agents) has effect as if references to the landlord were to the RTM company (and as if subsection (6) were omitted).

Right of first refusal

7 Where section 5 of the 1987 Act (right of first refusal: requirement that landlord serve offer notice on tenant) requires the landlord to serve an offer notice on the qualifying tenants of the flats contained in the premises, he must serve a copy of the offer notice on the RTM company.

Appointment of manager

8(1) Part 2 of the 1987 Act (appointment of manager by (a)... tribunal) has effect with the modifications provided by this paragraph.

(2) References to the landlord are to the RTM company.

(3) References to a tenant of a flat contained in the premises include a person who is landlord under a lease of the whole or any part of the premises.

(4) Section 21(3) (exception for premises where landlord is exempt or resident or where premises are functional land of a charity) does not apply.

(5) The references in paragraph (a)(i) of subsection (2) of section 24 to any obligation owed by the RTM company to the tenant under his tenancy include any obligations of the RTM company under this Act.

(6) And the circumstances in which [(b)the appropriate tribunal] may make an order under paragraph (b) of that subsection include any in which the RTM company no longer wishes the right to manage the premises to be exercisable by it.

(7) The power in section 24 to make an order appointing a manager to carry out functions includes a power (in the circumstances specified in subsection (2) of that section) to make an order that the right to manage the premises is to cease to be exercisable by the RTM company.

(8) And such an order may include provision with respect to incidental and ancillary matters (including, in particular, provision about contracts to which the RTM company is a party and the prosecution of claims in respect of causes of action, whether tortious or contractual, accruing before or after the right to manage ceases to be exercisable).

TEXTUAL AMENDMENTS

(a) Words in Sch 7 para 8(1) omitted (1.7.2013) by virtue of The Transfer of Tribunal Functions Order 2013 (SI 2013/1036), art 1, Sch 1 para 146(a) (with Sch 3)

(b) Words in Sch 7 para 8(6) substituted (1.7.2013) by The Transfer of Tribunal Functions Order 2013 (SI 2013/1036), art 1, Sch 1 para 146(b) (with Sch 3)

Right to acquire landlord's interest

9 Part 3 of the 1987 Act (compulsory acquisition by tenants of landlord's interest) does not apply.

Variation of leases

10 Sections 35, 36, 38 and 39 of the 1987 Act (variation of long leases relating to flats) have effect as if references to a party to a long lease (apart from those in section 38(8)) included the RTM company.

Service charges to be held in trust

11(1) Sections 42 to 42B of the 1987 Act (service charge contributions to be held in trust and in designated account) have effect with the modifications provided by this paragraph.

(2) References to the payee are to the RTM company.

(3) The definition of 'tenant' in section 42(1) does not apply.

(4) References to a tenant of a dwelling include a person who is landlord under a lease of the whole or any part of the premises.

(5) The reference in section 42(2) to sums paid to the payee by the contributing tenants by way of relevant service charges includes payments made to the RTM company under section 94 or 103 of this Act.

(6) Section 42A(5) applies as if paragraph (a) were omitted and the person referred to in paragraph (b) were a person who receives service charges on behalf of the RTM company.

Information to be furnished to tenants

12(1) Sections 46 to 48 of the 1987 Act (information to be furnished to tenants) have effect with the modifications provided by this paragraph.

(2) References to the landlord include the RTM company.

(3) References to a tenant include a person who is landlord under a lease of the whole or any part of the premises; and in relation to such a person the reference in section 47(4) to sums payable to the landlord under the terms of the tenancy are to sums paid by him under section 103 of this Act.

Statutory duties relating to certain covenants

13(1) The Landlord and Tenant Act 1988 (c. 26) (statutory duties in connection with covenants against assigning etc.) has effect with the modifications provided by this paragraph.

(2) The reference in section 1(2)(b) to the covenant is to the covenant as it has effect subject to section 98 of this Act.

(3) References in section 3(2), (4) and (5) to the landlord are to the RTM company.

Tenants' right to management audit

14(1) Chapter 5 of Part 1 (tenants' right to management audit by landlord) of the Leasehold Reform, Housing and Urban Development Act 1993 (c. 28) (referred to in this Part as 'the 1993 Act') has effect with the modifications provided by this paragraph.

(2) References to the landlord (other than the references in section 76(1) and (2) to 'the same landlord') are to the RTM company.

(3) References to a tenant include a person who is landlord under a lease of the whole or any part of the premises and has to make payments under section 103 of this Act.

(4) Section 80(5) applies as if the reference to a person who receives rent were to a person who receives service charges.

Right to appoint surveyor

15(1) Section 84 of the Housing Act 1996 (c. 52) and Schedule 4 to that Act (apart from paragraph 7) (right of recognised tenants' association to appoint surveyor to advise on matters relating to service charges) have effect as if references to the landlord were to the RTM company.

(2) Section 84(5) and paragraph 4(5) of Schedule 4 apply as if the reference to a person who receives rent were to a person who receives service charges.

Administration charges

16 Schedule 11 to this Act has effect as if references to the landlord (or a party to a lease) included the RTM company.

Index

References are to page numbers.